1

Proceedings of the Boston Area Colloquium in Ancient Philosophy

Proceedings of the Boston Area Colloquium in Ancient Philosophy

VOLUME XXXIV

Edited by

Gary M. Gurtler, S.J.
Daniel P. Maher

BRILL

LEIDEN | BOSTON

This hardback is also published in paperback under ISBN 978-90-04-40810-4.

Typeface for the Latin, Greek, and Cyrillic scripts: "Brill". See and download: brill.com/brill-typeface.

ISSN 1059-986X
ISBN 978-90-04-40812-8

Copyright 2019 by Koninklijke Brill NV, Leiden, The Netherlands.
Koninklijke Brill NV incorporates the imprints Brill, Brill Hes & De Graaf, Brill Nijhoff, Brill Rodopi, Brill Sense, Hotei Publishing, mentis Verlag, Verlag Ferdinand Schöningh and Wilhelm Fink Verlag.
All rights reserved. No part of this publication may be reproduced, translated, stored in a retrieval system, or transmitted in any form or by any means, electronic, mechanical, photocopying, recording or otherwise, without prior written permission from the publisher.
Authorization to photocopy items for internal or personal use is granted by Koninklijke Brill NV provided that the appropriate fees are paid directly to The Copyright Clearance Center, 222 Rosewood Drive, Suite 910, Danvers, MA 01923, USA. Fees are subject to change.

This book is printed on acid-free paper and produced in a sustainable manner.

Contents

Preface   VII
Notes on Contributors   IX

COLLOQUIUM 1
The Argumentative Unity of Plato's *Parmenides*   1
    David Horan
Commentary on Horan   33
    Darren Gardner
Horan/Gardner Bibliography   41

COLLOQUIUM 2
Genesis and the Priority of Activity in Aristotle's *Metaphysics* IX.8   43
    Mark Sentesy
Commentary on Sentesy   71
    Daniel Shartin
Sentesy/Shartin Bibliography   79

COLLOQUIUM 3
Language as *Technē* vs. Language as Technology: Plato's Critique of Sophistry   85
    D.C. Schindler
Commentary on Schindler   109
    Max J. Latona
Schindler/Latona Bibliography   116

COLLOQUIUM 4
Epicureans on Pity, Slavery, and Autonomy   119
    Kelly E. Arenson
Commentary on Arenson   137
    Susan A. Stark
Arenson/Stark Bibliography   147

COLLOQUIUM 5
Aristotle on What to Praise and What to Prize: An Interpretation of *Nicomachean Ethics* I.12   149
    Jan Szaif

Commentary on Szaif   179
   Colin Guthrie King
Szaif/King Bibliography   187

Index of Names   189

Preface

Volume 34 contains papers and commentaries presented to the Boston Area Colloquium in Ancient Philosophy during the academic year 2017–18. The colloquia for this year include two papers each on Plato and Aristotle, with one on the Epicureans. The commentators provided significant challenges to the presenters' theses.

The first paper examines the overall unity of Plato's *Parmenides*, with the dilemma of participation in the first and second hypotheses differentiating how *one* applied to sense objects differs from *one* applied to intelligible objects, explaining how an intelligible one can be participated in by many and remain undivided. The comment argues the alternative, that the two parts of the dialogue fall under one premise.

The second paper presents an equally intriguing examination of *Metaphysics* IX.8 about the relation of genesis and activity. First, Aristotle argues that τέλος is ἀρχή in the fullest sense, given the structure of genesis. Second, he answers three objections that take ἐνέργεια as τέλος. The comment proposes that the argument in *Met.* IX.8 can profit from an examination of substance and change in the *Categories* and middle books of the *Metaphysics*.

The third presentation returns to Plato's *Gorgias*, where philosophy and sophistry are contrasted in their use of language. To clarify the debate, it is helpful to look at the precise role of τέχνη in *Republic* I, as ordered to benefit, with the technical role of language, as ordered to truth outlined in the *Cratylus*. The comment surfaces some difficulties with considering language as like a craft, given its inherent epistemic ambiguity.

The fourth paper presents a pause with a consideration of whether Epicurean sages should pity rather than punish their slaves. Since pity elicits psychological pain, how can it form part of their hedonistic egoism? In answer, pity brings about the greater pleasure of social cohesion and avoids the greater pain of conflict. The comment challenges the notion of pity as morally problematic and prefers compassion as the proper term.

The fifth paper presents a very careful reading of a neglected chapter in *Nicomachean Ethics* I.12. With the distinction that happiness is prized while virtue is only praised, this chapter foreshadows the argument of *NE* X.6–8 and thus presents an unsuspected appreciation of the unity of the whole work. The comment counters with the claim that the unity actually rests with the extrinsic role of a metaphysical foundation.

The papers and commentaries appear in the order they were given at the different meetings of the Boston Area Colloquium in Ancient Philosophy at one of the following participating institutions: Assumption College, Boston College, the College of the Holy Cross, and St. Anselm College. The dialogical character of the colloquia is partially preserved by publishing both paper and commentary from each of the meetings. In many cases these oral presentations have been extensively revised, not to mention expanded, by their authors in the light of subsequent discussions, and especially in response to critical comments from our external referees. For their generous assistance as referees, I would like to thank the following scholars: Elizabeth Asmis, Owen Goldin, Paula Gottlieb, Douglass Reed, Eric Sanday.

At the end of the volume, together with the section 'About our Contributors,' readers will find a general index of names which was collated by our editorial assistant, Lydia Winn.

In conclusion, I wish to thank my colleagues on the BACAP committee, whose voluntary service structures the reality to which these Proceedings stand at one remove. Furthermore, I want to welcome Daniel Maher, who generously agreed to serve as co-editor. I would also like to welcome our new editorial assistant, Lydia Winn, and thank her for outstanding work in preparing the copy for this volume in the Philosophy Department at Boston College, and for her countless other efforts in assisting the editors and the contributors in the process of bringing the papers to finished form. Finally, I want to acknowledge the continued financial assistance provided by the administration at Boston College, whose support for this project has remained most generous over the years.

Gary Gurtler, S.J.
Boston College

Notes on Contributors

Kelly E. Arenson
is Assistant Professor of Philosophy at Duquesne University. She was educated at Boston College and Emory University. She has published articles concerning Epicurean hedonism as well as Plato's views on the nature and goodness of pleasure. She is the author of *Health and Hedonism in Plato and Epicurus* (forthcoming with Bloomsbury) and is currently editing the *Routledge Handbook of Hellenistic Philosophy*.

Darren Gardner
teaches at New York University in Liberal Studies and is a visiting scholar at Dartmouth College. He received his M.A. and Ph.D. from the New School for Social Research in New York City. His research focuses on Plato's Eleatic dialogues and on music as a philosophical enterprise in antiquity and early to late modernity. He is currently at work on *Philosophical Exercise in Plato's Parmenides*.

David Horan
is a member of the Trinity Plato Centre, Trinity College Dublin. He received his B.Sc. and M.B.A. degrees from University College Dublin and his Ph.D. from Trinity College Dublin. He has published on Plato's *Sophist* and *Parmenides* and their interrelation, and on Plotinus's use of the latter dialogue. He is currently engaged, with private support, upon the production a new translation of the complete works of Plato from ancient Greek into English. This project is scheduled for completion in 2020.

Colin Guthrie King
is Associate Professor of Philosophy at Providence College. He was educated at Colgate University and the Humboldt-Universität zu Berlin. He has published on various topics in the history of ancient philosophy and science, particularly on the history of logic and the theory of argumentation. He is currently working on a book on Aristotle's theory of dialectical argumentation.

Max J. Latona
is Associate Professor of Philosophy and the Richard L. Bready Chair of Ethics, Economics and the Common Good at Saint Anselm College. He was educated at Canisius College and Boston College, and has published articles on Parme-

nides, Plato, Aristotle, and various topics in ethics. He is currently working on a book-length project on the role of myth in Plato's thought.

D.C. Schindler

is Associate Professor of Metaphysics and Anthropology at The John Paul II Institute at The Catholic University of America, in Washington, D.C. His research falls mainly in the areas of ancient Greek philosophy (especially Plato), classical German philosophy, and 20th century Catholic philosophy. Among his many books and articles is *Plato's Critique of Impure Reason: On Goodness and Truth in the Republic* (CUA, 2008).

Mark Sentesy

is Assistant Professor of Philosophy and Classics and Ancient Mediterranean Studies at the Pennsylvania State University. He studied at Carleton University, KU Leuven, and Boston College. He has published on ancient philosophy, language, and technology, and on issues related to metaphysics, physics, philosophy of mind, and ethics. He has recently completed a book entitled *The Ontology of Change in Aristotle*.

Daniel Shartin

is Professor Emeritus of Philosophy at Worcester State University. He also taught at Vassar College, Clark University, and the College of the Holy Cross. He received his M.A. and Ph.D. from UCLA ages ago, where he studied with Montgomery Furth, Robert Yost, and Tyler Burge. Shartin taught courses in ancient philosophy, philosophy of religion, philosophy of science, and logic. He is proud to have been, along with John Cleary, one of the original editors of the *Proceedings of the Boston Area Colloquium in Ancient Philosophy*.

Susan Stark

is Associate Professor of Philosophy at Bates College. She received her B.A. from Brown University and her M.A. and Ph.D. from Georgetown University. She works in ethics, moral psychology, and social philosophy. She has published articles on virtue ethics, emotions and moral philosophy, implicit bias, and anti-racism. She is currently working on an article on emotions and empirical moral psychology and another article on responsibility and reparations for ongoing racism.

Jan Szaif

is Professor of Philosophy at the University of California, Davis. He was educated at the Freie Universität Berlin and the University of Cambridge. He has published books and articles on topics in Plato, Aristotle, and the Aristotelian tradition, including a book on Plato's concept of truth (*Platons Begriff der Wahrheit*, 1996/98) and a book on Aristotelian and Peripatetic conceptions of happiness and its foundation in human nature (*Gut des Menschen*, 2012).

COLLOQUIUM 1

The Argumentative Unity of Plato's *Parmenides*

David Horan
Trinity Plato Centre, Trinity College Dublin

Abstract

This paper argues that the resolution of the dilemma of participation presented in the first part of Plato's *Parmenides* is a central purpose of the arguments of the first hypothesis and the beginning of the second hypothesis in the second part of the dialogue. I maintain that the training demonstrated by Parmenides in the first and second hypotheses, by shifting the consideration away from sense objects to intelligible objects and away from forms to the one, enables Parmenides to develop an understanding of what it means for anything to be one. This understanding shows that multiplicity is not inimical to the one remaining one when participated in. It argues for an intelligible one that is divisible and still remains one when divided. The model of participation in the second part of the dialogue differs from that in the first part where the dilemma of participation initially arises, insofar as there is a strong ontological connection in part two between the one and whatever participates in the one, a connection that is not present in part one, where sense objects participate in intelligible forms. I conclude by taking stock of how far the resolution of the dilemma of participation has been progressed to resolution by 144e7 and what problems still remain to be analysed and resolved.

Keywords

Dilemma of Participation – divisibility – forms – one – Parmenides

I   Introduction

The purpose of this paper is to defend the claim that there is an argumentative unity connecting the *aporiai* in the first part of Plato's *Parmenides* and the hypotheses of the second part.[1] According to the view I shall defend, the

---

1   The question of the unity of the *Parmenides* has been debated for decades. Ryle (1965) famously argued that there is no unity between the two parts of the dialogue. A similar conclu-

hypotheses of part two progress the resolution of, or provide the tools either to resolve or perhaps avoid, the *aporiai* of the first part of the dialogue. This paper focuses upon a single *aporia*, which Allen calls The Dilemma of Participation, which arises in the first part of the dialogue (at 131c); this is the point at which Socrates accepts that it is not possible for a form to be in many places at the same time and still remain one.[2] However, twelve Stephanus pages later at 144d, it is accepted, in contrast, that the one can indeed be in many places at the same time and still remain one. I wish to make the case that Parmenides' intervening argument, beginning at 137b1 and concluding at 144d, is significantly concerned with the question of the ways in which something can be one or fail to be one, and is significantly dictated by the issues raised in the Dilemma of Participation. This argument, which Parmenides presents as a training, ends in the second part of the dialogue with the acceptance of a proposition similar in its wording to the one that had previously been rejected. This similarity, I argue, marks Parmenides' return to the 131c *aporia*. In revisiting the earlier *aporia* in this way, Socrates, or the reader, is equipped to appreciate why such a different answer to the earlier question might be justified and is in a better position to understand how to resolve or avoid the earlier *aporia*.

---

sion has been defended by Sayre (1983). Miller (1986) defends the unity of the dialogue, and, in fact, his contention that the first two hypotheses resolve the difficulties raised in the first part of the dialogue is similar in some respects to my own. Similarly Curd (1986) diagnoses the issues of participation addressed in the first part and proposes that "in the Second Hypothesis Parmenides himself suggests an account of participation ... given in terms of parts and wholes" (134). She remarks that this later model is acceptable because Plato has "begun to see his way through and solve the problem of the unity of forms" (134), but she does not elaborate upon this point. Halper (1990) is another example of someone who argues in favour of unity, but, in contrast to my approach, he argues that the deductions of the second part serve to raise additional problems that augment those levelled against forms in the first part. More recently, Brisson (2002) has defended another kind of unity, according to which the second part of the dialogue comes before the first, and represents an in-depth examination of Parmenides' own thesis, not the issues with forms raised in the first part. On Brisson's view, the theory of forms is introduced as a, perhaps the only, way of avoiding these contradictory conclusions.

2   See Allen (1997, 128ff.). Allen is, of course, not the first to recognize that the problem of participation is central to the dialogue. Walker (1938), for instance, admonishes previous scholars for not appreciating that the *Parmenides* provides "Plato's own solution to the problem of the One and Many" (489). A similar view is expressed by Beck (1947), who identifies what he calls "the theory of *Methexis*" as the true subject matter of the dialogue (233ff.).

11   The One in Many Places

Plato's *Parmenides*, in the second part of the dialogue, contains the following exchange:

> "So, **being one**, is it, as a whole, **in many places** at the same time? Look at this carefully." // "I am, and I see that it's impossible." // "Therefore as divided, if in fact not as a whole; for surely it will be present to all the parts of being at the same time only as divided." // "Yes."
> (ἆρα οὖν ἓν ὂν πολλαχοῦ ἅμα ὅλον ἐστί; τοῦτο ἄθρει. — Ἀλλ' ἀθρῶ καὶ ὁρῶ ὅτι ἀδύνατον. — Μεμερισμένον ἄρα, εἴπερ μὴ ὅλον· ἄλλως γάρ που οὐδαμῶς ἅμα ἅπασι τοῖς τῆς οὐσίας μέρεσιν παρέσται ἢ μεμερισμένον. — Ναί.)[3] (144c8–d4)

The "it" in question is the one, considered in relation to an unlimited multiplicity of the things that are; each of which is, thus, one "thing that is." This question is put to Aristoteles and he is asked to consider it carefully (τοῦτο ἄθρει), an injunction which, in itself, is striking. It is the sole occurrence of this verb in the *Parmenides*. The question is whether the one, being one, can be participated in, as a whole, by each of the things that are. Aristoteles answers "no," presumably because such an outcome would mean that the one is present, as a whole, in two or more things that are spatially separated. But why does this question require careful consideration? Surely it is quite obvious that nothing can, as a whole, be in many places at the same time. The question requiring careful consideration certainly cannot be whether anything can, as a whole, be in many places at the same time, because such a question does not require any consideration at all—the answer is obviously, no. The cogency of the question must revolve around the stipulation, "being one."

Nothing can, as a whole, be in many places at the same time, that is obvious; so if anything is to be in many places at the same time it must do so by being divided. But if it is divided, so as to be in many places at the same time, will it still be one? The second extract above seems to assume that it can be divided and still be one. In the case of 144c–d above, we are considering the participation of things that are in the one. Now the one is, presumably, intrinsically one by nature; it cannot be other than one and still be what it is, namely, one. Since it is intrinsically one, it must remain one, even if it is partaken of by numerous things that are, each of which occupies a distinct spatial location. Accordingly, if it can be in many places at the same time, it must still be one, since it is intrinsically one.

---
3   Trans. Gill and Ryan (1996). Greek text from the Burnet (1901) edition.

III Forms in Many Places

The above extract is from the second part of the *Parmenides*. But in an earlier passage in the first part of the dialogue (130e–131e), Socrates, under questioning by Parmenides, was not prepared to accept that a form, when participated in, could be divided and still be one (καὶ ἔτι ἓν ἔσται, 131c10). So, in the space of some twelve Stephanus pages, Socrates' earlier refusal to accept that what is divided so as to be in many places at the same time can still be one has given way to acceptance by Aristoteles: how so? This earlier argument (130e–131e), unlike the above argument, was not concerned specifically with the one but with forms in general. In the earlier part of the dialogue Socrates was at pains to defend a position according to which forms are one, and he was intent upon maintaining that they remain one, even when they are participated in by numerous things that are. To defend this position on forms remaining one when participated in, he resorts to the analogy of a single day which is one and the same in many places. Parmenides challenges this position and introduces, in its stead, the analogy of a sail covering many persons, to argue that forms must be divided in order to be participated in:

> "So the forms themselves are divisible, Socrates," he said, "and things that partake of them would partake of a part; no longer would a whole form, but only a part of it, be in each thing." // "It does appear that way." // **"Then are you willing to say, Socrates, that our one form is really divided? Will it still be one?"** // "Not at all," he replied.
> (Μεριστὰ ἄρα, φάναι, ὦ Σώκρατες, ἔστιν αὐτὰ τὰ εἴδη, καὶ τὰ μετέχοντα αὐτῶν μέρους ἂν μετέχοι, καὶ οὐκέτι ἐν ἑκάστῳ ὅλον, ἀλλὰ μέρος ἑκάστου ἂν εἴη. — Φαίνεται οὕτω γε. — Ἦ οὖν ἐθελήσεις, ὦ Σώκρατες, φάναι τὸ ἓν εἶδος ἡμῖν τῇ ἀληθείᾳ μερίζεσθαι, καὶ ἔτι ἓν ἔσται; — Οὐδαμῶς, εἰπεῖν.) (131c5–11)

I shall refer to this extract and the associated argument, hereafter, as the Day/Sail *aporia*.[4] According to this argument, being divisible or being divided so as

---

[4] For a detailed analysis of the relation between the day and sail analogies, see Panagiotou (1987). Panagiotou argues that Parmenides' transposition of Socrates' day analogy to the sail preserves the relevant features of the former, and, therefore, is not philosophically disingenuous. There has of course been great scholarly debate over the fairness of Parmenides' substitution of Socrates' Day analogy with his own Sail analogy. I take the view that Plato, as the writer, places his emphasis upon the problematic claim that forms cease being one on participation, rather than the fairness of the argumentative move by which this claim is asserted. If Socrates' Day analogy does indeed afford the basis of an argument against this claim, it does not seem, from Plato's text, that he himself wishes to explore the coherence of such a counterargument.

to be in many places at the same time is inimical to being one. If a form was divisible, but had not been participated in and had not been divided, would it still be one? Can a form be divisible and still be one? Can it be divided and still be one? The immediate question is: in what way are the forms, as introduced by Socrates, said to be one? Are they wholes with parts and thus divisible?[5] Or are they, in some sense, intrinsically one? And, if they are intrinsically one, how should that expression be understood? Or is there some other sense in which they can be one?

There is, of course, an *aporia* at this point, an *aporia* according to which there cannot be participation in forms without their ceasing to be one; and if forms by their nature must be one, there cannot be participation at all. According to Allen, "this dilemma is fundamental to everything in the *Parmenides* that follows."[6] Allen asserts that the argument above is a *reductio*, and he says:

> The Dilemma is in structure a *reductio*. If there is participation, there is participation either in the whole of an Idea or in part of it; there can be participation neither in the whole Idea nor in part of it; therefore, there is no participation.[7]

Socrates, as an advocate of the theory of forms, obviously cannot accept the impossibility of participation, nor is he prepared to deny that forms are one; these two essential commitments generate the dilemma.

IV Socrates' Defence of the Unity of Forms

Socrates himself first introduces the theory of forms in response to Zeno's arguments against the possibility of multiplicity. He asks Zeno:

> But tell me this: don't you acknowledge that there is a form, itself by itself, of likeness, and another form, opposite to this, which is what unlike is? Don't you and I and the other things we call 'many' get a share of those two entities? And don't things that get a share of likeness come to be like

---

5 It is implied throughout the section of the dialogue that we will analyse presently, that being a whole with parts is a manner of being one. However, it is only later in the dialogue that this is explicitly stated. Hence at 157d8–e1 we have a reference to "some one character and of some one [thing], **which we call** a 'whole,' since it has come to be one complete thing composed of all." (ἀλλὰ μιᾶς τινὸς ἰδέας καὶ ἑνός τινος ὃ καλοῦμεν ὅλον, ἐξ ἁπάντων ἓν τέλειον γεγονός.)

6 Allen (1997, 128).

7 Ibid.

in that way and to the extent that they get a share, whereas things that get a share of unlikeness come to be unlike, and things that get a share of both come to be both?

(οὐ νομίζεις εἶναι αὐτὸ καθ' αὑτὸ εἶδός τι ὁμοιότητος, καὶ τῷ τοιούτῳ αὖ ἄλλο τι ἐναντίον, ὅ ἔστιν ἀνόμοιον· τούτοιν δὲ δυοῖν ὄντοιν καὶ ἐμὲ καὶ σὲ καὶ τἆλλα ἃ δὴ πολλὰ καλοῦμεν μεταλαμβάνειν; καὶ τὰ μὲν τῆς ὁμοιότητος μεταλαμβάνοντα ὅμοια γίγνεσθαι ταύτῃ τε καὶ κατὰ τοσοῦτον ὅσον ἂν μεταλαμβάνῃ, τὰ δὲ τῆς ἀνομοιότητος ἀνόμοια, τὰ δὲ ἀμφοτέρων ἀμφότερα;) (128e6–129a6)

Here we have the form corresponding to some manifest characteristic, x, being defined as "x itself by itself," or "what x is." It is surely necessary that "what x is" must be just one thing. It would certainly be absurd to conclude that "what x is," is the form x designated as F_{x1}, and also another form F_{x2}, where F_{x1} and F_{x2} are different from one another. Such a conclusion would mean that "what x is," is two different things. It is surely reasonable therefore for Socrates to insist that forms, defined using the "what x is" formulation, must be one, in the sense of being unique, that is, "for any property F, there is exactly one form of F-ness."[8]

But in what other sense may we understand one and many in this context? We have already considered two possibilities, firstly that a form may be one in the sense that it is a whole with parts; this is surely the manner of being one that gave rise to the *aporiai* encountered by Socrates in the context of participation. Alternatively, a form may be intrinsically one or definitionally one; this is the manner of being one captured by the "what x is" formulation, as used to define forms. We should also allow that a form may be intrinsically one and, at the same time, be a whole with parts. In this latter case the form would not depend for its being one solely upon the fact that it is a whole with parts. If we are to understand how this issue of the one remaining one, when instantiated in multiple objects, is treated in the second hypothesis (H2) at 144b–c, we should first be as clear as we can about what Socrates means when he says that forms are one, in the early part of the dialogue. It is this conception of being one that leads to the series of *aporiai* concerning the possibility of forms remaining one when instantiated.

---

8 See Rickless (2007, xiii, 28, 73n.17). Rickless (187, 240) contends that the arguments of the *Parmenides* lead to the rejection of the principle of uniqueness of forms. I find no evidence in the arguments analysed in this paper to support such a contention.

V   The Relevant Manner of Being One

Perhaps the best immediate guide to what Socrates means by "one" when he maintains that forms are one lies in the propositions he refuses to accept when challenged by Parmenides. When Socrates proposes the Day analogy as a way of explaining how forms are one despite having multiple locations, he says:

> "No it wouldn't," Socrates said. "Not if it's like one and the same day. That is in many places at the same time and is nonetheless not separate from itself. If it's like that, each of the forms might be, at the same time, one and the same in all."
> (Οὐκ ἄν, εἴ γε, φάναι, οἷον [εἰ] ἡμέρα [εἴη] μία καὶ ἡ αὐτὴ οὖσα πολλαχοῦ ἅμα ἐστὶ καὶ οὐδέν τι μᾶλλον αὐτὴ αὑτῆς χωρίς ἐστιν, εἰ οὕτω καὶ ἕκαστον τῶν εἰδῶν ἓν ἐν πᾶσιν ἅμα ταὐτὸν εἴη.) (131b3–6)

Socrates, by introducing the analogy of "day," is here proposing that "each of the forms might be, at the same time, one and the same in all." However, we know from the further development of the "Day/Sail" in the *Parmenides* that Socrates, via the analogy of the "sail," is ultimately faced with the following question:

> "Then are you willing to say, Socrates, that our one form is really divided? Will it still be one?" // "Not at all," he replied.
> (Ἦ οὖν ἐθελήσεις, ὦ Σώκρατες, φάναι τὸ ἓν εἶδος ἡμῖν τῇ ἀληθείᾳ μερίζεσθαι, καὶ ἔτι ἓν ἔσται; Οὐδαμῶς, εἰπεῖν.) (131c9–11)

So Socrates, with the refutation of his Day argument, is faced with the prospect that the form, in order to be partaken of, must be divisible and be divided and thus no longer be one. Setting aside the fairness or unfairness of Parmenides himself in the conduct of the Day/Sail argument, we should simply note that Socrates accepts, in this exchange, that if the form is divided, it will, indeed, no longer be one.[9] Accordingly, it seems that, in response to Parmenides' challenge, Socrates, in the context of participation, envisages a manner of being one that is based upon wholeness, that is, x is one because x is a whole with parts. Socrates wishes to maintain that a form can be in many places at the same time and still be one, but if it is one only by being a whole with parts, it will no longer be one once it is divided in order to be in many places.

---

9   See my earlier n4 on the fairness of Parmenides' refutation of the Day argument.

A little later, at the conclusion of the so-called third man (really third large) argument, Parmenides faces Socrates with the conclusion that: "Each of your forms will no longer be one, but unlimited in multitude" (καὶ οὐκέτι δὴ ἓν ἕκαστόν σοι τῶν εἰδῶν ἔσται, ἀλλὰ ἄπειρα τὸ πλῆθος) (132b1–2). This conclusion, too, is unacceptable to Socrates not because the form is divided but because there are multiple occurrences of it. Accordingly, he seems to regard forms as one, in the sense of being unique, and so wishes to maintain that "there is exactly one (and hence, no more than one) form of largeness."[10] Allen's reading of the Largeness regress is that it does indeed threaten the uniqueness of forms, a core commitment of Socrates: "Given further that Largeness is what it is to be large, and excludes its opposite, and is unique, this regress is vicious, as implying multiple contradiction."[11] Therefore, from the position Socrates is defending in the first part of the dialogue, we can discern two elements of his conception of the oneness of forms. Firstly, a form is not one only as a whole with parts, which can cease to be one by being divided into its parts; it is intrinsically one. Secondly, a form is unique; there is exactly one, and no more than one form, in each case.

The difficulty faced by Socrates in this part of the dialogue is that, under questioning by Parmenides, he is unable to show how forms can be instantiated in multiple objects without the form either being divided, and thus no longer being one, or else losing its uniqueness. In the case of the Day/Sail argument forms cannot be participated in as wholes, so they must be divisible and be divided and thus, according to the argument in the first part of the dialogue, no longer be one. In the case of the third large argument, forms cannot be participated in without becoming unlimited in multiplicity, thus losing their uniqueness and ceasing to be one in that way.[12]

VI Training: Two Realms

The subsequent third large argument, the νοήματα argument, and the likeness regress, also demonstrate, in each case, that once there is participation in a

---

10 See Rickless (2007, 73). See also the earlier n8 pointing out that Rickless believes that the *Parmenides* mandates the rejection of the uniqueness of forms. I see no evidence to support his belief in the sections of the dialogue analysed here.

11 Allen (1997, 166).

12 Curd (1986) analyses the kind of multiplicity implied by the Day/Sail analogy as a predicational multiplicity—the instantiated form ends up possessing multiple and contradictory predicates—and the kind of multiplicity implied by the third large argument as a numerical multiplicity—there are many distinct forms of the same property.

form, the form ceases to be one. Parmenides next proceeds to emphasise the grave consequences of the failure, thus far, to resolve the various *aporiai*. He then highlights a further difficulty—indeed, the greatest difficulty—which follows from their failure to come up with a mechanism that allows forms to be instantiated and still remain one: the total separation between the realm of forms and "our realm," and the fact that the two realms are unable to interact with one another in any way at all. With this we approach the end of the first part of the dialogue and Parmenides prepares to move into the second part. Since my aim is to highlight what I regard as a single, particular connection between the first part of the dialogue and the second, I shall now focus upon the transition between these two parts. At this point Parmenides diagnoses the problem that has given rise to Socrates' *aporiai*, as follows:

> "Socrates, that's because you are trying to mark off something beautiful, and just, and good, and each one of the forms, too soon," he said, "before you have been properly trained...."
> (πρῴ γάρ, εἰπεῖν, πρὶν γυμνασθῆναι, ὦ Σώκρατες, ὁρίζεσθαι ἐπιχειρεῖς καλόν τέ τι καὶ δίκαιον καὶ ἀγαθὸν καὶ ἓν ἕκαστον τῶν εἰδῶν.) (135c8–d1)

So the problem is a lack of training,[13] and when pressed on the nature of the training, he first reminds Socrates of something he himself said to Zeno: the manner of the training involves consideration, not of what is visible, manifest, and apprehensible by the senses, but what is grasped by reason—namely, forms.

> "What manner of training is that, Parmenides?" he [Socrates] asked. //
> "The manner is just what you heard from Zeno," he [Parmenides] said. "Except I was also impressed by something you had to say to him: you didn't allow him to remain among visible things and observe their wandering. You asked him to observe it instead among those things that one might above all grasp by means of reason and might think to be forms."
> (Τίς οὖν ὁ τρόπος, φάναι, ὦ Παρμενίδη, τῆς γυμνασίας; Οὗτος, εἶπεν, ὅνπερ ἤκουσας Ζήνωνος. πλὴν τοῦτό γέ σου καὶ πρὸς τοῦτον ἠγάσθην εἰπόντος, ὅτι

---

13 This may also, in my view, explain why there is little emphasis by Plato upon the fairness of Parmenides' refutation of Socrates' Day analogy. Socrates' problem is lack of training, so if he really did fall foul of an unfair move by Parmenides, it is the overall training which will enable him to avoid such a failing.

οὐκ εἴας ἐν τοῖς ὁρωμένοις οὐδὲ περὶ ταῦτα τὴν πλάνην ἐπισκοπεῖν, ἀλλὰ περὶ ἐκεῖνα ἃ μάλιστά τις ἂν λόγῳ λάβοι καὶ εἴδη ἂν ἡγήσαιτο εἶναι.) (135d7–e4)[14]

We notice here that Parmenides does not focus directly upon the resolution of the *aporiai* themselves; he focuses instead upon the reason why they have arisen—namely, a lack of training on Socrates' part. Furthermore the first aspect of the training—that one should look to intelligibles rather than sensibles—is an aspect of which Socrates is already aware.

Socrates himself, as Parmenides says, has already emphasised this distinction between what is visible and grasped by the senses, and what is grasped by reason—forms themselves. Socrates himself drew this distinction and argued that it was a means of avoiding the *aporiai* presented by Zeno because such *aporiai* arise only among visibles and not among intelligibles:

> [B]ut I would, as I say, be much more impressed if someone were able to display this same difficulty, which you and Parmenides went through in the case of visible things, also similarly entwined in multifarious ways in the forms themselves, in things that are grasped by reasoning.
> (πολὺ μεντἂν ὧδε μᾶλλον, ὡς λέγω, ἀγασθείην εἴ τις ἔχοι τὴν αὐτὴν ταύτην ἀπορίαν ἐν αὐτοῖς τοῖς εἴδεσι παντοδαπῶς πλεκομένην, ὥσπερ ἐν τοῖς ὁρωμένοις διήλθετε, οὕτως καὶ ἐν τοῖς λογισμῷ λαμβανομένοις ἐπιδεῖξαι.) (129e5–130a2)

Socrates' earlier response to Zeno's *aporiai* was not to resolve them but to explain that they only occur in a particular realm, the visible realm, where they are commonplace. Thus, for example, Socrates himself is, of course, in a sense, one, as one person, and in another sense, many, as having many parts. Such *aporiai*, he claims, do not occur in the intelligible realm, among forms. Accordingly Socrates would be astonished if the one itself, what one is, could be shown to be many: "But if he should demonstrate this thing itself, what one is, to be many or, conversely, the many to be one; at this I'll be astonished" (ἀλλ' εἰ ὃ ἔστιν ἕν, αὐτὸ τοῦτο πολλὰ ἀποδείξει καὶ αὖ τὰ πολλὰ δὴ ἕν, τοῦτο ἤδη θαυμάσομαι) (129b6–c1). Socrates simply explained to Zeno that if he looked to the intelligibles there would, in his view, be no *aporiai* of the sort Zeno devised among sensibles. Is Parmenides making a similar point to Socrates? Is his point that the *aporiai* that Socrates has encountered would not arise if he confined himself to considering intelligibles? Or might he show that the behaviour in question arises in the intelligible realm, not aporetically, but as part of the

---

14   The translation is from Gill and Ryan (1996), adjusted to omit the words "between opposites" which do not occur in the Greek text.

ontological nature of the intelligible objects? Furthermore, our consideration of what Socrates means when he insists that forms must be one is a consideration that is confined to the intelligible realm. In the visible realm, whatever is one, is one as a whole with parts, and, as such, it is also multiple and divisible, and it can cease to be one if it is broken into its constituent parts. Is there a manner of being one in the intelligible realm, different from the manner of being one in the visible realm? Is it possible for intelligible objects to be divided so as to be instantiated, and yet remain one?

VII   Is the One a Form?

I wish to argue that the issue, crystallising towards the end of the first part of the dialogue, primarily concerns forms' being one. Accordingly I maintain that the question of what one is, or what it means to be one, naturally becomes the main focus of the second part of the dialogue. In the extract quoted above Socrates refers to the one using the very terminology by which he defines forms, referring to it as "this thing itself, what one is" (ὃ ἔστιν ἕν, αὐτὸ τοῦτο) (129b7). This is part of his immediate response to Zeno's *aporiai*. Shortly thereafter he explicitly includes the one among a list of "forms, themselves by themselves":

> But if someone first distinguishes as separate the forms, themselves by themselves, of the things I was talking about a moment ago, for example, likeness and unlikeness, multitude and the one ...
> (ἐὰν δέ τις ὧν νυνδὴ ἐγὼ ἔλεγον πρῶτον μὲν διαιρῆται χωρὶς αὐτὰ καθ' αὑτὰ τὰ εἴδη, οἷον ὁμοιότητά τε καὶ ἀνομοιότητα καὶ πλῆθος καὶ τὸ ἕν ...) (129d6-e1)[15]

A little later, Parmenides asks Socrates:

> Tell me. Have you yourself distinguished as separate, in the way you mention, certain forms themselves, and also as separate the things that partake of them? And do you think that likeness itself is something, separate from the likeness we have? And one and many ...?

---

15   The translation is from Gill and Ryan (1996) adjusted to render "oneness" as "the one" since the Greek reads τὸ ἕν. Unlike Gill and Ryan I prefer, throughout this paper, to avoid terms such as "unity" or "oneness," and consistently speak of "one" or "the one" since the Greek text consistently uses τὸ ἕν.

(καί μοι εἰπέ, αὐτὸς σὺ οὕτω διῄρησαι ὡς λέγεις, χωρὶς μὲν εἴδη αὐτὰ ἄττα, χωρὶς δὲ τὰ τούτων αὖ μετέχοντα; καί τί σοι δοκεῖ εἶναι αὐτὴ ὁμοιότης χωρὶς ἧς ἡμεῖς ὁμοιότητος ἔχομεν, καὶ ἓν δὴ καὶ πολλά ...;) (130b1–5)

Socrates accepts this, and so within the short space of a single Stephanus page Plato apparently includes the one among the forms three times. However, the relationship between the one, as a form, and the other forms, each of which is one, is not specified in the first part of the dialogue. Socrates insists that forms themselves must be one, and, furthermore, he speaks of the one using the terminology used to characterise forms. As Parmenides proceeds to describe the training which Socrates requires, we should expect the question of what it means for anything to be one, and the question of the different ways it can be one, to be addressed in a manner that allows us to revisit the part-one *aporiai*. Since each form must be one, and since the *aporiai* involve forms' no longer being one when instantiated, the question of what it means for anything, even a form, to be one, and how anything may cease to be one, will surely be crucial.

VIII   The Training and the One

We have seen that the training proposed by Parmenides involves consideration of intelligibles rather than sensibles, and we have also seen that the dilemma of participation revolves around the manner in which the intelligible forms may be participated in by sensibles while still remaining one. We have also noted that if the manner in which forms are one is only by being wholes with parts, they would, based solely upon that manner of being one, no longer be one when they are instantiated, because they are thus divided and no longer whole and no longer one in that sense. We have argued that forms must therefore be intrinsically, or definitionally, one. By this we mean that they cannot cease to be one; being one is inseparable, for them, from being what they are. But what exactly does it mean for a form to be one in such a way as to be intrinsically one, and therefore incapable of not being one and still being what it is? Apart from invoking phrases like "intrinsically one" or "definitionally one," which are, in the end, mere verbal formulations, this is not an easy question to answer. The dilemma of participation seems to be driven by some acceptance that forms are one in the sense of being wholes with parts, which are therefore no longer one when they are divided. If there is some other manner, besides this, in which forms can be one, it might be possible to avoid the *aporiai* associated with the dilemma of participation by allowing forms to be participated in while still remaining one. But what precisely is that other manner of being one? Should the training proposed by Parmenides help us to come up with an understanding of what it means to be one, an understanding that is different from the whole-with-parts model?[16]

We have noted the stress that Parmenides lays on the importance of considering intelligibles rather than sensibles. Could it be that in considering intelligibles rather than sensibles we arrive at an understanding of what it is to be one that does not rely upon being a whole with parts? This possibility receives some support from the fact that when Parmenides must choose a subject with which to illustrate the proposed training, the subject he chooses is the one itself: [17]

> Is it all right with you ... if I begin with myself and my own hypothesis? Shall I hypothesize about the one itself, and consider what the consequences must be, if it is one or if it is not one?
> (ἢ βούλεσθε ... ἀπ' ἐμαυτοῦ ἄρξωμαι καὶ τῆς ἐμαυτοῦ ὑποθέσεως, περὶ τοῦ ἑνὸς αὐτοῦ ὑποθέμενος, εἴτε ἕν ἐστιν εἴτε μὴ ἕν, τί χρὴ συμβαίνειν;) (137b1–4)

Now, Gill and Ryan mention that although the Greek text here reads, εἴτε ἕν ἐστιν εἴτε μὴ ἕν, some scholars have proposed emending the text so that they can translate: "if one is or if it is not."[18] Such an emendation makes Parmenides' hypothesis existential rather than predicative. Although there is no manuscript support for such an emendation the text is, in any case, arguably, ambiguous between the predicative and existential interpretations even without the emendation. Based upon the predicative reading, the question of whether the one is one, or not one, could be understood as asking whether the one is a whole with parts and therefore multiple and, in that sense, not one, or whether it is truly or strictly one, and therefore entirely devoid of multiplicity. Although the precise nature of this second way of being one might not be clear at this

---

16   Hence Walker (1938, 492): "For the problem of the One and the Many is not, basically, how one Idea may be composed of many Ideas or participated in by many things and still be one, but rather the essential significance of Unity and Plurality as such."
17   We should note that what Gill and Ryan (1996) translate here as "the one itself" is τὸ ἓν αὐτό, <u>not</u> αὐτὸ τὸ ἕν, the phrase used later to refer to the one of H1. In the above extract Parmenides says that he will hypothesise about τὸ ἓν αὐτό; I distinguish this from αὐτὸ τὸ ἕν by the comma punctuation used above.
18   Gill and Ryan (1996, 141n23). Cornford (1939, 108), influenced by Wundt (1935), does not translate per the received text. Allen (1997, 17) translates existentially and maintains (208 and n37) that no emendation is required as the text is ambiguous and that (209) "the existential meaning is fertile, in that it implies the predicative reading." Gill (2012, 59), responding to Allen, concedes "Grammatically he may be right, but idiomatically unlikely." See Meinwald (1991, 40–45) for an extensive discussion.

stage, we have, on the predicative reading, an indication that Parmenides may intend to present Socrates with this second way of being one, as part of the training which he is about to demonstrate. This might also explain Parmenides' strong emphasis upon considering intelligibles rather than sensibles. The latter are easily shown to be, in some way, multiple; Socrates has already made this point to Zeno:

> So if, in the case of stones and sticks and such things, someone tries to show that the same thing is many and one, we'll say that he is demonstrating something to be many and one, not the one to be many or the many one, and we'll say that he is saying nothing astonishing, but just what all of us would agree to.
> (ἐὰν οὖν τις τοιαῦτα ἐπιχειρῇ πολλὰ καὶ ἓν ταὐτὸν ἀποφαίνειν, λίθους καὶ ξύλα καὶ τὰ τοιαῦτα, τὶ φήσομεν αὐτὸν πολλὰ καὶ ἓν ἀποδεικνύναι, οὐ τὸ ἓν πολλὰ οὐδὲ τὰ πολλὰ ἕν, οὐδέ τι θαυμαστὸν λέγειν, ἀλλ' ἅπερ ἂν πάντες ὁμολογοῖμεν·) (129d2–6)

Scholars who favour an existential reading point to the consistency of such a reading with the hypotheses which constitute the second part of the dialogue. Although the *aporiai* of part one all relate to forms, Parmenides has now selected not forms but the one, as the subject which will constitute the basis of his training of Socrates. In any case, those who favour an existential reading and those who favour a predicative reading both accept that Socrates' earlier challenge in relation to the one itself is predicative: "But if he should demonstrate this thing itself, what one is, to be many, (εἰ ὃ ἔστιν ἕν, αὐτὸ τοῦτο πολλὰ ἀποδείξει) or, conversely, the many to be one; at this I'll be astonished" (129b6–c1). Can Parmenides respond to Socrates' challenge and present him with a way of being one, other than the way in which stones and sticks are one? Stones and sticks are "many and one," but they cease being one if they are divided so as to be in many places at the same time. Is there anything that does not cease being one if it is divided so as to be in many places at the same time? We do not find this among sensibles such as stones and sticks so, if there is such a one, it must be found in the other realm, among "the forms themselves, in things that are grasped by reasoning" (130a2).

I wish to avoid detailed consideration of how Parmenides' training, as a whole, is actually structured. This is set out in detail at 136a–c. However, I think that, for present purposes, this first step in Parmenides' demonstration of his proposed training for Socrates follows naturally from what I have said about the search for a one that does not cease being one if it is divided so as to be in many places at the same time. The first requirement is to consider intelligibles rather than sensibles because a one that does not cease being one if it is divided so as to be in many places at the same time does not occur in the sensible realm.

IX The First Hypothesis and Its Contribution

The training demonstrated by Parmenides in the case of the one begins with what is called the first hypothesis (H1). This overall demonstration of the training constitutes the second part, almost three quarters, of the dialogue. In this he begins, as we are led to expect from the first part of the dialogue, by considering the one and, I argue, immediately hypothesising a one that is not multiple and therefore not a whole with parts. We should also recall the important phrase already quoted above: Socrates has said that he would be astonished if someone could "demonstrate this thing itself, what one is, to be many." Such a demonstration would be impossible because he conceives "what one is" as entirely devoid of multiplicity. Parmenides, as if responding to Socrates' challenge, begins, I believe, by hypothesising that the one is indeed just one and not in any way multiple. His method of consequences will allow him to consider what the consequences will be if we assume that the one itself, what one is, is strictly non-multiple. So, we find that the first hypothesis begins by examining the consequences of denying all multiplicity to the one: "Very good," he said. "If it is one,[19] the one would not be many, would it?" (εἶεν δή, φάναι. εἰ ἕν ἐστιν, ἄλλο τι οὐκ ἂν εἴη πολλὰ τὸ ἕν;) (137c4–5). Hence, since this one is not many, we are hypothesising a one that is completely devoid of multiplicity. The first consequence, as we would anticipate from our earlier discussion, is that such a one will not be one by being a whole with parts. So, he says, "Then there cannot be a part of it nor can it be a whole (οὔτε ἄρα μέρος αὐτοῦ οὔτε ὅλον αὐτὸ δεῖ εἶναι) (137c5–6). He explains that this must be the case because, if such a one were to be a whole with parts, it would be multiple and no longer be just one. So, because all multiplicity is denied to the one, the subsequent argument leads to the consequences that it cannot be a whole with parts as a whole with parts is multiple. On the same basis, the argument continues, it is limitless because limits are parts, and this one does not have parts. It is also shown to

---

19   Gill and Ryan (1996) note that the Greek is underdetermined: the hypothesis could be rendered as "if it is one" or "if one is." The phrase can thus be read predicatively or existentially. However, the predicative reading leads to the existential reading. Rickless (2007, 114) thus makes the important point that the argument can proceed in exactly the same way based upon either rendering of the text here, because if the one is (existential reading), then the one is one (predicative reading).

enter into no relations whatsoever, either with itself or with anything else. This is because, as McCabe points out,[20] any relations would pluralise the one and it would thus no longer be just one. Consequently, it is not related to itself or to anything else as same, other, like, unlike, equal, unequal, greater, lesser, older, or younger; nor is it in time at all. Accordingly, it cannot even *be* and so, the argument suggests, it cannot even *be* one. Nor can it be known or spoken of or named, nor can it have any properties belonging to it.

Such a conclusion obviously presents interpretative challenges, and it is not surprising that Cornford concludes that "This cannot be a satisfactory account of Unity itself, but we must at least add "being" to unity, as we proceed to do in the next Hypothesis."[21] This strictly non-multiple one was, we thought, a way that Parmenides could present Socrates with a one that was not many and therefore not one merely by being a whole with parts. Socrates merely wished to deny multiplicity to the one, in making the quite reasonable claim that forms do not partake of their opposites: likeness does not partake of unlikeness; the one does not partake of multiplicity. As noted, Parmenides observes a similar principle at the start of the first hypothesis as quoted above: "Very good," he said. "If it is one, the one would not be many, would it?" (137c4–5). However the consequences that follow from Parmenides' repetition of Socrates' denial of any multiplicity to the one go far beyond what Socrates himself might have anticipated when he made his earlier claim. Rickless, in his comprehensive analysis of the argument of the first hypothesis, points out that the conclusions of the entire H1 argument are driven, for the most part, by this stricture, namely, that the one is not many.[22] Socrates' insistence on this in the first part of the dialogue demonstrates a connection between the argument of H1 in the second part and the proposition that forms are one, as defended by Socrates in the first part. As Rickless argues quite persuasively, once we accept the stipulation that the one is not many, the other consequences of H1 follow inevitably, including the conclusion that the one is not. These consequences were certainly not anticipated by Socrates when he insisted to Zeno that the one should not be many. However, H1 concludes with the following exchange: "Is it possible that these things are so for the one?" // "I certainly don't think so" (Ἢ δυνατὸν οὖν περὶ τὸ ἓν ταῦτα οὕτως ἔχειν;—Οὔκουν ἔμοιγε δοκεῖ) (142a6–8). Such a response to these strange conclusions, surely unexpected by Socrates, who is now a mere observer, is muted and somewhat ambiguous. In spite of the huge

---

20   McCabe (1994, 116): "relations ... are real features of the relata, and thus pluralise. But the one, as such, cannot be pluralised; and so it is precluded from all relations of identity."
21   Cornford (1939, 133).
22   Rickless (2007, 114ff).

range of possible interpretations of the first hypothesis and its status in relation to the dialogue as a whole, Parmenides has presented us with a one that is entirely devoid of multiplicity and is not one merely by being a whole with parts. Gill[23] argues that Socrates must now abandon his earlier thesis that the one is not multiple, but I do not think such a move is mandated by the argument thus far, nor am I convinced that the argument of H1 is a *reductio*. The thesis that the one is not multiple should nevertheless be rejected as a means of progressing our understanding of participation, since a one of this kind, however useful it may prove to be in exploring other issues that arise in the dialogue, will not further our understanding of participation, because such a one is not divisible and therefore cannot participate in anything. This, in my view, is a crucial point for the understanding of the role of the one of H1 in the context of our overall discussion here of the dilemma of participation and the extent to which it is progressed towards resolution in the *Parmenides*.

Parmenides opens H1 with the conclusion that a strictly non-multiple one does not have parts. But if it does not have parts, is it divisible? And if it is not divisible, how can it be divided? And if it cannot be divided, how can it be participated in? We should remind ourselves of Socrates' earlier acceptance that forms must be divisible in order to be participated in:

> "So the forms themselves are divisible,[24] Socrates," he said, "and things that partake of them would partake of a part; no longer would a whole form, but only a part of it, be in each thing." // "It does appear that way." (131c5–8)

In what I regard as a return, in the second part of the dialogue, to this issue of divisibility as a requirement for participation, we find this general claim, in the second hypothesis: "What is divisible must be as many as its parts. // Necessarily[25] (τό γε μεριστὸν πολλὴ ἀνάγκη εἶναι τοσαῦτα ὅσαπερ μέρη.—Ἀνάγκη) (144 d 4–5). This point, including the connection between part one and part two of the dialogue, is well made by Allen who also indicates the recurrence of the dilemma of participation in the *Philebus*:

> The Dilemma of Participation, therefore, though a reductio, issues in an implication by reason of the putative difference in modality of its

---

23 Gill (2012, 20–21).
24 Trans. Gill and Ryan (1996), rendering μεριστά as "divisible." They are not consistent in their translation of this adjective at 144d4.
25 Trans. Allen (1997), repeating the translation of μεριστόν as "divisible," as at 131c5.

disjuncts: if there is participation neither of whole nor part of an Idea, there is no participation; but if there is participation, it cannot be of whole but must be of part of an Idea. This difference in modality is explicitly marked at 144d2, and at *Philebus* 15b6–7, where the Dilemma is restated. The hinge effect of the Dilemma—no participation, or participation in parts—is important for arguments that follow.[26]

And so, if we were to revisit the part-one *aporiai* at this stage, expecting that a one of this nature might progress their resolution, we would surely be frustrated. The *aporiai* of part one arose because forms appeared to cease being one when instantiated in sensibles, because they are, thereby, divided and therefore no longer one. This strictly non-multiple one of H1 has no parts and is therefore not divisible, and so it cannot be instantiated in sensibles or be participated in. Accordingly, it cannot be the end of our search for a one that remains one when divided, because the one of H1 is not divisible.

The account of the one that the H1 argument presents establishes that such a one is other than being and, accordingly, does not include being. A comprehensive ontology therefore must include at least one further element in addition to this one of H1. There must be at least two elements, one and being, so that, as Cornford explains, this non-multiple one, or indeed anything else, can be (exist). The second hypothesis will make this addition. Consequently, I believe that Cornford's conclusion affords the most practical understanding for our present purposes: "This cannot be a satisfactory account of Unity itself, but we must at least add 'being' to unity, as we proceed to do in the next Hypothesis."[27]

x   The Second Hypothesis and its Contribution—Excluding Participation

The second hypothesis begins by proposing that the one *is* and by stating that if the one is to be, it must partake of being. This merely makes the now obvious point that the one, just by itself, cannot be; in order for it to be, we require another element, namely being. The one, partaking of being, constitutes a whole with two parts: one and being. This whole is called "the one that is" (τὸ ἓν ὄν). The one that is, the one of H2, being a whole with two parts, one and being, is therefore multiple, and indeed the argument will demonstrate that, as a result, it is unlimited in multiplicity (ἄπειρον τὸ πλῆθος). The one of H1, which is called

---

26   Allen (1997, 133).
27   Cornford (1939, 133).

the one itself, was, in contrast, denied all multiplicity and was therefore unable to constitute a whole with parts. Hence Parmenides presents a one that is many, the one of H2, the one that is: "'Do we say that the one partakes of being, and hence is?' // 'Yes.' 'And for this reason the one that is was shown to be many'" (Οὐσίας φαμὲν μετέχειν τὸ ἕν, διὸ ἔστιν;—Ναί.—Καὶ διὰ ταῦτα δὴ τὸ ἓν ὂν πολλὰ ἐφάνη) (143a4–6). We need not, for the purposes of this paper, enter into a discussion of the status of the one of H1 and whether Socrates must abandon his thesis or not. I will make the case, in due course, that the H1 argument does have a role to play in the development of the overall argument presented by Parmenides. The one of H2 is a one of a different kind; it is a whole with two parts, one and being, and is one in this way.[28] However, being a whole with parts, it is multiple or many, and so it is, I suggest, Parmenides' response to Socrates' challenge to show that "what one is" could indeed be many or multiple. The H2 argument therefore presents a one that can be many, because once we allow the one to be, and thus to partake of being, it will be multiple since it will be a whole with parts. The one that is (just) one is the one of H1—the one itself, the one that is devoid of multiplicity and therefore not divisible. The one of H2 is a whole with two parts—the one itself and being—and as such it is multiple or many. Now this one is a whole with parts, but is it one in the way in which stones and sticks are one? Stones and sticks can be divided, and, once divided, they are no longer one. Can we divide the one of H2? If so, what will happen to it?

If we assume that we can divide it into its two component parts, in the same way that any sensible object can be divided so as to be in many places at the same time, and thus no longer be one, we run into a problem. Let's refer to its two parts as the-one-part, and the-being-part. If we were actually to divide the one of H2 into these two parts, we would end up with the-one-part as one of the parts, but would it still be (exist)? Parmenides argues that it must, because being cannot be absent from any actual part of anything. Neither the one of H2, nor indeed anything else, could have a part that does not exist as one of its constituents. Furthermore, having performed this division, what would be the

---

28   Miller argues that the subject of the first hypothesis is the "One beyond the order of spatio-temporal existence"; the being that it has, if it has being at all, is the "timeless being of the forms." The subject of the second hypothesis is the One that is "subject to the categories, the basic kinds of character, proper to spatio-temporal existence" (1986, 96). Thus, Miller concludes, the consequences drawn in the first and second hypotheses are not contradictory because they apply to different subjects. His phrases "timeless being of the forms" (96) and "timeless forms" (90) are discussed extensively in nn 22 and 23 (241–242). He is referring to *Timaeus* 37e5ff, where Plato uses the phrase τὴν ἀίδιον οὐσίαν—eternal or everlasting being.

status of the-being-part? Would it still be one? Surely it would still be one; how could a part not be one part, and what would it mean for being (οὐσία), not to be one? Such an outcome would be absurd. Parmenides again confirms this by stating that if the one of H2 were divided, being would still be one. The above elaborates an argument, in the form of a regress, which runs from 142e to 143a. The argument does not actually make such divisions in the one of H2, but it does consider each part, one and being, and shows that the one can never be separated from being, or being from the one. It thus concludes that the one of H2 constitutes an unlimited multiplicity but still remains what it is, namely, one.

However this initial argument in H2 does not consider a situation in which there is any participation in the one of H2, the very process that gave rise to the part-one *aporiai*. The one of H2, at this stage in the argument, has been shown to be divisible because it has parts, but it has not yet been divided. Nevertheless Parmenides has, at this stage, presented Socrates with a one that remains one even though it constitutes an unlimited multiplicity, or more precisely, he has presented a one which, if it were to be divided, would yield another one that is only numerically distinct from the one that has been divided. Such a process of division could be carried out indefinitely, and so there is, potentially, an unlimited multiplicity of such ones, each of which is (exists) and is one. The one always is, and being is always one. We should note, however, as Allen puts it: "This suggests not that the presence of parts derives from the process of division, but that the process of division is possible because of the presence of parts."[29] This is a very important point for our present purposes. This one of H2 can be participated in because it is divisible, in contrast to the one of H1 which could not be participated in because it did not have parts and was not therefore divisible. We need not consider, for the purposes of this analysis, whether we should understand οὐσία, here translated as "being," in the purely existential sense, as this translation implies, or in the sense of essence. In either case the one of H2 is multiple, and yet it is one; it is divisible because it has parts, and it can be divided and still be one, and it is unlimited in multiplicity and still one. We now need to consider how such a one will fare when there is participation.

---

29   Allen (1997, 260).

XI The Second Hypothesis and Its Contribution—Including Participation

The part-one *aporiai* arose from consideration of the instantiation of intelligibles in sensibles or the participation of sensibles in intelligibles. The one introduced in the previous section would retain its unity were it to be divided. It is an intelligible one and, although it is multiple, and thus capable of being divided into its parts, it retains its unity even when divided. This is in contrast to sensible ones, which cease to be one when they are divided into their parts. Parmenides will now show how this intelligible one will fare when it is instantiated and he will, again, confine the consideration to the intelligible realm. So, in contrast to the participation arguments in part one, the participants here will be intelligible objects, not sensibles. Also, there will be a strong ontological connection between the one and its participants.

According to the previous argument, the-one-part of the one of H2 cannot be separated from being, for the-one-part must exist and it needs being so that it may exist. Neither can the-being-part of the one of H2 be separated from the one, since being would then no longer be one, which again is absurd. Parmenides next asks us to consider the-one-part, just by itself, without being. Because the one cannot actually be separated from being, this consideration must be done by way of a thought experiment, or τῇ διανοίᾳ, as Parmenides puts it. Parmenides refers to the-one-part of the one of H2 as "the one itself,"[30] and he introduces it as follows:

> "And what about the one itself, which we say partakes of being? If we grasp it in thought (τῇ διανοίᾳ) alone by itself, without that of which we say it partakes, will it appear to be only one, or will this same thing also appear to be many?" // "One, I should think." // "Let's see."
> (Τί δέ; αὐτὸ τὸ ἕν, ὃ δή φαμεν οὐσίας μετέχειν, ἐὰν αὐτὸ τῇ διανοίᾳ μόνον καθ' αὑτὸ λάβωμεν ἄνευ τούτου οὗ φαμεν μετέχειν, ἆρά γε ἓν μόνον φανήσεται ἢ καὶ πολλὰ τὸ αὐτὸ τοῦτο;—Ἕν, οἶμαι ἔγωγε.—Ἴδωμεν δή.) (143a6–b1)

The argument then proceeds to establish, by the non-identity principle, that, since there is participation, the one itself must be other than being, and being must be other than the one itself. However, these two are not different from

---

[30] We recall that this is the phrase used to describe the one of H1. Accordingly, Plato may intend us to regard this step as reverting to the one, as presented in the first hypothesis. See Allen (1997, 261) for such a consideration. We need not decide, finally, in this paper, whether such a back reference to the first hypothesis is indeed intended here, although it certainly seems likely to me.

each other because of their own nature. So, if there are these two—being and one—and they are different from each other, and they cannot be different by their own nature, there must be a third element, "difference," by which these two can indeed be different from each other. And so, we have three elements: being, difference and one. Once it is shown that there are these three, the argument establishes that all number(s) without exception, must exist. And since each number *is*, and since number is unlimited in multiplicity, being too is unlimited in multiplicity, having been divided by number. So, Parmenides' argument that being is infinitely divided runs as follows: because number is unlimited in multiplicity, and each number is (exists), there is an unlimited multiplicity of things that are, beings. Being is thus divided into as many things as there are numbers—it is divided into a multiplicity that is without limit.

We now come to the point in the argument with which we began this paper. We have seen that being is divided and is unlimited in multiplicity because, once there is being, one, and difference, there must be all number. And since number is unlimited in multiplicity, and every number *is*, or every number may be said to be, being must also be unlimited in multiplicity. But crucially for his consideration of the one, every number that may be said to be, exists as one number, and there is an unlimited multiplicity of these. Hence the argument continues:

> "Now, is there any of them [numbers] that is part of being, yet not one part?"
> "How could that happen?"
> "I take it, on the contrary, that if in fact it is, it must always, as long as it is, be some one thing; it cannot be nothing."
> "Necessarily."
> "So the one is added to every part of being and is not absent from a smaller or a larger, or any other, part."
> "Just so."
> "So, being one, is it, as a whole, in many places at the same time? Look at this carefully."
> "I am, and I see that it's impossible."
> "Therefore as divided, if in fact not as a whole; for surely it will be present to all the parts of being at the same time only as divided."
> (Τί οὖν; ἔστι τι αὐτῶν ὃ ἔστι μὲν μέρος τῆς οὐσίας, οὐδὲν μέντοι μέρος;—Καὶ πῶς ἄν τοι τοῦτο γένοιτο;—Ἀλλ᾽ εἴπερ γε οἶμαι ἔστιν, ἀνάγκη αὐτὸ ἀεί, ἕωσπερ ἂν ᾖ, ἕν γέ τι εἶναι, μηδὲν δὲ ἀδύνατον.—Ἀνάγκη.—πρὸς ἅπαντι ἄρα ἑκάστῳ τῷ τῆς οὐσίας μέρει πρόσεστιν τὸ ἕν, οὐκ ἀπολειπόμενον οὔτε σμικροτέρου οὔτε μείζονος μέρους οὔτε ἄλλου οὐδενός.—Οὕτω.—ἆρα οὖν ἓν ὂν πολλαχοῦ

ἅμα ὅλον ἐστί; τοῦτο ἄθρει.—Ἀλλ' ἀθρῶ καὶ ὁρῶ ὅτι ἀδύνατον.—Μεμερισμένον ἄρα, εἴπερ μὴ ὅλον· ἄλλως γάρ που οὐδαμῶς ἅμα ἅπασι τοῖς τῆς οὐσίας μέρεσιν παρέσται ἢ μεμερισμένον). (144c2–d4)[31]

This part of the H2 argument may be summarised as follows: once there is the one itself, being, and difference, there is number, unlimited in multiplicity. Once there is number, unlimited in multiplicity, being is unlimited in multiplicity because each number partakes of being and there is an unlimited multiplicity of numbers. But since each number exists as one number, and whatever is, is one (thing), the one itself is therefore divided by being and is unlimited in multiplicity. Parmenides summarises his conclusions as follows:

> "Furthermore, what is divisible[32] certainly must be as numerous as its parts."
> "Necessarily."
> "So we were not speaking truly just now, when we said that being had been distributed into the most numerous parts. It is not distributed into more parts than the one, but, as it seems, into parts equal to the one, since neither is being absent from the one, nor is the one absent from being. On the contrary, being two, they are always equal throughout all things."
> "It appears absolutely so."
> "Therefore, the one itself, chopped up by being, is many and unlimited in multitude."
> "Apparently."
> "So not only is it the case that the one being is many, but also the one itself, completely distributed by being, must be many."
> "Absolutely."
> (Οὐκ ἄρα ἀληθῆ ἄρτι ἐλέγομεν λέγοντες ὡς πλεῖστα μέρη ἡ οὐσία νενεμημένη εἴη. οὐδὲ γὰρ πλείω τοῦ ἑνὸς νενέμηται, ἀλλ' ἴσα, ὡς ἔοικε, τῷ ἑνί· οὔτε γὰρ τὸ ὂν τοῦ ἑνὸς ἀπολείπεται οὔτε τὸ ἓν τοῦ ὄντος, ἀλλ' ἐξισοῦσθον δύο ὄντε ἀεὶ παρὰ πάντα.—Παντάπασιν οὕτω φαίνεται.—Τὸ ἓν ἄρα αὐτὸ κεκερματισμένον ὑπὸ τῆς οὐσίας πολλά τε καὶ ἄπειρα τὸ πλῆθός ἐστιν.—Φαίνεται.—Οὐ μόνον ἄρα τὸ ὂν ἓν πολλά ἐστιν, ἀλλὰ καὶ αὐτὸ τὸ ἓν ὑπὸ τοῦ ὄντος διανενεμημένον πολλὰ ἀνάγκη εἶναι.—Παντάπασι μὲν οὖν). (144d5–e7)

---

31 Gill and Ryan (1996) translation adjusted to render πρόσειμι as 'added to' rather than 'attached to.' Note 'present to' at 144d4—πάρειμι.
32 I adjust Gill and Ryan's (1996) translation of μεριστόν here to be consistent with 131c5.

In concluding this argument, Parmenides emphasises that it is not just the one of H2, the one being, that is divided into an unlimited multiplicity and still remains one. The one of H2 has already been shown to retain its unity upon division. But this latter argument leads to the conclusion that even the one itself, considered τῇ διανοίᾳ, becomes unlimited in multiplicity, because being is unlimited in multiplicity, and the one is coextensive with being, in the sense that, "being two, they are always equal throughout all things" (ἐξισοῦσθον δύο ὄντε ἀεὶ παρὰ πάντα). We now have participation in the one, and so the one is not just divisible, as at 142d9–143a1, but is actually divided as a consequence of being present to all numbers, while still remaining one.

The one itself is divided by being—this is Parmenides' somewhat terse conclusion to the argument here. I think we must understand him to be saying that the one of H1 was not divisible and so there could be no participation in such a one. But once being was added, and one and being were shown to be coextensive, it then became possible for the one itself to be as divided as being is, and therefore unlimited in multiplicity. This is the sense in which I think we should understand the conclusion that the one itself is divided by being: the addition of being, and the fact that one and being are thus coextensive, and the fact that being is divided among the unlimited multiplicity of things that are, are what allow the one to be divided. In this sense the one itself is divided by being.

We should note at this stage that the relationship between the one and the numbers in which it is instantiated is captured here by the verb πρόσεστιν ("added to") rather than the verbs μετέχειν or μεταλαμβάνειν that were translated as "participate" or "share in," in the first part of the dialogue. As the later argument continues, the verb πάρεστι ("present to") is used. In due course, we shall consider what significance this usage may have.

XII   What This Argument Establishes—the One Must Be Divisible

So, let us now review the argument and clarify what it establishes in terms of the dilemma of participation. In order to provide Socrates with the training he lacked, Parmenides undertook to hypothesise "about the one itself." According to Parmenides, lack of training on Socrates' part lay behind the *aporiai* that he encountered in expounding his theory of forms. Although we have not analysed every aspect of Parmenides' training, we have considered the first hypothesis, and part of the second hypothesis, up to the point where, I suggest, the *aporia* from the Day/Sail argument in part one is revisited and, I believe, progressed in the direction of diagnosis and resolution. I would like to revisit some of what Socrates said in the first part and see if Parmenides' training, as considered thus far, enables us to find out where the roots of the *aporiai* may lie, in the very arguments that Socrates uses. Let's begin before the *aporiai*, with Socrates' commitment to forms' being one. He says: "But if he should demonstrate this thing itself, what one is, to be many, or, conversely, the many to be one; at this I'll be astonished. (ἀλλ᾽ εἰ ὃ ἔστιν ἕν, αὐτὸ τοῦτο πολλὰ ἀποδείξει καὶ αὖ τὰ πολλὰ δὴ ἕν, τοῦτο ἤδη θαυμάσομαι) (129b6–c1). This is part of an overall argument in which Socrates makes the general, and quite reasonable point that forms should not themselves exhibit qualities opposite to those of which they are the forms; likeness itself will never be unlike; the one will never be many. But when Parmenides, in the first hypothesis, takes the one and excludes all multiplicity from it, we see that the consequences of hypothesising such strict non-multiplicity include the conclusions that the one cannot enter into any relations, cannot partake of being, and hence cannot even exist. More significantly for the dilemma of participation, it does not have parts, is therefore not divisible and, as a consequence, cannot be divided in order to be participated in.

Does the H1 argument, as Gill argues, prompt Socrates to abandon the idea that the one must not be many or multiple?[33] For the purposes of our present analysis I think we may conclude that the dilemma of participation from the Day/Sail *aporia* of part one, will be progressed in part two only through the one of H2, because the one of H1 cannot enter into any relations and cannot therefore be participated in. However, based upon our analysis thus far, I think the one of H1 certainly serves an argumentative purpose here in allowing Parmenides to show Socrates that any strict insistence that the one should not be multiple in any way, far from resolving the *aporiai*, gives rise to additional problems.

Accordingly, the very first argument in Parmenides' training shows that if all multiplicity is denied to the one, it cannot have parts and thus be divisible, and not being divisible, it cannot be divided in order to be participated in. Socrates may, perhaps, be able to hold to the claim that there is indeed a one that is not multiple in any way, but he must admit that such a one will not help him resolve the dilemma of participation. Some multiplicity must be allowed to the one and, in the next hypothesis, this will involve allowing it to partake of being and thus be (exist). The training, by the end of the first hypothesis, has already shown Socrates that it is not possible to deny all multiplicity to the one and still have participation. He therefore needs to consider the exact nature of this

---

33   Gill (2012, 20–21).

multiple one and the extent to which this will resolve any of the difficulties with forms from the first part.

XIII   What This Argument Establishes—the One Must Be Divided

The *aporiai* of part one involve forms, each of which must be one, turning out to be many under the circumstances of participation. We noted that the one was spoken of in the first part of the dialogue using the ὃ ἔστιν x formulation that Socrates uses to describe forms. However, if the one is a form, it is a form in which all of the other forms must participate since each of them is one. If we were to ask why each form is one, we could simply respond, based upon Socrates' introduction of forms at 129a, that it is one because it participates in "the one," another form. But we have already surmised that Socrates' unstated argument as to why a form must be one must be stronger than this. Since a form is defined as "what x is," the form must be unique; "for any property F, there is exactly one form of F-ness,"[34] or there is at most one Form of G, for every G.[35] So, he does not need to invoke participation of the form in another form, the one, in order to account for the fact that any form is one; the form, by its very nature, is necessarily unique and therefore one in that sense. Being a form and being one are inseparable.

Some such argument as this seems to lie behind Socrates' persistent commitment to forms' being one. The difficulty Parmenides poses to him arises when there is participation in this unique form and it is divided so as to be in many places at the same time. Socrates must accept that, for participation, the form must be divisible, and, with participation, the form apparently ceases to be one because it is divided. He thus encounters the dilemma of participation, a dilemma that centres upon forms' being one and remaining one. We have seen that the first stage of Parmenides' training of Socrates was to direct him away from sensible objects towards intelligible objects. Accordingly, to give a demonstration of the training, Parmenides undertook to hypothesise about an intelligible object, the one.

When Parmenides introduced "the one that is," the existent one, he showed that this one was divisible and could indeed be divided and still be one. Divisibility into its two component parts was not inimical to its remaining one. Because it was divisible, and any part of it could, in turn, be divided once more,

---

34   See Rickless (2007, xiii, 28, and 73n.17).
35   See Fitelson and Zalta. $\forall x,y,G[(IsAFormOf(x,G)\ \&\ IsAFormOf(y,G)) \rightarrow x=y]$. Theorem 1b: There is at most one Form of G, for every G.

without limit, such a one was unlimited in multiplicity. Unlike sensible objects, which no longer remain one when divided into the parts that constitute them, this intelligible object, the existent one, remains one when it is divided. Socrates now has some basis on which to accept that something can be divided and still be one, a possibility he strongly denied at 131c11. This denial was central to the dilemma of participation in the first part, but Parmenides has now demonstrated that the one can be divided into an unlimited multiplicity, and still be one, and we should recall Allen's point that "the process of division is possible because of the presence of parts."[36] So such a one is unlimited in multiplicity, and it is infinitely divisible[37] because of the presence of this unlimited plurality of parts. It has infinitely many parts, and yet it is still one. But we have not yet mentioned participation, or some means whereby there could be multiple instances of this "one that is." If Parmenides is to revisit the dilemma of participation he now needs to consider how this one may actually be divided, and how anything else other than the one can thus be one.

xiv What This Argument Establishes—How the One Itself Gets Divided

Since the part-one *aporiai* centre upon forms' remaining one when participated in, we should expect Parmenides to revisit this issue. In the second part of the dialogue, the issue of participation may be reduced to the following question: how can anything else, other than the one, be one? The above argument concludes that the one of H2 is unlimited in multiplicity; it consists of an infinite number of parts. Gill describes these parts as what Harte calls, "property-parts," the parts being of just two sorts: one-parts and being-parts.[38] Allen summarises this argument as showing that the one that is constitutes an infinite multiplicity, which "has the dense plurality characteristic of a continuum."[39] Based upon either understanding of the argument, such an account of the multiplicity of the one is not particularly useful for understanding participation because the one has only a single instance, being.

However, Parmenides does go on, via the second argument for unlimited multiplicity, to indicate that there can indeed be multiple instances of the one, all numbers. Thus, as Allen succinctly puts it, "the existence of a plurality with

---

36   Allen (1997, 260).
37   See Allen (1997, 252ff) for a detailed discussion of this issue.
38   See Gill (2012, 79). Gill's reference is to Harte (2002, 70).
39   Allen (1997, 261).

three members [one, being and difference] implies the existence of plurality with infinitely many members, namely, the plurality of numbers."[40] This latter argument establishes that there can be multiple instances of the one, indeed an unlimited multiplicity thereof. Allen's formulation of the purpose of this particular argument is very precise:

> But the aim of the argument is not to show that if the numbers are one, they partake of Unity conceived apart from its own being. It is to show that Unity, conceived apart from its own being, has parts if the numbers are one.[41]

Parmenides has now shown that the one "considered apart from its own being" has parts[42] and is in many places at the same time because it is present to each member of this plurality of numbers, and so he has shown how the one gets divided so as to be in many places at the same time. If we wish to explore the question of how anything else other than the one can be one, we are now equipped to do so using the example of number. In what way is each number belonging to this unlimited multiplicity of numbers one?

xv What This Argument Establishes—How Anything Other Than the One Can Be One

We have already noted above, in the case of forms, that because they are by definition unique and therefore one, we do not need to suppose that they participate in the one in order to account for the fact that they are one. They are necessarily one and cannot be other than one. We have also noted that in the second hypothesis when he speaks of numbers' being one, Parmenides is careful to avoid the earlier term, participation, which translates μετέχειν in the first part of the dialogue. Instead πρόσεστιν (added to) is the first verb he uses, rather than the verbs μετέχειν or μεταλαμβάνειν, which were used in the first part of

---

40 Allen (1997, 266), bracketed words mine.
41 See Allen (1997, 277).
42 These parts may be regarded as what Harte (2002, 70) calls "instance-parts"; each number is an instance of the one. In the first H2 argument for the unlimited multiplicity of the one, the multiplicity of parts are all property-parts and there is only a single instance part of the one, namely being. Allen (1997, 275) also discusses this issue: "Previously, if Unity partook of Being, its own being was part of it. We now find a use in which a given number is part of number, and the being of that number part of Being. These are distinguishable uses."

the dialogue. As the later argument continues, the verb πάρεστι (present to) is used, and so he says: "for surely it [the one] will be present to all the parts of being at the same time only as divided" (ἄλλως γάρ που οὐδαμῶς ἅμα ἅπασι τοῖς τῆς οὐσίας μέρεσιν παρέσται ἢ μεμερισμένον) (144d3–4). This usage is a further indication that the model of participation employed in the early part of the dialogue, and described by Socrates at 129a in the context of sensible objects, may not apply to the consideration of intelligible objects in the later argument. Let's repeat Allen's formulation: "the existence of a plurality with three members (one, being and difference) implies the existence of plurality with infinitely many members, namely, the plurality of numbers."[43] Every number in this plurality must be and must be one; one and being are inseparable, in this argument, from what it is to be a number. A number must be *a* number, and any number that is *a* number must be one number. This point is emphasized by Parmenides: "I take it, on the contrary, that if in fact it is, it must always, as long as it is, be some one thing; it cannot be nothing" (ἀλλ᾽ εἴπερ γε οἶμαι ἔστιν, ἀνάγκη αὐτὸ ἀεί, ἕωσπερ ἂν ᾖ, ἕν γέ τι εἶναι, μηδὲν δὲ ἀδύνατον) (144c4–5).[44] Either it is "some one thing" (ἕν τι), or it is nothing. Therefore, it is not possible, except by way of a thought experiment, or τῇ διανοίᾳ, as Parmenides put it, to separate any number from being or from the one; every number necessarily is and is one. The one is present to them, or added to them, because of what they are in themselves as these intelligible objects. The concept of participation in the one, as presented in the first part of the dialogue, does not seem to be required in order to account for the fact that they are one.[45] The verb "added to" or "present to" better reflects what actually takes place. In the case of these intelligible objects, such as numbers, whatever is (exists) is one, and whatever is one is (exists), because the one and being are coextensive, or as Parmenides puts it: "Since neither is being absent from the one, nor is the one absent from being. On the contrary, being two, they are always equal throughout all things" (οὔτε γὰρ τὸ ὂν τοῦ ἑνὸς ἀπολείπεται οὔτε τὸ ἓν τοῦ ὄντος, ἀλλ᾽ ἐξισοῦσθον δύο ὄντε ἀεὶ παρὰ πάντα) (144e1–3). In the first argument for the multiplicity of the one of H2, the one was inseparable from its own being, and its own being was spoken of as part of the one. In this latter argument about numbers, every particular number is part of number, and the being of any number is part of that number and also part of being, while the oneness of any part of being is part of the one itself. So intelligible objects such as numbers are one by their own nature or

---

43 Allen (1997, 266), bracketed words mine.
44 See Allen (1997, 275) for a similar point in Aristotle, *Metaph.* x, 1054a 18: "to be one is just to be a particular thing."
45 Allen (1997, 276–277), in commenting upon this passage continues to use the language of participation and does not refer to the change in the verbs used.

ontological origin; being (existing) and being one are each inseparable from what they are. Such objects are inseparably related to being and to the one insofar as they are (exist) and are one.[46]

XVI The Training—What Has Been Accomplished and What Remains?

There are four headings above under which I have attempted to summarise what Parmenides' argument, presented as part of Socrates' training, establishes: that the one cannot be entirely devoid of multiplicity in such a way that it is not divisible, if there is to be participation; how the one can be many and divisible and still remain one; how the one gets divided; and how anything other than the one can be one. Parmenides' entire argument is governed by his overall principle of preferring intelligible objects over sensible objects. He adheres to this principle by confining all of the arguments, up to the point in H2 (144e7) where our discussion ended, to the intelligible realm, and by first considering the consequences that follow if the one is just one and strictly non-multiple and then the consequences that follow if the one is allowed to be multiple.

I have argued that the purpose of this training was to allow Socrates to avoid the part-one *aporiai* in relation to forms' remaining one when they are participated in, and thus divided. I have made the case, through analysis of his arguments, that Parmenides clearly revisits the 131b–c Day/Sail *aporia* once more in the second part of the dialogue at 144c–d and progresses its resolution. In addition, I believe that further textual evidence that he is revisiting the earlier *aporia* is very strong, insofar as he asks Aristoteles to give careful consideration to a relatively straightforward question,[47] the answer to which, without the earlier context, appears quite obvious. Furthermore, the question faced by Aristoteles in relation to the one, at 144c8, is substantially the same as the question faced earlier by Socrates, in relation to forms, at 131c9: can a form, or the one, be in many places at the same time (πολλαχοῦ ἅμα) and still be one? In the earlier case, Socrates responds with an emphatic "not at all"; later, in the case of Aristoteles, it is presumed, without question, that the answer is yes.

---

46   See previous footnote quoting Allen (1997, 275).
47   As pointed out earlier, the wording of the injunction to Aristoteles to consider the question carefully (τοῦτο ἄθρει), is, itself, striking as it is the sole occurrence of this verb in the *Parmenides*.

Indeed, the phrase πολλαχοῦ ἅμα, meaning "in many places at the same time," is conspicuous in itself, because it occurs only three times in the dialogue: twice in the Day/Sail argument and once, at 144d1, when Parmenides revisits the Day/Sail argument again in H2. This later occurrence is certainly noteworthy; the two earlier uses related to manifest objects, which are indeed, literally, in many places. But the last use of the word relates to intelligible objects, namely, numbers, which, of course, do not have physical location; numbers must, therefore, be understood as having an intelligible location. Hence the phrase πολλαχοῦ ἅμα cannot retain its literal meaning, and its use by Parmenides in an unusual context seems to be another way of indicating a return to the Day/Sail argument where the phrase was used twice previously.

I think we can be quite satisfied from the textual evidence, summarised above, that Parmenides intends us to reconsider the Day/Sail *aporia*, once we are armed with materials from the training that has intervened. I also believe we should note the occurrence of the word μεριστά (divisible, as applied to forms) at 131c5 and its recurrence at 144d4 in the general statement connecting divisibility with the presence of parts. These are the only two occurrences of the word in the dialogue and I regard this as a significant indication that Plato intends us to have evolved our understanding of divisibility and its role in participation through the intervening arguments.

The dialogue has not spelled out, by this point (144e7) in H2, how the preceding principles and the conduct of the hypotheses should be directly applied to that earlier *aporia*. Parmenides leaves that to Socrates; Plato leaves it to the reader. Parmenides simply presents us with the acceptance in H2 of something that was denied as an impossibility in the first part of the dialogue. The argument that intervenes between the initial denial in part one and the subsequent acceptance in part two does indeed, I have argued, afford the basis for such acceptance, and I have attempted to explore, in this paper, how Parmenides' arguments accomplish this.

Those arguments and their associated principles, guidelines, and hypotheses have now been analysed and summarised above. However, the initial *aporia* concerned the participation of sensible objects in intelligible forms, whereas Parmenides' subsequent hypotheses and the later conclusions relate entirely to intelligible objects. Furthermore, the part-one *aporiai* concerned forms' remaining one when participated in by multiple sensible objects, whereas the conclusions at 144c-d relate to the one's remaining one when present to multiple intelligible objects, namely numbers. We should also note that in the second part of the dialogue there is a strong ontological connection between the participants, the numbers, and what they participate in, the one. Yet, in part one there was no such strong connection because we were considering forms, which are intelligible objects, being instantiated in sensible particulars. By "ontological connection" here I mean, as Allen puts it,[48] that the existence of the one "implies the existence of the number series." So, there is an ontological dependence of the number series upon the one, in the sense described by Aristotle and attributed by him to Plato: "a thing is prior in respect of its nature and substance when it is possible for it to *be* without other things but not them without it: this division was used by Plato."[49] To revisit the earlier *aporia* in full, in the light of the unfolding of the argument as far as 144c–d, we would need to return to the consideration of forms rather than the one. To do so, we would need to clarify the precise relationship between forms and the one or unity. We would also need to return to the consideration of sensible objects and their participation in the one and in forms. All of these considerations present huge challenges, but the real work with Plato's *Parmenides*, in my opinion, lies in taking up such challenges set by Parmenides and Plato and in engaging with the associated issues, using the approach taught by Parmenides in training Socrates. And so, Allen, referring to the dilemma of participation, says:

> It is not too much to say that this dilemma is fundamental to everything in the *Parmenides* that follows; it is the only criticism that Plato will afterwards, in the *Philebus* (15b–c), repeat. The *Philebus* suggests that the dilemma is *aporetic*, a source of perplexity if the wrong admissions are made, and of easy passage, given the right ones. This statement is a sufficient reason to suppose that the Dilemma of Participation, and the criticisms of Ideas in the *Parmenides* that depend on it, are put neither as trivial fallacies nor fatal objections, but as problems to be solved.[50]

I hope that this article has made some contribution to the solution of these problems.

---

48 Allen (1997, 266).
49 Kirwan's translation (1971, 45) of *Metaph.* v, 1019a 1–4: τὰ δὲ [sc. λέγεται πρότερα καὶ ὕστερα] κατὰ φύσιν καὶ οὐσίαν, ὅσα ἐνδέχεται εἶναι ἄνευ ἄλλων, ἐκεῖνα δὲ ἄνευ ἐκείνων μή· ᾗ διαιρέσει ἐχρήσατο Πλάτων.
50 Allen (1997, 128).

COLLOQUIUM 1

Commentary on Horan

Darren Gardner
New York University

Abstract

This commentary examines several key points in David Horan's paper "The Argumentative Unity of Plato's *Parmenides*." First, I discuss the general view of the paper, which engages with the first two hypotheses and in particular, the thought experiment passage in hypothesis 2 that is seen as a key to resolving the dilemma of participation. I consider the proposed view that hypothesis 1 takes up from its premise a strictly unitary, or non-multiple "one," and hypothesis 2 takes up from its premise a one that admits of multiplicity, not a non-multiple "one." I argue for an alternative reading whereby the premise of hypothesis 1 is not "if one is one" and hypothesis 2 is "if one is not one," but rather that both hypotheses fall under the premise "if one is."

Keywords

Parmenides – one – hypotheses – *aporia* – participation

It is not immediately clear how the problems about forms that arise in the first part of the *Parmenides* are addressed by the hypotheses in the second part. So much is this the case that some scholarship has famously focused on the narrative concerning the refutation of Socrates' notion of forms without fully addressing the point of Socrates' youth and inexperience. Socrates, however, is depicted here as quite young and, according to Parmenides, his view about forms is unexercised and underdeveloped. In addition, the arguments in the second part of the dialogue can and have been considered in many different ways. Some see them as merely aporetic, some see them as ironic, and others see them as productive or educational. Horan, if I understand him correctly, argues that the hypotheses are in fact educational for Socrates, which helps him sustain his view of an argumentative unity throughout the dialogue. His position is that while the arguments in the second part of the dialogue may seem to be contradictory, they can also be understood to contribute to solving some of the problems that are raised in the first part of the dialogue. This position, in general, is quite laudable, departing from the battles about the status of the apparent refutation of Socrates' forms by Parmenides.

In particular, Horan argues that the major *aporia* about forms in the first part of the dialogue is directly addressed in the second hypothesis of the second part. This *aporia*, called by Allen the "dilemma of participation,"[1] sets up a two-part *reductio* whereby if Socrates contends that there is participation in a form, then the consequence is that the form turns out to be multiple, having instances in many participants. The form, being many, would then no longer be "one," which is definitionally essential to a form. And on the other hand, if the form is taken to be essentially "one," then there can be no participation, which is also an essential aspect of a form relative to participant things.[2] Horan argues that overcoming this *aporia*, at least to some extent, is possible in light of a passage in the second hypothesis where Parmenides addresses the problem of the divisibility of the "one." If Socrates can understand how a "one" can be intrinsically "one" but nevertheless a multiplicity or an aggregate, then such a "one" could be a model for a form without falling victim to the *aporia* above. Such a model of a "one" could range over its participants as somehow divisible while still remaining intrinsically "one."

In support of this position, Horan briefly looks at the first hypothesis, then moves on to the important thought experiment passage in the second hypothesis. It is argued that the dialogue presents a non-multiple subject in the first hypothesis: a "one" as it is strictly one and in no way a multiplicity. This subject "one" holds no predicates, has no being, and in the end cannot even be considered a "one." Horan proposes that this hypothesis establishes for Socrates that a strictly non-multiple "one" holds unacceptable consequences, and therefore the form "one" cannot be strictly "one," at least not in this way. The consequence of this argument therefore undermines what Socrates had initially proposed, namely, that a form is by itself, which is to say, a form is strictly "one." The second hypothesis then reorients the inquiry about the "one" from the first failed attempt by taking up and examining a "one" that is *not non-multiple*. This second "one" has being (unlike the first) and is thereby subject to all sorts of multiplicity and divisibility.

While the "one" of the second hypothesis might appear to be a "one" that is like a sensible thing, or a divisible whole composed of parts, following Horan,

---

[1] Horan (2019, 2); Allen (1997, 128).
[2] Horan (2019, 5): "There is, of course, an *aporia* at this point, an *aporia* according to which there cannot be participation in forms without them ceasing to be one; and if forms, by their nature, must be one, there cannot be participation at all."

it is also and perhaps most essentially an intelligible "one" that admits of multiplicity while still remaining "one." This "one" is composed of "one" and "being," and therefore it is a multiple (minimally being of two parts: "one" and "being" [142e]). But more to the point, the second hypothesis has within it this very curious thought experiment at 143a-ff, whereby Parmenides pauses to examine just the "one" aspect of the two predicates "one" and "being"; he takes up in thought just the "one" part all by itself.

It is argued that the "one" part by itself can be understood to be multiple and still remain intrinsically "one." The unity of this "one"—which has "being" and is "one" despite having parts into which it can be divided—is somehow a model or a lesson to help disarm the dilemma of participation. If this view is viable, Socrates could learn from the thought experiment how an intelligible "one" can be understood as multiple while remaining intrinsically "one." Such a view would contribute to understanding how a form is likewise a "one" that can also be distributed among many participants. The goal rings true, but how to achieve it in this way remains unclear.

Horan's argument requires that the subject of the first hypothesis, the premise from which the argument follows, is understood from 137b where Parmenides introduces taking up his hypothesis as the subject for the demonstration of exercises, which we generally refer to as the hypotheses. It is proposed that the exercises will consider a "one" if it is one, and a "one" if it is not. The first "one" (if it is one) would correlate to the first hypothesis, and the second (if it is not one) would correlate to the second hypothesis. And it is argued that 137b provides just these two distinctions, justifying the reading of the two hypotheses as having two premises: if "one" is one, and if "one" is not one. However, there is an alternative reading of 137b that challenges Horan's view and is, I believe, preferable.

But before we consider the alternative reading, Horan's view ought to be appreciated for several very important points. First, Socrates' notion of forms is not cast aside, but rather Socrates' forms are understood as necessary. Second, it takes seriously that the hypotheses are genuinely pedagogical, following Parmenides' description of the training offered to Socrates.[3] And third, the hypotheses are taken as exercises provided to the young Socrates to help him disarm the *aporia(s)* that emerge from Parmenides' critique, the disarming of which would help to sustain or perhaps even strengthen Socrates' notion of forms.

There are, however, also important points that would benefit from further scrutiny. For instance, there is the issue of the analogy of the day at 131b. Here,

---

3   *Parm.* 136a–137b.

Socrates offers up a possible way that a form can be one or whole while not being divided in virtue of having participants (131b). Parmenides replaces Socrates' example of the day with the image of a sail covering over many people. Once replaced, Socrates has to accept that the sail is divisible into discrete parts which cover the many people underneath. If the replacement is a fair one, then Socrates has been shown that a form must be divisible like a sail, setting up the dilemma of participation. If it is an unfair replacement, then Socrates can be characterized as not yet able fully to understand his own example, perhaps because he needs to develop his insight a bit more.

Horan sees that the salient features of the day remain in play when replaced with the sail and therefore he maintains that a form must be divided in order to account for participation. This is why, as I understand Horan, the training for Socrates ought to show him how a "one" can be intrinsically one all the while being divisible. Nevertheless, both the view of the equivalence of the day and the sail, and the consequent goal of the hypotheses remain quite controversial.

The use of the "day" is an ambiguous example that could be suggestive of a time interval, like, say, morning, or it could be suggestive of day as in day-light. The day understood as a time interval can be distributed among many without being itself divided. Many people eat supper at suppertime. And, even if the day is understood in terms of day-light, there are no discrete indications of divisible parts, for where are the parts and where are the joints? The sail, on the contrary, is physically divisible in a spatial and extended way: it can be cut up and divided into discrete sail parts, such as the head, the foot, the clew, and all the rest. This suggests that, although the analogy of the day may fail to fully represent, robustly, the notion of a form, it is disingenuous to replace it with the image of the sail. Moreover, it is plausible that Parmenides makes this substitution in order to test Socrates' understanding of his idea. Think of it like a challenge presented to Socrates for the sake of diagnosing his ability at this point to fully and rightly conceive of the necessary nature of a form. Even if the day has promise—and I believe it does—Parmenides shows that Socrates is not yet keyed into the strength of his own example because he does not object to the substitution.

At this point, Socrates, tellingly, hesitates to agree with Parmenides when the sail is given as a substitute; he replies only with a meek "maybe" (131c) and does not force the issue any further. Once Parmenides continues with the example of the sail in place of the day as if it were fully agreed upon, Socrates is forced to concede that a form distributed over participants like a sail is not a unified one. Would the older, more trained Socrates allow for the sail to be substituted for the day without a fight?

Parmenides also seems to suggest that his criticism of Socrates' articulation of forms offers some possibility of relief, which would mean that the dilemma of participation may not be as comprehensive as it appears. For example, at 131a Parmenides pauses to ask Socrates if there is another way for a many to participate in a form, hinting at the thought that the *aporia* could be avoided. Parmenides says: "So does each thing that gets a share get as its share the form as a whole or a part of it? Or could there be some other means of getting a share apart from these two?"[4] Parmenides' challenge could be honestly provocative, motivating Socrates to think more carefully about the nature of a form, particularly if Socrates might see how a sail, as a spatially determined extended thing, cannot possibly represent important aspects that are definitional to a form.

My second perplexity concerns the nature of the subject "one," which is instrumental for Horan's argument, and moreover, to understanding the arguments in the *Parmenides* in general. If the first hypothesis articulates a "one" that is strictly one, is that particular kind of "one" carried over to the second hypothesis either in the premise or through the conclusions? Or are they altogether different "ones"? And if they are not the same, are they different because there are two different premises, or is it because the conclusions drawn are different? And can the "ones" be somehow not altogether different so as to exclude each other?

It was suggested that the first hypothesis "one" is an intelligible "one," and it is that intelligible kind of "one" that is at least momentarily operative in the second hypothesis in the important thought experiment at 143a. In this way, if I understand Horan correctly, the isolated "one" part in the thought experiment could be understood to serve as the example for how in general a "one" could be intrinsically "one" while nevertheless also a multitude. This proposal however remains opaque because the "one," isolated in thought, could and in my view should be understood just as the isolated unitary aspect of a one-of-many (that is, the oneness taken by itself in thought from a divisible or aggregate kind of "one") without needing to be understood as intrinsically "one," let alone a "one" considered as a form.

Another and perhaps preferable way to consider the differences between the two "ones" would be to take the view that hypotheses 1 and 2 depict different types of "ones" only insofar as they conclude in different ways. From this perspective, the premise from which the differing conclusions all can be, and I argue should be, simply: "if one is." Nothing precludes the view that hypotheses 1 and 2 could examine the same preliminary subject "one" and conclude in

---

4   Gill and Ryan (1996) translation.

opposite ways, namely, that the subject "one" is not, and then that the subject "one" is.

Let us take a closer look at Parmenides' premise at 137b. Parmenides says: "Shall I hypothesize about the one itself and consider what the consequences must be, if it is one or if it is not one?" ἢ βούλεσθε, ἀπ' ἐμαυτοῦ ἄρξωμαι καὶ τῆς ἐμαυτοῦ ὑποθέσεως, περὶ τοῦ ἑνὸς αὐτοῦ ὑποθέμενος, εἴτε ἕν ἐστιν εἴτε μὴ ἕν, τί χρὴ συμβαίνειν; (Gill and Ryan 1996 tr.). Horan argues that the phrase εἴτε ἕν ἐστιν εἴτε μὴ ἕν should be rendered as "if it is one or if it is not one," contending that the alternative translation "if it is one or if it is not" or perhaps "if one is or if one is not" is possible only through emending the text. This point is crucial because it allows for his reading of the first and second hypotheses as following from one another. The first hypothesis appears to Horan to be about a "one" that is non-multiple following from the reading "if it [one] is one," and the conclusions therefore show that this kind of non-multiple "one" is untenable. And the second, then, takes the "one" as divisible or multiple "if it [one] is not [one]" and shows how it can potentially be a helpful model for thinking about a form. While divisibility and multiplicity are in fact attributes that follow from some of the conclusions, they are not the defining features of the subject "one" from the get-go.

There is good reason to reconsider the phrase at 137b to mean that the subject "one" must be considered "if one is" and "if one is not" emphasizing the existence and the non-existence of the proposed subject rather than the unity or non-unity view, reading "if it [the one] is one," or "if it [the one] is not [one]." In support of the existence and non-existence view we can look carefully at the plan Parmenides lays out for the work ahead. Parmenides tells Socrates at 136a: "If you want to be trained more thoroughly, you must not only hypothesize, if each thing is, and examine the consequences of that hypothesis; you must also hypothesize if the same thing is not." Parmenides then reinforces the plan and takes by way of an example the subject "many" filling in the schema if many things are or if many things are not. He then follows with another example, "likeness," and finally generalizes the plan, claiming that any subject one might examine ought to be examined first if it is, and then if it is not. This sets the context for 137b when Parmenides asks to employ the "one" as the subject.

The schema for the hypotheses is revealed to be a four-part process depicted at 136a5 and following. First, the subject should be examined, if it is, and considered with respect to itself and its correlative other(s) (all that the subject is not). Second, the correlative other should be considered, if it is, with respect to itself and to the original subject. Then Parmenides explains that not only should the subject be considered as extant, if it is, but that the subject should also be considered if it is not. Following this, the third line of inquiry should take the subject, if it is not, and it should be examined with respect to itself and its correlative other. And in the fourth the correlative other is taken and considered with respect to itself and with respect to the original subject (if it is not). The eight hypotheses in the dialogue, we find out, are a performance of these four lines of inquiry, with "one" employed as the subject. But in demonstrating the arguments, the inquiry is doubled. Each line of inquiry is actually demonstrated twice, with opposed sets of conclusions drawn about the "one." Hence, there is some baked-in confusion whether or not hypothesis 1 and 2 take the premises "if one is not" and "if one is," or if they both take the premise "if one is" and conclude in opposite ways.

It is important to see the doubling of each hypothesis because it reinforces the view that the subject is the same for both the first and second hypothesis. Following the schema, the first and second hypotheses fall under one line of inquiry, having the same premise "if one is." The conclusion might well be drawn that the "one" of the premise is the same for both hypotheses. That "one" however must be a somewhat ambiguous "one," and therefore it ought not to be seen right off the bat as either a strictly monadic "one" or a compound "one" as Horan argues. Rather, those conclusions (if and when true) are drawn *only after* the arguments have been worked out.

So the sentence at 137b has a strong contextual basis to be understood as "if one *is*" or "if one *is not*" rather than "if one is one" or "if one is not one" because it follows the schema that Parmenides tells Socrates and because it bears out in the pattern of the hypotheses that are demonstrated. If 137b is read along the lines suggested by Horan, it neither aligns with the schema at 136a nor with what we see in the pattern of the hypotheses taken as a whole. But, on the other hand, if we follow my view, the text would apparently need emending.

Horan, following Gill and Ryan (1996), claims that to have the reading that follows the schema, the text must be altered, for instance, by inserting ἐστιν to read εἴτε ἕν ἐστιν εἴτε ἕν μὴ ἐστιν, or following Meinwald (1991), by replacing the second ἕν with ἐστιν.[5] These emendations certainly give the sentence the possibility of the same meaning that I propose. But, I suggest that it hardly requires any emendation to the text at all. If ἐστιν is read as an enclitic ἔστιν then it gives existential rather than predicative force to the verb. Since ancient texts did not typically contain accents, it is not a stretch to consider this option as valid and in fact a preferred reading: it aligns not only with the description of the exercises but also with the general plan of the hypotheses as demonstrated.

On my reading, the subject of the hypotheses is examined in two ways, existing and not existing, and therefore the subject of the first two hypotheses is not

---

5   Gill and Ryan (1996, 141 n23); Meinwald (1991, 40–45); Gill (2012, 59–60).

so easily read as a different subject due to the failure of the view of the non-multiple "one." They should be considered as the same subject "one" since the same premise is given for both.[6] Rather, the two sets of conclusions are opposed. The first hypothesis and the second both take the same subject "one," albeit they conclude in opposite ways about that one. The premise for both is "if one is." In a similar way, the fifth and sixth hypotheses correspondingly consider the "one" if it is *not* (160b/163b).[7]

The general idea, I contend, is that it is really through the course of the arguments within the hypotheses that the "one" comes to be determined. Such determinations come after the premise: they are hit upon from thinking through what must follow from the initial premise. And in our case, hypothesis 1 and 2 offer up the same premise "if one is," but nevertheless provide conclusions that depict a "one" that is not, and a "one" that is. The upshot of this view is that Socrates, or the trainee going through the hypotheses, is invited to try and understand how these seemingly contradictory depictions of the "one" under the same premise can be resolved. The goal as I see it is to begin to comprehend how the "one" that is determined to hold no predicates and to admit no temporal modes of being, and the "one" that is determined to be inclusive of predicates and modes of temporal being can be conceived of together without contradiction. This task would be a propaedeutic for considering the way in which a form-like "one" and a participant-like "one" can be comprehended without contradiction. If rightly understood, this would help Socrates and students of the *Parmenides* dispel the *aporia* of participation.

---

6   Hypothesis 1: εἰ ἕν ἐστιν, ἄλλο τι οὐκ ἂν εἴη πολλὰ τὸ ἕν; (137c3); Hypothesis 2: ἓν εἰ ἔστιν, ἆρα οἷόν τε αὐτὸ εἶναι μέν, οὐσίας δὲ μὴ μετέχειν; (142b5–6).
7   Hypothesis 5: τίς οὖν ἂν εἴη αὕτη ἡ ὑπόθεσις, εἰ ἓν μὴ ἔστιν; (160b7); Hypothesis 6: οὐκοῦν ἓν εἰ μὴ ἔστι, φαμέν, τί χρὴ περὶ αὐτοῦ συμβαίνειν; (163b8–c1).

COLLOQUIUM 1

Horan/Gardner Bibliography

Allen, R.E. 1997. *Plato's* Parmenides. *Translated with Comment. Revised edition.* New Haven: Yale University Press.
Beck, M. 1947. Plato's Problem in the *Parmenides*. *Journal of the History of Ideas* 8: 232–36.
Brisson, L. 2002. 'Is the World One?' A New Interpretation of Plato's *Parmenides*. *Oxford Studies in Ancient Philosophy* 22: 1–20.
Burnet, J. 1901. *Platonis Opera. Tomus II*. Oxford: Clarendon Press.
Cornford, F.M. 1939. *Plato and Parmenides*. London: Routledge & Kegan Paul.
Curd, P.K. 1986. *Parmenides* 131c–132b: Unity and Participation. *History of Philosophy Quarterly* 3: 125–36.
Fitelson & Zalta. The Theory of Forms <http://fitelson.org/cm/forms/>. Accessed August 2017.
Gill, M.L. & Ryan, P. 1996. *Plato: Parmenides*. Indianapolis: Hackett.
Gill, M.L. 2012. *Philosophos: Plato's Missing Dialogue*. Oxford: Oxford University Press.
Halper, E. 1990. A Note on the Unity of the *Parmenides*. *Hermes* 118: 31–42.
Harte, V. 2002. *Plato on Parts and Wholes*. Oxford: Oxford University Press.
Kirwan, C. 1971. *Aristotle's* Metaphysics *Books* Γ, Δ, *and* E. *Translated with Notes.* Oxford: Clarendon Press.
McCabe, M.M. 1994. *Plato's Individuals*. Princeton, NJ: Princeton University Press.
Meinwald, C.C. 1991. *Plato's* Parmenides. Oxford: Oxford University Press.
Miller, M. 1986. *Plato's* Parmenides*: The Conversion of the Soul*. University Park: Penn State University Press.
Panagiotou, S. 1987. The Day and Sail Analogies in Plato's *Parmenides*. *Phoenix* 41: 10–24.
Rickless, S. 2007. *Plato's Forms in Transition: A Reading of the* Parmenides. Cambridge: Cambridge University Press.
Ryle, G. 1965. Plato's *Parmenides*. Reprinted in *Studies in Studies in Plato's Metaphysics*, ed. R.E. Allen, 97–148. London: Routledge & Kegan Paul. Originally published in 1939 in *Mind* 48: 129–151 & 302–325.
Sayre, K. 1983. *Plato's Later Ontology: A Riddle Resolved*. Princeton: Princeton University Press.
Walker, M. 1938. The One and Many in Plato's *Parmenides*. *The Philosophical Review* 47: 488–516.
Wundt, M. 1935. *Platons Parmenides*. Stuttgart: Kohlhammer.

COLLOQUIUM 2

Genesis and the Priority of Activity in Aristotle's *Metaphysics* IX.8

Mark Sentesy
The Pennsylvania State University

Abstract

This paper clarifies the way Aristotle uses generation (γένεσις) to establish the priority of activity (ἐνέργεια) in time and in being. It opens by examining the concept of genetic priority. The argument for priority in beinghood has two parts. The first part is a synthetic argument that accomplishment (τέλος) is the primary kind of source (ἀρχή), an argument based on the structure of generation. The second part engages three critical objections to the claim that activity could be an accomplishment: (i) activity appears to lack its own structure; (ii) activity is different in kind from the object it accomplishes; and (iii) activity is external to its accomplishment. Aristotle responds to these objections by analyzing the structure of generation. In the course of the argument, Aristotle establishes that beinghood and form are activity.

Keywords

Aristotle – genesis – actuality – telos – *Metaphysics*

1 Introduction

Aristotle declares that his aim in *Metaphysics* IX.8 is to show that being-at-work or activity (ἐνέργεια) has priority over potency (δύναμις), nature (φύσις), and other similar sources, presumably desire (ὄρεξις) and choice (προαίρεσις) (*Metaph.* IX.5, 1048a4–14).[1] He argues that it is prior in four ways: in speech (*Metaph.* IX.8, 1049b12–16), in time (1049b17–1050a3), in beinghood (οὐσία)[2]

---

[1] All quotations from the *Metaphysics* are from the Sachs (1999) translation, unless otherwise noted.
[2] I shall not render οὐσία as "substance," the word most often used in translations and secondary scholarship, because that is not a translation of οὐσία but of ὑποκείμενον. Scholars continue to

(1050a4–b5), and in independent being (1050b6–1051a1; also see Panayides 1999).

The most contentious argument is that being-at-work (ἐνέργεια) is prior in beinghood (οὐσία). But the basis for the argument is not very clear. It does not obviously proceed, for example, by applying a clear, pre-established analysis of priority in beinghood.[3] That Aristotle does not simply appeal to the concept of beinghood to decide the case is clear from the fact that in making the argument he overshoots his target, establishing not just the claim that being-at-work (ἐνέργεια) is primary in relation to beinghood, but also the much more significant claim—the banner claim—that beinghood and form (εἶδος) are at-work (*Metaph.* IX.8, 1050b2). The extent of this overshoot is significant: it is as though, instead of showing that trees are the tallest plants, he showed that all plants are trees.

There are two problems that this paper aims to address. First, it aims to discern the basis of the argument of the passage. Second, it aims to show how this basis can plausibly justify the claim that beinghood (οὐσία) and form (εἶδος) are at-work (ἐνέργεια).

In *Metaphysics* IX.8, I aim to show, Aristotle does not apply a pre-existing account of priority to the case of potency and being-at-work; he makes an immanent argument: since potency is paradigmatically a source (ἀρχή), his method is to examine the structure of sources.[4] The argument proceeds by

---

use the word in an attempt to maintain continuity with earlier scholarship and the Latin tradition of commentary. But this means, for example, that when it is translated "primary substance," as it frequently is, both words refer to features of the concept, while neither translates the word. So I shall render οὐσία as "being," "beinghood," or "thinghood," and append or simply use the transliterated word itself.

3   Aristotle's general list of kinds of priority varies from text to text, but they can be divided into two types: those ordered by an ἀρχή (*Metaph.* v.11, 1018b9–29, *Categories* 12, 14a26-b8), and asymmetrical dependence (Plato's Criterion) (*Metaph.* v.11, 1019a2–5, XIII.2, 1077b1–12, *Cat.* 12, 14b10–23, *Physics* VIII.7, 260b17–19). Scholars worry that the general criteria for priority to which Aristotle refers do not provide an adequate basis for his claims to priority in *Metaph.* IX.8. Witt claims, in response, that the priority of ἐνέργεια is established because potency depends for its existence on the existence of ἐνέργεια, but not vice-versa, in other words Plato's Criterion (*Metaph.* v.11, 1019a2–5) (Witt 1994 and 1998). Menn and Beere hold that this criterion is not successful (Menn forthcoming, 111α3, 11; Beere 2009, 289). Broadie argues that Plato's Criterion cannot be found in *Metaph.* IX.8, and that the attempt to assimilate IX.8 to it should be abandoned (Broadie 2010, 201). Peramatzis defends a reading of priority that he thinks can assign ontological primacy to ἐνέργεια in cases of potency-ἐνέργεια relations (Peramatzis 2011). Panayides notes that in *Phys.* VIII.7, 261a12–20 Aristotle distinguishes between priority in οὐσία and priority due to independent existence, and shows that this distinction obtains in *Metaph.* IX.8 (Panayides 1999).
4   In *Metaph.* v.11, 1019a4–8, Aristotle says that in a way all things are said to precede or follow according to the order determined by potency and being-complete (ἐντελέχεια). Parts are prior

establishing, first, that there is another kind of source alongside potency-like sources, namely being an accomplishment (τέλος), and second, that ἐνέργεια can in fact be such a source. Again, the core claim is that accomplishment is the primary kind of source, and then that being-at-work (ἐνέργεια) is an accomplishment. The basis for the argument, then, is an analysis of the structure of sources (ἀρχαί).

Now, the paradigm Aristotle uses to work out the structure of sources is generation (γένεσις). Aristotle uses generation in two ways in first philosophy: (1) γένεσις names the coming to be of any sort of form in underlying material, and thereby the coming to be of beings (οὐσίαι), as children come to be in material (for examples, see *Phys.* I, 7–9 and *Metaph.* VIII.5, 1044b21–29). Generation is an important indicator of priority in οὐσία, since it is the process by which non-eternal beings (and their attributes) are constituted. In addition, (2) γένεσις names the coming to be of activities (ἐνέργειαι) from potencies, as flute-playing comes from the flute-playing potency (for instance at *Metaph.* IX.8, 1050a24–31). It thereby covers all changes whatsoever and events that do not count as changes.

Generation is an intuitive basis for the banner claim in the passage, because a process only counts as generation if a being (οὐσία) with a form or structure (εἶδος) emerges from it. The source responsible for such an emergence will be, thereby, the source of beinghood and form. Because first philosophy seeks the primary sources (ἀρχαί) of being, it makes sense for it to study generation in order to find out what the sources of such things are.[5]

I follow Menn (Menn forthcoming) in holding that the subject of *Metaph.* IX.8 is sources (ἀρχαί) and their accomplishment (τελεία). But there are two ways that my account differs from existing scholarship. First, some scholars hold that γένεσις is not the basis for priority in this passage, but that categorical being (οὐσία) has a structure of priority built into it: they say that by definition a man is prior in being to a boy (for example, see Makin 2006, 195 and Beere 2009, Ch. 8). As noted, I aim to show that γένεσις is, throughout the passage, the basis for the claim to the priority of being-at-work. Second, while I think

---

in potency since they continue once the whole has been dismantled, but wholes are prior in being-complete, since the whole has some independence, e.g., it can remain though the parts change, and it guides the assembly of the parts.

5 Studying sources in this way does not amount to doing physics: first philosophy studies all things, including change and changing things, not insofar as they change, but insofar as they are. Moreover, being a source is being in the primary sense, and being a source of change and generation is the primary way of being a source (*Metaph.* I.3, 983a25–7, *Metaph.* IV.2, 1003b16–19, and *Metaph.* XII.8, 1073a23-b2). Menn argues that the purpose of *Metaph.* IX is to prepare the concept of ἀρχή to play its role in the culmination of the *Metaph.* in the account of God in *Metaph.* XII (Menn forthcoming).

Broadie's assessment of the stakes of the Location Argument (*Metaph*. IX.8, 1050a23–b2) is correct, I think she does not go far enough (Broadie 2010). I shall argue that, while it is true that one of the stakes of the passage is the intelligibility of the natural world, as she argues, the stakes are, more immediately, to show how being-at-work (ἐνέργεια) can be an accomplishment (τέλος).

This paper has the structure of a commentary. First it clarifies the way Aristotle uses generation (γένεσις) in the passage on priority in time, then it divides the argument for priority in being into its parts. The first part argues that the accomplishment (τέλος) is the primary kind of source (ἀρχή). I aim to show how this is not an analytic argument, but a synthetic one, made on the basis of the structure of generation.[6] The second part argues that being-at-work (ἐνέργεια) is an accomplishment (τέλος). I aim to show that, through analyzing the structure of generation, Aristotle answers three critical objections to this claim, namely that being-at-work appears to lack its own structure, to be different in kind from the object it accomplishes, and to be external to its accomplishment. The paper closes by showing how the argument has in fact established that beinghood and form are being-at-work using the structure of generation.

11 Two Bases for Priority: Time and Genesis (*Metaph*. IX.8, 1049b17–1050a4)

The role of priority of sources first becomes clear in the chapter's lengthy discussion of priority in time. To clarify the way Aristotle is approaching generation (γένεσις), it is necessary to examine his lengthy treatment of genetic priority in this section. To sort out the priority of potency and being-at-work (ἐνέργεια) in time, Aristotle examines genetic sequence. In mounting his argument, he gives not one but *two* ways of understanding the organization of genetic processes.

In the first, potency precedes activity in time: for example, in time, an individual's ability to run (that is, being a runner) precedes actively running, so potency temporally precedes activity.[7] A capacity to act comes to be before

---

6 This analytic-synthetic distinction is borrowed from Kant's *Critique of Pure Reason* (Kant 1998, A6–7). I use it here only to indicate the structure of the argument.

7 E.g., "there must be something burnable before being burned and something that can set it on fire before setting it on fire" (*Phys*. VIII.1, 251a15–16). Add to this that actively being the case implies the capacity to be the case, while potency continues even when the activity is not there, and the case for the priority of potency over ἐνέργεια looks extremely strong. Cf. *Metaph*. IX.3, 1046b2–1047a10 and XII.6, 1071b24–1072a18. On Menn's argument, the physicists and

the action; a thing is potentially a particular *this* before it comes to be at-work being *this*. But it is only when the investigation is limited to individual (τόδε) beings, that is, when the analysis of priority is limited to the *Individual Sequence*, that potency is prior to being-at-work. The limitation to an individual being excludes the γένεσις of the being in question, and prevents such a view of priority from being fundamental.

When the restriction to individuals is lifted, however, and we look at a complete being along with its γένεσις, then it is not potency but activity that takes precedence. In this more basic sense of temporal precedence, activity precedes potency:

> preceding these in time, there are other things that are at work, out of which these particular ones are *generated*.... Some *mover* is always first, and what causes change is already *at work*. (*Metaph.* IX. 8, 1049b17–24, translation modified)

Before this individual was either potential or at work, there was a source of change, which was "the same in form, though not numerically the same" (*Metaph.* IX.8, 1049b18–19). Parents come first, and babies come later. But if the analysis is no longer limited to a particular temporal extent, there is no reason to stop at the parents. Why not continue back to their childhood, to their parents, and on and on? What is it about parents that makes them primary? It is that, while children precede parents, parents are *sources* of children. Their priority is established by being sources of generation, and generation of a child, because it brings a new being into the world, is a more fundamental kind of generation than the growth of a child into an adult. Parents are prior in this way insofar as they *actively* generate, not insofar as they are capable of generating.[8]

The temporal order of events is the same in the Individual Sequence, but now, no longer constrained to the temporal limits of an individual life, the inter-generational pattern of coming-to-be establishes the fundamentality of γένεσις. We shall call this a *Genetic Priority*, a term Aristotle adds to the last line of the argument: "being-at-work is also in this way prior to potency in genesis *and* time" (*Metaph.* IX.8, 1050a2–3, my translation). Genetic Priority is not, in fact, the same as temporal priority, but overlies and governs temporal priority.

Platonists hold that if the cosmos came to be, potency must come first or have ontological primacy (Menn forthcoming, IIIα1, 9–11).

8   Moreover, Aristotle adds, activity generates dispositional potencies: to be a builder, in other words, to be-a-builder-in-potency, one must first build (*Metaph.* IX.8, 1049b29).

Three remarks are necessary: first, activity is prior in time in a more governing way than potency. It takes precedence because Genetic Priority encompasses the narrower view of priority. For potency to be prior in time simply, we would need to distort what is genetically primary by interpreting it through the temporal framework of an individual, that is, through abstraction from the conditions of the individual's emergence. Second, the wider view allows individual sources of generation (parents, for example) to become visible as what they are, namely sources, while the Individual Sequence does not. They have been generated, and in addition they are sources of generation. This means Genetic Priority gives us evidence for the structure of priority proper to sources (ἀρχαί) in general, namely that generated things are sources. Third, unlike the Individual Sequence, which accounts for the development of capacities and activities of *already* existing beings, Genetic Priority accounts for the birth and existence of individual beings themselves.[9] This means priority in coming-to-be is already priority in being.

III   Priority in Being: Division of the Argument

Having worked out this distinction between temporal and genetic priority, Aristotle turns to a discussion of priority in being (οὐσία). This argument divides into two parts. Part One, running from *Metaph.* IX.8, 1050a4–15, is an argument that being-at-work (ἐνέργεια) is prior to potency because the accomplishment or result (τέλος) is a source in a more governing way than the capacity that is its precondition. Part Two, running from 1050a15–1050b2, is an argument that being-at-work (ἐνέργεια) is indeed a kind of accomplishment (τέλος). It has a form or structure (εἶδος) (1050a15–16), this form or structure is determined by the accomplishment (τέλος) (1050a21–23), and it is in the same location as the accomplishment. With few exceptions, the tendency among scholars is to think that nothing much is at stake in this latter trio of arguments, which is taken to be fairly self-evident (Broadie 2010 and Charles 2010 are the notable exceptions). To remedy this, after providing a synopsis of the first half of the

---

[9] Note also that because the phenomena are structured by genetic priority, both the being that generates and the being that is generated already appear to be mature adults or skilled agents. This is clear from the way Aristotle describes the case: once he has established that the center of a genetic analysis is not the seed or the child, but the mature being who can and actively does generate, he does not say that a child comes to be from an adult, but that a man comes to be from a man. Even the being that is generated is, ultimately and properly, the one who can generate, that is, the source of being.

argument in this section, I will in the detailed discussion of its steps try to clarify the stakes involved in its core claims.

In Part One, the main thing I aim to establish is that in moving from an argument for priority in time to priority in οὐσία, we are not leaving Genetic Priority behind. The argument as a whole is quite clearly an analysis of the structure of γένεσις, in the sense indicated by Genetic Priority:

> But surely [being-at-work] takes precedence in thinghood too, first because
> (1) things that are later[10] in *coming into being* take precedence in form and in οὐσία, as a man does over a boy, or a human being over the germinal fluid, since the one already has the form, and the other does not, and also because
> (2) everything that *comes into being* goes up to a source and an end,
>   a. since that for the sake of which something *is* is a source, and
>   b. *coming into being* is *for the sake of the end*, but
> (3) being-at-work is an end, and it is for the enjoyment of this that the potency is taken on. (*Metaph.* IX.8, 1050a4–10, translation modified)

Step (1) claims that the outcome of γένεσις is a form and οὐσία. Step (2) identifies the accomplishment of such a genetic process as a source (which means that the form and οὐσία in (1) is an ἀρχή of γένεσις). Step (3) is to argue that potency, likewise, *comes-to-be for the sake of activity*. Therefore being-at-work is prior in beinghood.

I introduce the second part by examining the reasons why it seems that being-at-work (ἐνέργεια) cannot be an accomplishment (τέλος), and why accomplishment seems to be a bad criterion for establishing its priority. Aristotle responds:

> (4) Furthermore, material is in-potency (δυνάμει) because it comes to (ἔλθοι) a form; and when it is at-work (ἐνεργείᾳ), then it is *in* the form. And it is similar in other cases, including those in which the accomplishment is change, and that is why teachers display (ἀποδιδόναι) a student at work, thinking that they are delivering up the accomplishment, and nature does likewise.
> (5) For the work (ἔργον) is an accomplishment (τέλος), and *being at work* (ἐνέργεια) is the work, and this is why the name *being at work* is said

---

10   Sachs has translated *hustera* correctly as "later," since it refers to the Individual Genetic Sequence, rather than Genetic Priority simply.

through the work and stretches toward (συντείνειν) being-complete (ἐντελέχεια). (*Metaph.* IX.8, 1050a15–23, my translation)

(6) Whenever only the exercise (χρῆσις) comes to be (γένεσις), the being-at-work or exercise is just as much an accomplishment (τέλος) as the potency. And whenever from what is potent both the exercise and a work-object come to be (γένεσις), since the being-at-work or exercise of the potency, that is, the work-act or ἐνέργεια, is *in* the work-object with the τέλος, the ἐν-έργ-εια is *more* a τέλος, in other words more ἐντελέχεια, than the potency. (*Metaph.* IX.8, 1050a23–b2, paraphrased for brevity)

(7) And so it is clear that beinghood (οὐσία) and form (εἶδος) are being-at-work (ἐνέργεια). So as a result of this argument it is obvious that being-at-work takes precedence over potency in beinghood. (*Metaph.* IX.8, 1050b2–3, translation modified)

Each premise has for its evidence and its basis the internal structure of coming-to-be (γένεσις). Because γένεσις is *for* its accomplishment, because the accomplishment of γένεσις is the primary way of being a source, and because ἐνέργεια is an accomplishment, it is therefore a source. Each step examines an aspect of the structure of γένεσις. The structure of genetic sources thereby constitutes a claim about ontological primacy.

IV The Argument that Accomplishment Is a Source

A. *The Generation Argument* (Metaph. *IX.8, 1050a4–6*). The first step of the argument that τέλος is an ἀρχή relies on the idea that τέλος means an outcome or result:

(1) things that are later in coming into being take precedence in form and in οὐσία, as a man does over a boy, or a human being over the germinal fluid, since the one already has the form, and the other does not. (*Metaph.* IX.8, 1050a4–6, translation modified)[11]

What comes later is prior because it is the form and being (οὐσία) that results from generation (γένεσις).

Beere argues that the phrase "things that are later in coming into being take precedence in form and in οὐσία (as a man does over a boy)" (1050a4–5),

---

11   In the phrase ἤδη ἔχει τὸ εἶδος, ἔχειν is used as a being-replacing word.

opposes priority in γένεσις to priority in οὐσία. This motivates him to maintain the hypothesis that the argument has moved beyond change to being (Beere 2009, 304–312). But the contrast Aristotle draws here is clearly between precedence in οὐσία and the *Individual Sequence*: in the Individual Sequence, as here, what is prior is the capability of a seed or a child. If Aristotle were referring to Genetic Priority, however, what is prior would be the active adult, which would make nonsense of the contrast. To make the claim that Aristotle leaves γένεσις behind, then, Beere has to overlook the distinction Aristotle has just made between the Individual Sequence and Genetic Priority.[12]

On my argument, this sentence continues the previous discussion of source-based priority. The idea that the mature being (οὐσία) is a source is already on the table, and the discovery of Genetic Priority put it there.[13] In addition, this clause is the first in an argument seven lines long, the rest of which establishes that ἐνέργεια is a source (ἀρχή). Not only is the active source of generation prior in the sense of coming *before* and *giving rise to* a particular being, but the source of generation is also prior within the development of the individual.

Aristotle usually formulates this claim by saying that what comes later is prior since then it has its nature (*Metaph.* V.4, 1015a3–12; *Politics* I.2, 1252b34–6; *Parts of Animals* I.1, 640a19–26, 641b23–642a1, and II.1, 646a25–27; *Generation of Animals* II.1, 734a16–32, II.6). If Aristotle is indeed making the same argument here in *Metaph.* IX.8 as he does elsewhere, then the form at the end of a genetic process will be prior in being to earlier phases of γένεσις because it has come to be a nature, that is, a natural source of change and rest.

B. *The Source Argument* (Metaph. IX.8, 1050a6–8). If the centrality of the concept of γένεσις and ἀρχή was only implicit in claim (1), it is inescapable in claim (2), which argues that coming-to-be results in a *source*, which is some goal or τέλος: "everything that comes to be comes up to (ἔλθοι) a source (ἀρχή) and accomplishment (τέλος)" (*Metaph.* IX.8, 1050a6–8, my translation). This is a descriptive statement: γένεσις "comes up to" something because things that count as coming to be *accomplish* or *yield* something. *Genesis* yields, Aristotle says,

---

[12] Even Beere's claim that the basis for substantial priority is a constitutive, normative non-reciprocity between stages of generation (meaning that "man" constitutes the being of the boy in a way that "boy" does not constitute the being of the man), turns out to depend on γένεσις, because being *from* something ultimately depends on what the structure of γένεσις is (thus, the relevant ways of being *from* something in *Metaph.* V.24 depend on the structure of γένεσις in *Metaph.* IX.8) (Beere 2009, 304–312).

[13] Cf. *Phys.* I.5, 188b26–8, where the source-like character of form is explicit: "the sources must come neither from one another nor from anything else, and everything else must come from them" (my translation).

something that is a source. To establish this as a general claim, Aristotle offers two premises:

> [Premise 1] generation (γένεσις) is for the sake of (= goes up to) an accomplishment (τέλος)
> [Premise 2] being 'what something is for the sake of' is being a source (ἀρχή). (*Metaph.* IX.8, 1050a6–8, argument reversed and paraphrased; also see Ross 1924, 262)

These premises interpret the "coming up to" that we perceive in a process of generation as its being *for* something, and on this basis they establish that the accomplishment of generation is a way of being a source.

It is important to note here that this is not an analytic argument: Aristotle does not claim that to be a τέλος just means to be a source (ἀρχή). It is not obviously the same thing for something to be *for* something and for it to have an accomplishment (τέλος).[14] The argument is, instead, synthetic: it identifies the terms with one another through a proper medium, namely the process of γένεσις: the accomplishment is a source because they are both "that for the sake of which," in other words that up to which coming-to-be comes. Τέλος is ἀρχή, then, because coming-to-be has the structure of being *for the sake of something* (ἕνεκα). It is only because γένεσις is *directed at* something determinate that Aristotle can claim that the "for which" is an accomplishment. The "going toward" evident in a process of generation is its being-for-the-sake of something.

Crucially, among all changes (alteration, change in size, motion in place, generation), γένεσις is the one that most obviously is *for* something, because it most obviously yields something, because a distinct thing *emerges*. Of changes that are *for* something, γένεσις is the paradigm. Thus, Aristotle reads the *for-*structure off of γένεσις, and thereby establishes his claim that to be a τέλος is to be an ἀρχή.[15]

---

14   I can aim to run a whole marathon, but if I am out of shape, I can try instead to run as much of a marathon as I can. If being *for the sake of* something is going to mean being for an accomplishment (τέλος), we need to specify what it is an accomplishment of. In this case, the accomplishment is the activity or use of a potency. In this example, in both cases, I am completing or exercising my being a marathon runner, or my incomplete ability to run.

15   Note that in saying that γένεσις is *for* something, no claim is made about the nature of the parts of the process. Γένεσις is not described as having a set morphological pathway or even an inherent character, only that it aims at an accomplishment.

On this basis Aristotle introduces a completely new way of being a source: unlike potency-like sources, for being-at-work (ἐνέργεια) to be a source is for it to be the accomplishment sought or aimed at.

By supplying the implicit premise we can actually deduce the Generation Argument that precedes it:

> [implicit premise] Being a source of γένεσις is being (οὐσία) in the primary sense
> (1) Therefore, what completes the genetic process is being (οὐσία) in the primary sense

Thus, (1) what comes later in γένεσις is prior in οὐσία, and this is because what comes later is the source of the γένεσις. The man into which the boy is growing is that for which he is growing, namely his accomplishment, and thereby the source of his being and generation.

C. *The Exercise Argument* (Metaph. IX.8, 1050a9–16). Now that Aristotle has shown formally how a τέλος can be a source of γένεσις, he has an easy argument at hand, which both confirms the claim about τέλος being a source, and gives him an important argument for the ontological primacy of ἐνέργεια over δύναμις: (2) "But the ἐνέργεια is an end, and it is for the enjoyment of this that the potency is taken on" (*Metaph.* IX.8, 1050a9–10, translation modified). We take up potency in order to exercise it; potency comes to be for activity. This appears to be a very straightforward and, on the face of it, a sufficient argument to establish the primacy of activity over potency. It is so intuitive that it makes the rest of the argument seem pointless: why belabor the details of the relationships between being a source, being for something, and being an accomplishment?

On its own, this argument is not, however, sufficient: it requires the preceding argument to establish the priority and sourcehood of the accomplishment through an analysis of the structure of generation:

- Coming to be (γένεσις) is for the sake of an accomplishment (τέλος)
- The accomplishment of a process of coming to be is a source (ἀρχή)
- Being a source is prior in beinghood (οὐσία) to the process of coming to be of which it is the source
- Potency comes into being for the sake of being-at-work
    a. The accomplishment of potency (δύναμις) is being-at-work (ἐνέργεια)
- Therefore, being-at-work is the source of potency.

If this argument is successful, saying that potency comes to be *for* activity would be sufficient to establish that activity is prior.

D. *Remarks.* Let us take a step back to look at Aristotle's chapter as a whole: what is its philosophical accomplishment? He announced that his purpose was to show that ἐνέργεια is prior to "every source of change or rest in general" (*Metaph.* IX.8, 1049b7, translation modified). This category includes nature, potency, choice, and desire, that is, everything that aims at an accomplishment. Here he establishes that ἐνέργεια is prior to such sources because it is the source of potency. In what way is it prior? By being a *more governing kind of source*. Potency comes to be for it, since the reason we come to have a potency is to use it. The accomplishment of this passage is first of all to establish, on the basis of γένεσις, a new, primary way of being a source (ἀρχή), namely being a τέλος, and, second, to establish that ἐνέργεια is a τέλος in just this way.

Aristotle has now argued that both potency and its activity are sources. They are not, however, sources in the same way. Being a potency means being the kind of source that sets to work changing an other or being changed by an other when the conditions are right. Potency is what generates the accomplishment (τέλος); it is the potency that makes both the product and the activity come to be, like the house-building potency that generates both the house and the activity of building (*Metaph.* IX.8, 1050a30–2). This argument does not establish activity as self-sufficient. In this passage, activity requires potency in order to come to be, and potency persists even while the activity is not there (*Metaph.* IX.3, 1046b29–1047a10).[16]

On the other hand, what the potency is, that is, its being (οὐσία) refers to and is directed toward its activity. But this means the being of the potency depends on its proper activity: it is generated for and, thereby, it *is* at all *for the sake of* the activity.

Potency, then, has two sorts of accomplishment (τέλος): the complete potency (for example being a builder), and the accomplishment it sets to work doing (for example building). Thus, potency is neither essentially incomplete, nor is it a state of lacking the activity. The fact that potency is *for* activity does not make it inherently incomplete. To the contrary, it is when a potency is complete that its "being-for" is also complete, since it is then that it is the most ready to set to work.[17]

---

[16]   If there are kinds of activity that have no corresponding potency, then the claim is limited to the sort of activity that does involve potency.

[17]   In this respect, I disagree with Panayides' interpretation of the argument. He claims that the growing boy is potent because he is intrinsically lacking his end, whereas the end is by definition complete (Panayides 1999). My claim is that the boy is not yet fully in-potency,

Once we supply Aristotle's pivotal assumption, the conclusion follows:

- [implicit premise] Sources of *coming-to-be* are prior in beinghood (οὐσία)
- Therefore, the accomplishment is prior in beinghood
- Therefore, being-at-work is prior to potency in beinghood.

After this argument, the only major premise that Aristotle must establish—and it is not an easy one—is that ἐνέργεια can in fact be a τέλος. This, too, Aristotle works out by examining γένεσις. He must argue that, in each sort of γένεσις, ἐνέργεια is indeed a τέλος (*Metaph.* IX.8, 1050a23–b2).

V   The Argument that Activity is Accomplishment

A. *The Problem of Telos.* Having established that potency is *for* the activity, Aristotle appears to have given a complete argument for the priority of being-at-work over potency, since ἐνέργεια is its telic source. Now we face a second question: why, after completing this argument, is Aristotle not finished? Aristotle is not even halfway through the argument. What remains to be said, and why does he devote so much work to it?

Most commentators do not take the second half of this argument to address a single coherent problem.[18] Broadie (2010) takes up this question in the following way: Aristotle examines the location of activity in transitive and intransitive activities at *Metaphysics* IX.8, 1050a23–b2. Transitive activities are those that occur in a further object, such as a house, or the learning of a student, while intransitive activities do not, as in theoretical thinking and seeing. Why does it matter, she asks, where the activity (ἐνέργεια) is located? She gives three

---

that is, that his potency is not complete until he has grown. Thus, potency's lacking its activity is not the relevant sort of incompleteness.

[18] Cf. Makin, who takes the worries to be (1) how to include the case of material potency in the argument for priority, and (2) how to relate the capacity to its exercise teleologically (a problem that I take Aristotle to have solved in the first half of the argument for priority in οὐσία) (Makin 2006, 197–204). Beere, similarly, presents the purpose of the passage to be chasing down individual cases to show that the capacity is *for* the ἐνέργεια (Beere 2009, 310–313). Witt takes this passage to clear up the difference between potency for activity and potency for the hylomorphic product of the activity (Witt 2003, 88–89). By contrast, I take the extension of potency and ἐνέργεια to material and form and of ἐνέργεια to ἐντελέχεια to depend on the way that the product is evidently a τέλος to show that ἐνέργεια is in fact a τέλος.

reasons: First, activity's claim to priority appears problematic because, while activity comes and goes, potency remains. Second, she argues, since transitive activities aim at something else beyond them, in the case of the house, the house, rather than the activity, appears to be the accomplishment. Thus activity's claim to priority is undermined. Third, she says, Aristotle is pushing back on Plato's claim that activity is impermanent and unintelligible in itself, and that it must be directed at a transcendent idea beyond individual beings. Her argument for this point hinges on her claim that form is activity and potency is indeterminate matter. On this supposition, if activity is primary, then we can know the distinctive forms of things by examining their activity, but if potency is primary, then because it is indeterminate, she avers, the sources of things in the world will be unknowable.

Broadie is right to raise this concern about the location of ἐνέργεια, and I will extend and add to her argument. But my position differs from hers in the following way: while it is true that Aristotle is concerned to show how activity and change are intelligible, his concern does not seem to be quite the same as Broadie makes out. For one, the physicists of Aristotle's time hold the position that making sources material makes them more intelligible rather than less. Moreover, if I am right that for Aristotle potency has its own forms, then it is intelligible in its own right, even if it is also directed at activity (*Metaph.* IX.5, 1048a16–22). Aristotle is concerned not with the intelligibility of underlying processes, but with whether the beings that emerge from them in nature truly are beings. Broadie's concerns overlap with this problem, but do not raise it. Still, Aristotle is, as Broadie says, resisting Plato's solution, namely, the argument that changing beings point to an intelligible transcendent being.

Second, Broadie thinks Aristotle's worry about location occupies the passage from *Metaphysics* IX.8, 1050a23-b2, whereas, as I aim to show, the fundamental worry occupies the whole three-part argument from *Metaphysics* IX.8, 1050a15-b4. As a result of concentrating on only part of the passage, she does not present the problem as sharply as I think it should be presented in context. I think the worry is not only whether activity (ἐνέργεια) is prior, but whether it has a solid claim to being a τέλος at all. Even more critical is the question whether calling something a τέλος is in fact a legitimate basis for priority.

Potency appears to make all activity (ἐνέργεια) transitive. If this is the case, activity cannot be a τέλος. If ἐνέργεια is the use or activity *of potency*, it will inherit the structure of potency.[19] Potency is an other-directed, that is, a disper-

---

19   Cf. *Phys.* III.3. The relationship between activity and use is prominent: "living and acting are a using [χρῆσις] and a being-at-work" (*EE* II.1, 1219b1–2, my translation). Cf. *Protrepticus* B79, B80, (Beere 2009, 161–6), and (Menn 1994).

sive, transitive structure: it is the source of change in *another thing* or the same thing *as other*, and this other is where its τέλος is located. Thus, the τέλος of an agent is in the patient; in the example of a builder the τέλος is the change in the buildable things, while the τέλος of a patient seems to be in the agent; in the example of buildable things the τέλος seems to be the builder's activity of building.[20]

The dispersive structure of potency, meaning its transitive character, is apparent in the word "work" (ἔργον). "Work" (ἔργον) has two meanings: a deed or act, such as the activity of working, and its product, such as the works of Shakespeare. It forms the root word of activity, or being-at-work (ἐνέργεια). Not only is the activity of the worker temporary, it is not ultimately located in the worker, but beyond the worker at the work object. Moreover, the work object appears to be primary, since it is the product and τέλος of working. So the work and its τέλος appear to be different and in different places, and being-at-work appears secondary.

From this we can see a reason to doubt that activity can be a τέλος at all. First, activity does not seem to have its own character: on the one hand, it appears merely to be the exercise of potency, so everything determinate about it seems to derive from potency. But to be τέλος and, indeed, to be primary at all appears to require that something has its own character, that is, that it be in a way something definite. On the other hand, if potency and activity are fundamentally other-directed, we might worry that neither of them has an inherent determinate character. As it stands, there is nothing, or nearly nothing, about activity that would justify us calling it a τέλος. For it seems false to say that either the capacity to work or the activity of working are accomplishments. Since a τέλος is that at which other things are directed, then both potency and activity are means, and neither is an end in itself.

Moreover, two things undermine the idea that an accomplishment could indicate primacy. First, Aristotle has established that both potency and activity depend on one another in order to be: potency depends on activity because activity is the aim or purpose of the potency, while activity depends on potency because without it, no activity would occur.[21] But activity is tempo-

---

20   A further worry, not addressed in this *Metaph.* IX.8 passage, but featuring decisively in the argument for the primacy of eternal beings (*Metaph.* IX.8, 1050b6–1051a2), is whether potency in fact has a single accomplishment, since only part of what something is capable of being can actively be at a time. Aristotle could respond to this by saying that this is not the case for natural or dispositional completed potencies.

21   In the first half of this *Metaph.* IX.8 passage, Aristotle argued that the way potency is a source is secondary to activity, since it comes to be only for the activity. Thus, it appears that both activity and potency depend on one another in different ways in order for them to come to be. The argument so far concerning priority in beinghood (οὐσία) appears to

rary: the builder stops and starts building (*Metaph.* IX.3, 1046b29–1047a10). Thus, potency's permanence seems to anchor the ongoing possibility of activity and thereby override the claim of τέλος to decide which is primary.

Second, since transitive potencies and activities do not seem to coincide with their own accomplishment (τέλος), they seem to be related to their accomplishment externally or accidentally, rather than through themselves (καθ' αὐτό) or essentially. It is therefore unclear why the accomplishment would decide whether potency or being-at-work is primary: from the fact that the potency and activity of building give rise to an existing house, it does not obviously follow that activity is prior to potency. Both appear to be equally necessary.

It is possible to present these problems under one heading. Change comes to an end in other things: the ends of change are always elsewhere than where the source and/or activity of change sets to work. Change is dispersive: a moving thing scatters others like a bowling ball does pins. Dispersion is an interpretation of the structure of change as a whole. The very activity of changing spreads things out in a continuum of place and time, rather than collecting or concentrating in one whole, so change itself appears to be the very contradiction of τέλος.[22] It seems that, based on the character of potency and activity, neither can give us a genuine accomplishment (τέλος), because on their own neither appears to be an end in itself, but each is directed beyond itself. Thus, the attempt to show that change has an accomplishment, and that ἐνέργεια is an accomplishment, is pulled apart.

Aristotle provides three arguments to establish the possibility that activity could be an accomplishment, which we shall go through in the order in which they occur in the text. First, he needs to show that activity is something, that it has its own character. He will do this by drawing on the way potency extends to the concept of material, and activity to form. This extension will show that both potency and activity are definite, knowable, and articulable. The same is true, he adds, in the case of change. I shall call this the Structure Argument.

---

have drawn potency and activity to a stalemate concerning Plato's Criterion. But potency still appears to have a claim to primacy because of its permanence: the parts of some things are more primary in being, at least in the sense that they remain when the whole is destroyed (*Metaph.* V.11, 1019a8–15, VII.15, 1040a22–24). Moreover, since potency is the *source* of change, while ἐνέργεια *is* change, potency remains while ἐνέργεια comes and goes (*Metaph.* IX.3, 1046b29–1047a10).

22 This is one of the strongest arguments Plato has against the being of change (e.g., Plato, *Timaeus* 38b). But in fact the criticism only applies to the quantity of change, e.g., the space or distance it covers, and not to the change itself, which is itself a source of unity: "what is called continuous is that of which the change is one in its own right" (*Metaph.* V.6, 1016a4–5, my translation).

Second, Aristotle needs to show that activity has an even more fundamental structure than dispersion. He will show this by arguing that activity is aimed at, and converges with, τέλος. In fact, it is only being *for* something, that is, having its own directed character, that makes it possible for change to be dispersive. For the outcome of activity could not be in some other thing unless the activity of change *also* and primarily *aims* and is *directed somewhere*. Thus, change is directed at a τέλος, which means that activity is intrinsically related to τέλος. This will remove the worry that being merely the use of potency and therefore being fundamentally other-directed might mean that activity is not the τέλος. I shall call this the Etymological Argument. It sets the table for the claim that activity is τελεία, but does not clinch it, since the transitive activities still appear to be in different locations from their products.

Note that the claims that change is dispersive and that there is a τέλος of change are not mutually contradictory. Change contains asymmetric structures: one of othering or dispersion and the other of direction and accomplishment.

Third, to show that activity can, through itself, be an accomplishment, Aristotle needs to show that the activity is in the same place as the accomplishment, not apart from it. He will show this by distinguishing between intransitive and transitive activities. Thus, he distinguishes between two senses of τέλος: (i) the fulfillment of a *potency*, as in the builder's activity of building, or the buildable's activity of being built, and (ii) the product as the fulfillment of *changes* (which is to say of the activity of a being in potency), such as the house that comes to be. I shall call this the Location Argument.

B. *The Structure Argument* (Metaph. IX.8, 1050a15–16). Aristotle's task is to establish that being-at-work (ἐνέργεια) can be an accomplishment (τέλος) after all. But he first needs to show that activity is structured. The worry is twofold. On the one hand, insofar as it is the use of potency, being-at-work seems not to have its own form, but to derive whatever structure it has from potency. Similarly, on the other hand, to the extent that it is transitive, its structure could be entirely derivative from what it produces. He shows that activity is structured by specifying how the concept of potency extends to material and activity extends to form.[23] In the Structure Argument (*Metaph.* IX.8, 1050a15–16), I aim to

---

23 Aristotle announced that potency and activity could be extended to material and οὐσία in *Metaph.* IX.6, 1048a32-b9, but he describes the extension through examples, and characterizes the relationship between the change-related terms and the material-οὐσία-related terms as analogous. Since in the *Rhetoric* being analogous (ἀνάλογον) means being the same (ὁμοῖος), Anagnostopoulos argues that between the two senses of the terms there is a single shared relation between potency and activity, that is, that the terms apply in the

show, the claim is that the internal structure of the relation between material and form is actually a relation between potency and ἐνέργεια. The defining characteristics of this relation are that material/potency tends toward its counterpart, and that when it is at work, it has the structure of the form. By doing this, he shows that potency and activity are definite in every sense of those words, notably including senses referring to change.

Aristotle defines material in terms of potency in several places (*Metaph.* VIII.1, 1042a26–8; VIII.2, 1043a15–17; VIII.6, 1045b18–19). To describe a house insofar as it is potent is, first, to describe its bricks and wood (that is the level of material immediately relevant to being a house), not to describe its elemental constituents (compare *Metaph.* VIII.4, 1044a33–b3 and IX.7, 1049a19–b1). Second, it is to describe this material *exactly insofar as it is capable of being a house*.[24] If you describe a particular whole thing by describing it insofar as it is potent, you are describing material parts as capable of being a particular whole thing. But in these passages, while Aristotle clearly indicates that potency and material are related to one another, he does not describe the relationship between potency and activity, nor does he say explicitly what it is about material that makes it useful to call it potency. The same goes for form. But in the passage that concerns us now, he does just this: "Furthermore, (1) material is in-potency [δυνάμει] because it comes to [ἔλθοι] a form; and (2) when it is at-work [ἐνεργείᾳ], then it is *in* the form" (*Metaph.* IX.8, 1050a15–16, my translation). This passage describes the relationship between potency and activity very clearly, namely that material comes to form in the way potency comes to activity. Let us examine claims (1) and (2) in order.

Claim (1) expresses the relationship between potency and material. As a source, potency immediately sets to work in an other or is set to work by an other when the conditions are right (*Metaph.* IX.7, 1049a5–18). This means that material immediately takes a form when the conditions are right, as metal flakes snap into a certain arrangement when a magnet is present. Material comes to the form the way potency sets to work when the conditions are right. For material to be in potency means, for something natural, that it will be on

---

same way to both cases (Anagnostopoulos 2010, 416–424). Pointing out the identity of the relation between potency and activity and other uses of the words, Anagnostopoulos claims that the dative case (being-in-potency, δυνάμει and being-in-work, ἐνεργείᾳ) and the nominative case (potency, δύναμις, and being-at-work, ἐνέργεια) are interchangeable, meaning that the dative case offers no special "ontological" sense of the terms.

24 Note that, *contra* Panayides (1999), material is not related to form as a lack (στέρησις) is related to form, as Aristotle explicitly warns: "For we say that material and lack are different things, and of these the one is a non-being incidentally, namely the material, while the lack is so in its own right, and the one, the material, is almost, and in a certain respect is, an οὐσία, which the other is not at all" (*Phys.* I.9, 192a3; Sachs 1999 translation).

its own unless something gets in its way and, for something artificial, that it will be if the artificer desires it (*Metaph.* IX.7, 1049a5–18). To come to a form, then, is to be in that form unless something gets in the way, that is, to be at work, ἐνέργεια. Thus, claim (1) both characterizes the relationship between potency and activity, and in addition says what it is about material that relates it to the form.

But the argument from γένεσις that we examined earlier in this paper enriches the description of this structure: potency is on the way to activity because its being is *what* it is for the sake of *generating* activity, so material, too, is *what* it is for the sake of *giving rise to* a form. Thus trees are cut into planks, and these planks are what they are for the sake of generating a house or a table; the organs of the body come to be what they are for the sake of generating the activity of the living animal.

The word "come to" (ἔρχομαι) cannot mean that material moves toward form in a literal sense, nor that it changes into form in an ontological sense. For material and form are not the poles that define the continuous magnitude between the opposites involved in change—those poles are form and its privation (στέρησις) (*Phys.* I.7, 190b30–191a2). For the same reason, it cannot mean that potency moves toward activity or is converted into activity. Instead, the word ἔρχομαι indicates that material is active in its relationship with form, that it tends to generate a form. Genesis shows this tendency more clearly than any other phenomenon: a thing's progression from the absence of form F into the organized form F exhibits the tendency, that is, the potency, and potency is, thus, apparent in the way that coming-to-be is *for* its τέλος.

Claim (2) answers the worry that activity is indeterminate with the argument that activity is itself something distinct, meaning that it has a form. To argue that the material is *in* the form when it is active amounts to arguing that it has come to have a certain active shape. What is the basis for this claim? The preceding argument from γένεσις suggests one, namely, that what *comes to be* is something definite. This is a reasonably intuitive claim: we say γένεσις has occurred when something definite has arisen, that is, something with a distinct form, but if nothing definite has arisen, we do not say γένεσις has occurred.

The tendency of potency and material to set to work when conditions are right implies that when it is at work it has come to have a definite structure or form. Through this identification of material and form with potency and activity, Aristotle does not just gain a way to indicate the active, source-like aspect of material and form. He also makes it quite clear that activity is structured.

But it was not the case of material and form that led to the worry about indefiniteness; it was the transitive and other-directed character of changes. This is why Aristotle immediately turns back to change:

(1) material is in-potency [δυνάμει] because it comes to [ἔλθοι] a form; and (2) when it is at-work [ἐνεργείᾳ], then it is *in* the form. And (3) it is similar in other cases, including those in which the accomplishment is change, and that is why teachers display [ἀποδεδωκέναι] a student at work, thinking that they are delivering up the accomplishment, and nature does likewise. (*Metaph.* IX.8, 1050a15–19, my translation)

Aristotle explicitly marks change as an accomplishment. Change is *not* essentially incomplete, for *change is itself an accomplishment, an accomplishment of potency.*[25] In this case, the student's being-at-work is a change, and being-at-work is being in the form. As the τέλος of potency, change has a form, an organization and order. It is because change has a form that it can maintain the organization of material, as what is seen with a body staying the same through continuous change.[26] Applying it here means that changes, not just objects, have structures, patterns, and forms that we can grasp and articulate.

C. *The Etymological Argument* (Metaph. *IX.8, 1050a21–23*). The Structure Argument has shown that potency and activity are definite, but it did not deal directly with the problem of dispersion. Since potency and activity seem other-directed (potency by being a source of change in an other, the activity of potency by being a change in an other), they seem always to differ from their τέλος. In the Etymological Argument, Aristotle dismantles this problem by showing that the way genetic processes and other changes are oriented, namely, their directedness, actually bolsters activity's claim to being a τέλος.

The Etymological Argument connects the root words that make up ἐνέγεια and ἐντελέχεια. Although it has the form of an etymological argument, it also has philosophical content. Aristotle uses the word "work" (ἔργον) to show that ἐνέργεια is naturally related to τέλος:

For (1) the work [ἔργον] is an accomplishment [τέλος], and (2) *being-at-work* [ἐνέργεια] is the work, and (3) this is why the name *being at work* is said through the work and (4) stretches toward [συντείνειν] being-complete [ἐντελέχεια]. (*Metaph.* IX.8, 1050a21–23, my translation)

---

25 Only the parts of changes are incomplete. The whole change is complete (*NE* X.4, 1174a13–b23).

26 As Socrates suggests, drawing on Heraclitus: "Doesn't the condition of bodies get destroyed by quiet and idleness, but get preserved for the most part by exercises and motion?" (*Theaetetus* 153b, Benardete 1984 translation).

The path joining ἐνέργεια to τέλος is the path from ἐν-έργ-εια to ἐν-τελ-έχ-εια.[27] To join the two together, Aristotle appeals to the idea that the root word "work" (ἔργον) evidently names an accomplishment, completion, or outcome (τέλος). Once this gets established, his goal is to substitute accomplishment (τέλος) for work (ἔργον). We can map out the path, supplying ἐντελεία as a step in the etymological pathway.

Word	Meaning	Argument
(1) ἔργον	ἔργον-object = a work, possessions, subject matter	ἔργον-object = τέλος
	ἔργον-act = an act, deed, work	
(2) ἐν-έργ-εια	ἐνέργεια = *being at work*, being-in-act, activity, doing, being-in-the-work	ἐν-έργ-εια = ἔργον-object OR ἐν-έργ-εια = ἔργον-act
(3) ἐν-έργ-εια		ἐν-έργ-εια aims at the ἔργον-object
		OR ἐν-έργ-εια means being *in* the ἔργον-object
		OR ἐνέργεια is named after the ἔργον in either sense of the word
+ ἐν-τέλ-εια	completed, accomplished	The ἔργον-object is the τέλος.
		τέλος replaces ἔργον.
(4) ἐν-τελ-έχ-εια	being-complete, having-the-accomplishment, being-in-accomplishment	ἐντελεία + ἔχειν, have or possess, hold on, be, lead or point toward. This reintroduces ἔργον-act.

---

27 Aristotle coined both ἐνέργεια and ἐντελέχεια to have this philosophical relationship, which is one reason translating them less literally (e.g., rendering both as "actuality," one or the other as "reality," "activity," etc.) prevents the words from functioning as resources for understanding the concepts.

The argument is difficult to grasp, for two reasons: "work" could mean either the work-act or the work-object, and to say that being-at-work "stretches toward," "strains toward," "converges with," or "draws tight to" (συντείνειν) being-complete could mean either that it aims at being-complete, or that being-at-work (ἐνέργεια) and being-complete (ἐντελέχεια) ultimately mean the same thing.

The clear point of departure is that (1) both the work-object and certain kinds of work-acts are accomplishments (τέλος), like a carpenter's table and a singer's act of singing. Step (2) would then be the claim that the being-at-work is the work-object (this would be the activity of a table holding itself together), or the potency at-work (as in the cases of the activity of building or singing). Steps (1) and (2) set up the claim that being-at-work is a τέλος.

But steps (3) and (4) do not straightforwardly draw this conclusion.[28] They argue that the source of the structure of being-at-work is the work that it brings into being.[29] For the claim (3) that being-at-work is named through (κατά) the

---

28   There is a difference between saying that (2) being-at-work *is* the work and saying that (3) being-at-*work* is named through or by the work, since the latter could be a different thing. This conflict could be resolved by claiming that being-at-work only means the work-act, and that claim (2) is about priority instead of identity and says that being-at-work is the work *more* than the work-object. The problem with this is that it conflicts with another of Aristotle's positions, namely that the transcendent work-object takes priority over the act of production.

29   At first, it seems that the argument could amount to the claim that ἐνέργεια means being-*in*-the-τέλος: the claim (3) that being-at-work is named through the work could draw both on the root ἔργον and also on the ἐν-prefix. On this reading, the ἐν- prefix of ἐν-έργ-εια would mean "in," recalling the claim that being-in-ἐνέργεια is being *in* the form (ὅταν δὲ γε ἐνεργείᾳ ᾖ, τότε ἐν τῷ εἴδει ἐστίν) from the Structure Argument (*Metaph.* IX.8, 1050a15–16). Thus, being ἐν-έργ-εια would mean being-*in*-the-work in the sense of being *in* an accomplished form, whether the work/τέλος is a table or a song. This makes step (4) a strong claim, that being-in-work *just is* being-in-the-τέλος. For example, the activity of the builder is *in* the work-object or form, the activity of a runner has the form "running," which is to say the movement of running is its ἐντελέχεια, and the activity of thinking is *in* the form "thinking." This is quite a literal interpretation of ἐνέργεια. What is at-work is *in* the τέλος. This leads directly to the Location Argument, which we shall turn to in a moment. But there are two worries with this reading. First, it seems to define ἐνέργεια as something static, whereas Aristotle uses it in the surrounding passages as a synonym for the activity of use (χρῆσις). The solution is to make both being-in and the work into activities, for example, because a living animal and a table both are actively being what they are. But we might hold back from reading the passage this way for a more serious reason: because there is a conflict between saying that the ἔργον is the τέλος (*Metaph.* IX.8, 1050a21) or that ἐνέργεια is the τέλος of potency (*Metaph.* IX.8, 1050a9–10) and saying that ἐνέργεια means being *in* the τέλος (*Metaph.* IX.8, 1050a15–16), since the latter seems to make the τέλος something else than the ἐνέργεια. The problem is that, however literal a rendering it is of ἐνέργεια, being-in-the-work-τέλος seems to substitute the *relation between* potency and

work means that the being-at-work takes its name from the work-object that it accomplishes. For the activity to aim at the work is for it to be organized by the work, for its structure to come from the work. This is why the building-act takes its name from the building-object that emerges from it, even though the building-act is definitely *not* the same as its object.[30] Thus (4) being-at-work stretches, strains, or extends toward, and draws tight with (all translations of συντείνειν) its accomplishment.

On this reading, the Etymological Argument does not equate being-at-work (ἐνέργεια) with being-complete (ἐντελέχεια). Instead, the builder's activity is what brings the building into being; the being-at-work is what *accomplishes* the accomplishment. This is what is expressed in the word συντείνειν.

In sum: I contend that the Etymological Argument addresses an objection to the possibility that being-at-work could be an accomplishment (τέλος), namely, that since the activity was directed at an *other*, it could not itself be a τέλος. If I am right, the argument shows, by contrast, that because being-at-work stretches toward and brings about a τέλος, it is the *source* of this τέλος. Because being-at-work brings the accomplishment into being, we call being-at-work an accomplishment as well (in the sense of accomplish*ing*), and we give it a name derived from the whole accomplishment.

D. *The Location Argument* (Metaph. IX.8, 1050a23–b2). But there is still a crucial problem: the claim that being-at-work is continuous with, and the source of, the τέλος that it accomplishes falls apart if the two are in different locations. If the activity belongs to a different being, then it seems that the relationship between the source and what it generates will be accidental. If so, it seems that everything caused by potent beings would be accidental: since the activity would be external to the effects it generates, there would be no *per se* causes.[31]

The Location Argument solves this problem by distinguishing the location of the accomplishment that belongs to each sort of potency, and it shows that in each case being-at-work is alongside its accomplishment, in the very same being. At the same time, Aristotle distinguishes the being-at-work of a potency

---

ἐνέργεια, or material and form, for the definition of ἐνέργεια itself. The problem is particularly acute, since what is at stake is τέλος. Saying that this is what ἐνέργεια itself is produces an infinite regress. To finesse this problem by restricting the Etymological Argument to cases in which ἐνέργεια has a further product means to resort to an *ad hoc* solution, and it is thin on textual support.

30   It is worth noting that, at the time, activities of production would have been recognizably related to their products. This is far less clear in an industrialized manufacturing process, especially with the advent of modular parts.

31   For a way to solve this problem, see Kelsey's argument that for a change to be by nature just means that the change is happening to a being that is its proper subject (Kelsey 2003).

from the product of the work. Thus, the activity of the builder is an accomplishment in a different way from the house: the activity of the builder is an accomplishment of the capacity to build, whereas the house is the accomplishment of the activity of building. But the working is *in* the thing that is complete, not apart from it. Thus, Aristotle's distinction between two senses of τέλος—the fulfillment of a potency and the work-object—allows him to show that they are located in the same place as the activity (ἐνέργεια), which means the two are related to one another internally, through themselves.

There are two rounds of argument at *Metaph.* IX.8, 1050a23–b2, each of which deals with two cases, where activities are themselves ultimate (ἔσχατον) and where activities are productive: in the first round, Aristotle works out the status of "putting to use" (χρῆσις), and in the second round, he locates the activity where the accomplishment is. Instead of quoting directly, I here paraphrase to show the structure of the argument:

(1) The potent thing, for example, the seer, the house-building capacity, is responsible for what comes to be, as we saw, but potency relates to the accomplishment it generates in two ways:
(2) The paradigms of the first structure are seeing, contemplating, life, and happiness, that is, natural potencies. Whenever only the exercise (χρῆσις) comes to be (γένεσις),
   a. The exercise or being-at-work is the last thing, the τέλος.
   b. Furthermore, the accomplishment of what is potent arises *in* what is potent.
   c. Therefore, by being active, the potent being is *in* the accomplishment. The ἐν-έργ-εια is ἐν-τελ-έχ-εια.
   d. Therefore the being-at-work or exercise is just as much an accomplishment (τέλος) as the potency.
(3) The paradigms of the second structure are building, weaving, and changes in general, in other words, productive potencies. Whenever from what is potent both the exercise and a work-object come to be (γένεσις),
   a. the being-at-work of the builder is *in the thing made*, the change is *in* what is moved [see also *Phys* III.3]
   b. The being-at-work is therefore together with the work-object, which is to say the accomplishment (τέλος), namely, *in* what is moved, at the same time as it is there. For example, the house-building occurs in the house, and comes to be and *is* at the same time as the house.

c. Therefore, since the being-at-work or exercise of the potency, that is, the work-act or ἐνέργεια, is *in* the work-object with the τέλος, the ἐν-έργ-εια is *more* a τέλος, more ἐντελέχεια than the potency [since the potency to act is *not* in the same being as the τέλος]. (*Metaph.* IX.8, 1050a23–b2, paraphrased for brevity)

First, transitive activities are directed beyond themselves at another thing. Being-at-work in this case is γένεσις: when building is the activity, it brings into being its τέλος and is directed toward it. Thus, the basis for the claim that ἐνέργεια aims at ἐντελέχεια is (the structure of) γένεσις. Second, for intransitive activities like singing, seeing, and thinking, since there is no further object generated by the activity of working, it appears that the τέλος is a work in the sense of an act, rather than an object (*Metaph.* IX.8, 1050a23–24).[32] In this case, since the *potency* brings the activity into being, it is still γένεσις, in the sense marked out above, that is the basis for its priority.

To draw out the import of the argument and its relationship to change, we need to note several things. First, being-at-work is clearly synonymous with exercise (χρῆσις). Γένεσις here covers every sort of change that has a potency-like source. Second, as noted, Aristotle uses γένεσις in two ways: the potency brings into being both the activity of building and the house or any other sort of change. Third, the exercise of the capacity to build, in other words the activity of building, and the house ultimately exist at the same time, once the house has taken hold of its shape.[33] This follows from the claim in the Etymological

---

32 It is misguided to read Aristotle as giving an account of activities like singing, seeing, and thinking as producing their objects. But it seems possible to allow a work-act to play the role of a work-object in the sense that it has a definite form. This makes these activities implicitly transitive, that is, intentional: singing stretches out toward the song, thinking toward its object, seeing toward what is visible. An important caveat here is that Aristotle takes thinking and seeing to be affected by their objects, rather than extending toward them: even though the knower can put her knowing to work on her own, this means she allows herself to be affected (*An.* II.4, 429a14–18, b6–9).

33 Some scholars are vexed by the claim that house-building comes to be and is at the same time as the house, since it conflicts with their view that the potency for building is extinguished when the house comes to be (which is the Potent Actuality reading inaugurated by Kosman). Kosman requires potencies for change, like building, to annihilate themselves by completing themselves (Kosman 1969 and 2013). The problem is not removed by saying that something of the τέλος has already come into being along the way (*Metaph.* IX.8, 1049b35–1050a2), because what has come to be already is not the complete thing, e.g., when the foundation of the house has come to be, but the house has not yet (*Phys.* VI.6, 237b10–24, cf. Chapter 5). To solve the apparent conflict, Charles argues that γένεσις constitutes two potencies at once: one for becoming a house, the other for being a house, but that the claim in this context "may mean no more than that the house building occurs

Argument that activity is continuous with its accomplishment. Fourth, potency always has an accomplishment, τέλος, in the same place the ἐνέργεια is. This gives us a very literal use of ἐντελέχεια: the being-at-work is, in fact, *in* the accomplishment, and bound up with it (συντείνειν).

Fifth, and most importantly, the reasoning seems to be that activity is prior to potency in cases of production because productive activities are located in the τέλος they produce, whereas the productive potency is located in the producer. But the same criterion yields no priority in the intransitive cases. We would expect ἐνέργεια to be more τέλος than potency in every case, and in particular, we might expect the intransitive activities like contemplation to be *more* τελεία than potency.[34] But Aristotle claims merely that the exercise of intransitive potencies is *at least as much* a τέλος as the potency. This shows that the decisive criterion is not simply τέλος, but, I argue, ἀρχή.[35]

VI Aristotle's Conclusion

Let us summarize the argument, before turning to the conclusion Aristotle draws from it. Since we only count γένεσις to have occurred when a definite thing emerges, generation is used as the paradigm of structures that are *for* something. The argument that being-at-work (ἐνέργεια) is prior to potency in beinghood (οὐσία) uses the structure of generation (γένεσις) to show that an accomplishment (τέλος) is a source (ἀρχή) in the most governing way and then analyzes its structure to show that ἐνέργεια can, in fact, be an accomplishment, meaning a definite structure whose identity derives from and is located in the product.

Part One of the argument aimed to establish that the accomplishment (τέλος) that results from a genetic process has a privileged status: since the process is *for* something, the principal source (ἀρχή) of the process is its

---

in the same place as the house" (Charles 2010, 184n, 189–190). On my reading, this is straightforward and correct. For her part, Broadie argues that ἐνέργεια has two senses: the ongoing activity of building that occurs for the sake of the house and the perfect aspect having-been-completed, that is, the ἐντελέχεια, which coincides with the house (Broadie 2010, 208).

34 Broadie appears to treat the intransitive activities as obviously prior to their potencies, whereas the productive activities are the ones that are problematic (Broadie 2010).

35 Many scholars characterize potency explicitly as a lack (see Sentesy 2018). The concept of complete potencies makes sense of the difficulty we have distinguishing between potency and ἐντελέχεια, e.g., at *An.* II.5, 417a22–24.

accomplishment (τέλος). Since even the potency is generated for it, the accomplishment must be primary.

Part Two of the argument aimed to show that being-at-work has the characteristics required for it to be an accomplishment: it has its own definite structure, this structure derives in each case from the accomplishment, and because it is in the same place as the accomplishment, the two can be internally related to each other.

To make these claims, Aristotle throughout uses γένεσις, coming-to-be, as the paradigm for sources. In particular, γένεσις provides the teleological structure of sources in general. It makes it possible to distinguish potency-like sources from τέλος-like sources and relates them to each other. The claim that an accomplishment has to sourcehood is based on the fact that things come-to-be *for it*. Without γένεσις, the claim has no basis or content.

Aristotle draws from this argument a conclusion that is, on the face of it, surprising. The stated aim of *Metaphysics* IX.8 was to show that activity is prior to potency in speech, time, οὐσία, and in independent existence. But the argument culminates in a claim (Claim 1) that goes well beyond the task of merely establishing the relative priority of activity, to the extent that the original claim (Claim 2) is merely tacked onto it:

> And so (1) it is clear that beinghood [οὐσία] and form [εἶδος] are being-at-work [ἐνέργεια]. So (2) as a result of this argument it is obvious that being-at-work takes precedence over potency in οὐσία. (*Metaph.* IX.8, 1050b2–3, translation modified)

The claim goes far beyond the explicit goals of the chapter: to claim that ἐνέργεια takes precedence in οὐσία does not require saying that οὐσία *and* εἶδος are essentially ἐνέργεια. Aristotle did not signal along the way that he was going to draw this conclusion. Some scholars think that this is because the claim is obvious.[36] If I am right, however, this conclusion is a genuine accomplishment.

This claim is justified by the landmark arguments we have examined: the argument is based on the claim that being *for* something (ἕνεκα) has the structure of generation (γένεσις). From this, Aristotle argues that in anything with a for-structure the accomplishment (τέλος) is the source (ἀρχή), that the way a thing is a source determines its primacy in beinghood (οὐσία), that the relation

---

36 For example, Beere makes this conclusion a premise in an earlier argument, suggesting that Aristotle failed to mention it there because it was too obvious (Beere 2009, 311, 313). Makin does not mention the conclusion in his commentary, presumably for the same reason (Makin 2006). Ross says that it follows from the whole argument for priority in οὐσία, noting in particular what I have called the Structure Argument (Ross 1924).

of a potency coming up to what it generates is the structure of the relation between material (ὕλη) and form (εἶδος), that being-at-work (ἐνέργεια) has its own form or structure, that this structure is determined by what it accomplishes, that both the being-at-work and the work-object are accomplishments, and that they both occur in the same being.

COLLOQUIUM 2

Commentary on Sentesy

Daniel Shartin
Worcester State University

Abstract

As Aristotle's treatments of substance and change develop from the *Categories* through the middle books of the *Metaphysics,* his interest in living things as the best examples of substances becomes more evident. Reading *Metaphysics* IX.8 against the background of these developments can help us better understand that chapter's discussion of the priority of actuality to potentiality.

Keywords

substance – potentiality – actuality – priority – organism

∴

> At the very beginnings of science, the striking dissimilarities between living and nonliving things became obvious. Two tendencies can be discerned in the attempts to arrive at a unified view of our world. One tendency is to use the living thing as the model system. This tendency is exemplified by Aristotle. For him, the son of a physician and the keen observer of many forms of life, it was obvious that things develop according to plans. Every animal and plant is generated in some definite way, runs through a cycle of development in which it unfolds its inherent plan, and succumbs to death and decay. For Aristotle, this very obvious feature of the world which surrounds us is the model for understanding the (sublunary) world.
>
> MAX DELBRÜCK, 20th-century biophysicist, Nobel laureate

∴

1   **Introduction**

What does Aristotle mean by saying that actuality is prior *in substance* to potentiality? What, indeed, does it mean for any kind of thing to be prior *in substance* to another? And why does Aristotle care about these questions? I think the general answer has to do with Aristotle's abiding interests in *substance* (particularly in living things) and in the differences between alteration and coming-to-be. Prof. Sentesy's emphasis on *genesis* in his thorough and stimulating paper, "*Genesis* and the Priority of *Energeia* in Aristotle's *Metaphysics* IX.8," may indicate that he would agree with me on some of these points.

Metaphysics IX.8 argues that actuality is prior to potentiality in formula, in time (in one sense), and in substance.[1] The bulk of the chapter is spent on the issue of priority in *substance*, and Sentesy's paper appropriately focusses almost exclusively on this issue, which he identifies as the "most contentious."

Aristotle begins the chapter with the confident claims: "(i) We have distinguished the various senses of 'prior', and (ii) it is clear that actuality is prior to potentiality" (1049b4–5), and the discussion that follows appears to be a series of arguments for claim (ii). But, as Sentesy tells us in his introduction, "the basis for the argument is not very clear. It does not obviously proceed, for example, by applying a clear, pre-established analysis of priority in beinghood" (Sentesy 2019, 44).

Sentesy's strategy is to show that, in IX.8, rather than applying "a pre-existing account of priority to the case of potency and being-at-work, [Aristotle] makes an immanent argument" (Sentesy 2019, 44) that examines the structure of sources. I agree that IX.8 does not proceed by providing an explicit account of priority *in substance* and then applying that account to the case at hand, but in my brief comments I'll aim to show that Aristotle does indeed have a previously developed account of priority *in substance*—and that account can help in understanding IX.8.

In part II of these comments, I'll cite some brief, representative passages from the *Categories*, *On Generation and Corruption*, the *Generation of Animals*, and the *Metaphysics*, to establish a context for my understanding of IX.8. I'll then return, in part III, to a closer examination of some of passages of IX.8. My aim will never be to show that Sentesy is mistaken in his analysis, as I believe him to be largely correct; I'll try instead possibly to supplement some aspects of his paper.

---

1   Aristotle cites this same trio of types of priority at *Metaphysics* VII.13, 1038b27–29: "Neither in formula nor in time nor in coming to be can the affections be prior to substance, for then they would be separable from it."

11   Some Background on *Substance*

The *Categories* offers Aristotle's opening thoughts on the concept of *substance*, thoughts he develops in additional texts. It's helpful in following the trail of those developments to have an initial understanding of the *Categories*' theory.

In the *Categories*, there are just four types of things: primary substances, secondary substances, primary non-substances, and secondary non-substances. The primary substances are individual things (for example: Socrates, Callias, or this particular book); the other three sorts of things are all universals (the sorts of things that can be predicates in subject-predicate sentences). In addition to (or rather, because of) the fact that primary substances are the only things in the *Categories*' world that can never be predicated of anything, they occupy a special place within this limited ontology:

- It seems most distinctive of [primary] substance that what is numerically one and the same is able to receive contraries. In no other case could one bring forward anything, numerically one, which is able to receive contraries. (*Cat.* 4a10–13)
- If the primary substances did not exist it would be impossible for any of the other things to exist. (*Cat.* 2b5–6)

Further, when a secondary substance is predicated of a primary substance (as in a sentence such as "Socrates is a man"), "man" is said of the individual man as subject but is not in a subject: "man is not *in* the individual man" (*Cat.* 3a14). When a predicate from outside the category of substance is predicated of Socrates (as when, "Socrates is bald"), the paronym of the predicate *inheres in* the subject (for example, baldness inheres in Socrates). The important point here is that cross-categorial predication expresses a relationship between two separable things, but this isn't the case for intra-categorial predication. Whatever the relationship is between Socrates and his being a man, it isn't one between two conceptually separable things. This fact reflects, I think, Aristotle's early understanding that, while Socrates may change from being bald to being hairy while continuing to be the same thing numerically, he could not analogously survive the change from being a man to being a goat; for Socrates to cease to be a man is for him to cease to be. I think this relationship between an individual and its species is one Aristotle continues to examine through *Metaphysics* IX.8.

So, the concepts of *change* and *substance* are importantly related to each other in the *Categories* (primary substances are distinguished as the only kinds of things that can undergo change), but the only kind of change recognized in the *Categories* is the kind Aristotle later calls "alteration." In later works Aristotle distinguishes alteration from coming-to-be and passing away:

> We must inquire what each of them is and whether alteration has the same nature as coming-to-be, or whether to these different names there correspond two different processes with different natures. (GC I.1, 314a4–6)

In beginning to explain the difference between alteration and coming to be, he maintains:

> In one sense things come to be out of that which has no being without qualification; yet in another they come to be always out of what is. For there must pre-exist something which *potentially* is, but *actually* is not; and this something is spoken of both as being and as not-being. (GC I.3, 317b15–18)

We know at this point that primary substances are individual things, that they alone are able to undergo alteration, and that coming-to-be involves progressing from potentiality to actuality—but we don't yet know which things are substances. My late mentor and friend Montgomery Furth distinguished what he called the 'metaphysical problem' about substance from the 'population problem': (1) What *makes* something a substance? (2) Which things *are* the substances? (Furth 1989, 54–58). These two questions cannot, of course, be answered independently of each other; knowing which things Aristotle regarded as substances will greatly help in understanding what it was about those things that made them substances. Several passages from the middle books of the *Metaphysics* and elsewhere indicate fairly clearly Aristotle's answer to this population problem: living things are the clearest cases of substances. Some of these passages follow:

> ***Metaph.* VII.7, 1032a15–19**: "Now natural comings to be are the comings to be of those things which come to be by nature; and that out of which they come to be is what we call matter; and that by which they come to be is something which exists naturally; and *the something which they come to be is a man or a plant or one of the things of this kind, which we say are substances if anything is.*" [Italics added]

> ***Metaph.* VII.8, 1033b29–33**: "In some cases it is even obvious that the producer is the same kind as the produced (not, however, the same or one in

COMMENTARY ON SENTESY

number, but in form), e.g. in the case of natural products (for man produces man), unless something happens contrary to nature, e.g. the production of a mule by a horse."

Metaph. VII.8, 1034a4: "for these [living things] are substances if anything is so."

Metaph. VII.9, 1034a11–13: "In some cases the matter which determines the production ... is such as to be set in motion by itself ... and can move itself in the particular way required."

Metaph. VII.9, 1034a33–b1: "Things formed by nature are in the same case as these products of art. For the seed produces them as the artist produces the works of art, for it has the form potentially."

Everything *that comes to be* (for we'll be reminded in IX.8 that there are some existent things that don't come to be) is produced by another (or others), but what's unique about a living thing is that once the production of the thing is set in motion by a seed or by the action of the parents, the rest of the process is guided by something within the offspring itself. In building a house, by contrast, the builders have to stick around and work until the house is completed; but in producing a new human body, once the act of conception is complete, the matter can, as Aristotle puts it at *Metaphysics* VII.9, 1034a13, "move itself in the particular way required." And Aristotle is especially interested in the fact that living things reproduce in kind (see "for man produces man" in *Metaphysics* VII.9, 1033b32 passage quoted above). The fact that human copulation produces only humans, if it produces anything at all (and the same with equines producing only horses, etc.) indicates to Aristotle that in conception some *information* must be passed from the parents to the conceptus in addition to whatever matter carries that information.[2] This information (or form) contains the "instructions" for making a new member of the same species as the parents, and that offspring will, as it were, "construct itself" from those instructions that are now in it.

---

2   In the quote at the beginning of these comments, Max Delbrück calls this information a "plan," and he suggests elsewhere that Aristotle's thought on this topic contained a precursor of the notion of DNA.

III   Topics for Further Discussion

Reading the arguments of *Metaphysics* IX.8 against the background of Aristotle's earlier and often-repeated contention that it's living things that are "substances most of all" leads to a somewhat different understanding of those arguments. I think that this different understanding and Professor Sentesy's may complement each other. I'll end by posing three issues to which I'd be interested in hearing his response.

(1) I agree completely with Sentesy that the opening paragraph of IX.8, 1049b3–12 sets the structure of the chapter: There are three senses in which one thing may be prior to another—in time, in formula, and in substance—and the chapter will argue that actuality is prior to potentiality in each of these ways. Sentesy does an excellent job of analyzing those arguments. But much of that opening paragraph is spent, I'd maintain, explaining that Aristotle's primary interest in talking about actuality and potentiality arises from his interest in living things. "For nature also is the same kind of thing as potentiality; *for it is a principle of movement— not, however, in something else but in the thing itself qua itself*" ([Italics added.] *Metaph.* IX.8, 1049b8–10). What's unique about living things for Aristotle is that they contain within themselves the principle that directs the development from potentiality to actuality. The thing that is only potentially a man (that is, the conceptus, or the embryo, or the boy) contains within itself the entire plan for making a man.

I maintain that this has been Aristotle's position for some time before *Metaphysics* IX.8, and if I'm right, Aristotle may take the chapter to be working out a position that he has held for some time. As Delbrück says,

> Every plant and animal is generated in some definite way, runs through a cycle of development in which it unfolds its inherent plan, and succumbs to death and decay. For Aristotle, this very obvious feature of the world which surrounds us is the model for understanding the (sublunary) world. (Delbrück 1972, 1312)

Sentesy is no doubt correct in suggesting that Aristotle does not, in IX.8, trot out senses of "priority" that have been established earlier; but I mean to suggest that he is using an argument that has deep roots in his other works.

(2) The 'biological' view I've been promoting also suggests a response to the "Location Argument" (*Metaph.* IX.8, 1050a23–b2) that Sentesy discusses. I understand Aristotle to be maintaining a line consistent with what I take to be his general view about the coming-to-be of living things: they contain within themselves the formal instructions for their own actualization, so they are the

same in location.[3] Sentesy comes, I think, to a similar conclusion when he says, about the question of location:

> the working is *in* the thing that is complete, not apart from it. Thus, Aristotle's distinction between two senses of τέλος—the fulfillment of a potency, and a work object—allows him to show that they are located in the same place as the activity (ἐνέργεια), which means the two are related to one another internally, through themselves. (Sentesy 2019, 66)

I'd be interested to know what Sentesy thinks about the relation between his view and the "biological" one.

(3) The hard work of *Metaphysics* IX.8 is finished by 1050b5, but the chapter goes on to a discussion Aristotle opens by saying, "But actuality is prior in a higher sense also; for eternal things are prior in substance to perishable things, and no eternal thing exists potentially" (*Metaph.* IX.8, 1050b6–7). Since these eternal things don't come into or pass out of existence, they don't fit into Sentesy's (or Aristotle's) discussion of *genesis*, but I think this final section of the chapter can nevertheless be instructive concerning some features of Aristotle's understanding of priority.

Eternal things cannot pass from potentiality to actuality since they cannot be potential, as "Every potentiality is at one and the same time a potentiality for the opposite" (*Metaph.* IX.8, 1050b8–9) and an eternal thing cannot come to be what it is not now. These eternal, imperishable things are universals; to use the language of the *Categories*, they are all of the things that can be predicated of other things, that is, everything but the primary substances. For Socrates, a primary substance, to exist is to be undergoing changes, but *man*, which is predicated of him, can't undergo any changes at all.

So far, all of this is consistent with the theory of the *Categories*, but in that earlier work, the primary substances have ontological priority (without them nothing else could exist), while in *Metaphysics* IX.8, Aristotle says of the universals that "these things are primary; for if these did not exist, nothing would exist" (1050b19). The primary things in the *Categories* were precisely those things that could "receive contraries," but we've learned by IX.8 that being able to receive contraries means that a thing *is* only potentially. Aristotle's position about which are the primary things has changed from the *Categories* to *Metaphysics* IX.8, but at least one criterion for assigning ontological priority

---

3   There are not, in fact, two separable things that could be in different locations. This is a point that may have been foreshadowed even in the *Categories'* insistence that intra-categorial predication could not be understood as a relationship between two separable things.

seems to remain intact: If A can exist without B, but B cannot exist without A, then A is prior in substance to B. Even though, as Professor Sentesy maintains, Aristotle does not explicitly base his arguments in the earlier parts of *Metaphysics* IX.8 on this criterion for *priority in substance*, the fact that he cites it repeatedly, and even in the latter part of *Metaphysics* IX.8, may indicate that the criterion provides at least one basis for the priority of actuality over potentiality.

COLLOQUIUM 2

Sentesy/Shartin Bibliography

Ackrill, J.L., tr. 1961. *Aristotle's Categories and De Interpretatione*. Oxford: Oxford University Press.

Ackrill, J.L. 1965. Aristotle's Distinction between *Energeia* and *Kinēsis*. In *New Essays on Plato and Aristotle* ed. R. Bambrough, 121–141. New York: Humanities Press.

Anagnostopoulos, A. 2010. Change in Aristotle's Physics 3. *Oxford Studies in Ancient Philosophy* 39:33–79.

Anagnostopoulos, G. ed. 2009. *A Companion to Aristotle*. Malden: Blackwell Publishing.

Balme, D.M. 1962. Development of Biology in Aristotle and Theophrastus: Theory of Spontaneous Generation. *Phronesis* 7.1:91–104.

Balme, D.M. 1965. Aristotle's Use of Teleological Explanation. Paper presented at the Inaugural Lecture, Queen Mary College, University of London, London.

Barnes, J., ed. 1984. *Aristotle, The Collected Works*, (2 Vols.). Princeton: Princeton University Press.

Beere, J. 2009. *Doing and Being: An Interpretation of Aristotle's Metaphysics Theta*. Oxford: Oxford University Press.

Benardete, S., tr. 1984. *Plato, Theaetetus*. In *The Being of the Beautiful*. Chicago: University of Chicago Press.

Bianchi, E. 2006. Material Vicissitudes and Technical Wonders: The Ambiguous Figure of Automaton in Aristotle's Metaphysics of Sexual Difference. *Epoche* 11.1:109–139.

Blair, G.A. 1967. The Meaning of 'Energeia' and 'Entelecheia' in Aristotle. *International Philosophical Quarterly* 7.1:101–17.

Blair, G.A. 1992. *Energeia and Entelecheia: "Act" in Aristotle*. Ottawa: University of Ottawa Press.

Blair, G.A. 1995. Unfortunately, It Is a Bit More Complex: Reflections on Ἐνέργεια. *Ancient Philosophy* 15: 92–93.

Blair, G.A. 2011. Aristotle on Entelexeia: A Reply to Daniel Graham. *The American Journal of Philology* 114.1:91–97.

Bradie, M. and Miller, F.D. 1984. Teleology and Natural Necessity in Aristotle. *History of Philosophy Quarterly* 1.2:133–146.

Brentano, F. 1975. *On the Several Senses of Being in Aristotle*. Translated by Rolf George. Berkeley: University of California Press.

Broadie (Waterlow), S. 1982. *Nature, Change and Agency in Aristotle's Physics*. Oxford: Oxford University Press.

Broadie, S. 2010. Where is the Activity? (An Aristotelian worry about the telic status of energeia). In *Being, Nature, and Life in Aristotle: Essays in Honor of Allan Gotthelf*, eds. J. Lennox and R. Bolton, 198–211. Cambridge: Cambridge University Press.

Burnyeat, M. 2008. Kinêsis vs. Energeia: A Much-Read Passage in (But Not Of) Aristotle's Metaphysics. *Oxford Studies in Ancient Philosophy* 6:219–92.

Charles, D. 2010. Actuality and Potentiality in Metaphysics Θ.7–8: Some issues concerning actuality and potentiality. In *Being, Nature, and Life in Aristotle: Essays in Honor of Allan Gotthelf*, eds. J. Lennox and R. Bolton, 168–197. Cambridge: Cambridge University Press.

Charles, D. 2015. Aristotle's Processes. In *Aristotle's Physics: A Critical Guide*, ed. M. Leunissen, 186–205. Cambridge: Cambridge University Press.

Charlton, W., tr. 1970. *Aristotle, Physics Book I and II*. Oxford: Oxford University Press.

Charlton, W. 1987. Aristotelian Powers. *Phronesis* 32.3:277–89.

Charlton, W. 1989. Aristotle on the Uses of Actuality. *Proceedings of the Boston Area Colloquium in Ancient Philosophy* 5:1–22.

Chen, C-H. 1956. Different Meanings of the Term *Energeia* in the Philosophy of Aristotle *Philosophy and Phenomenological Research* 17.1:56–65.

Code, A. 2003. Changes, Powers and Potentialities in Aristotle. In *Desire, Identity, and Existence: Essays in Honor of T.M. Penner*, ed. N. Reshotko, 253–71. Kelowna: Academic Printing & Publishing.

Connell, S.M. 2016. *Aristotle on Female Animals: A Study of the Generation of Animals.* Cambridge: Cambridge University Press.

Coope, U. 2015. Self-motion as other-motion in Aristotle's Physics. In *Aristotle's Physics: A Critical Guide*, ed. M. Leunissen, 245–264. Cambridge: Cambridge University Press.

Cooper, J. 1982. Aristotle on Natural Teleology. In *Language and Logos* eds. M. Schofield and M.C. Nussbaum, 197–222. Cambridge: Cambridge University Press.

Crombie, X.M. 1967. Review of *New Essays on Plato and Aristotle*. *Classical Review* N.S. 17:32.

Delbrück, M. 1970. A Physicist's Renewed Look at Biology: Twenty Years Later. *Science* 168:1312–15.

Dudley, J. 2011. *Aristotle's Concept of Chance: Accidents, Cause, Necessity, and Determinism.* Albany: State University of New York Press.

Ferejohn, M. 1994. Matter, Definition and Generation in Aristotle's *Metaphysics*. In *Proceedings of the Boston Area Colloquium in Ancient Philosophy, Vol. x*, eds. J.J. Cleary and W. Wians, 35–65. University Press of America.

Frede, M. 1994. Aristotle's Notion of Potentiality in Metaphysics Theta. In *Unity, Identity, and Explanation in Aristotle's Metaphysics*, eds. T. Scaltsas, D. Charles, and M.L. Gill, 173–93. Oxford: Oxford University Press.

Freeland, C. 1986. Aristotle on Possibilities and Capacities. *Ancient Philosophy* 6: 69–89.

Furth, M., tr. 1985. *Aristotle, Metaphysics: Books Zeta, Eta, Theta, Iota (VII-X)*. Indianapolis: Hackett.

Furth, M. 1989. *Substance, Form, and Psyche: An Aristotelian Metaphysics*. Cambridge: Cambridge University Press.

Gill, M.L. 1980. Aristotle's Theory of Causal Action in Physics III 3. *Phronesis* 25.1: 129–147.

Gotthelf, A. 1976. Aristotle's Conception of Final Causality. *Review of Metaphysics*, 30(2), 226–254.

Gotthelf, A. 1989. Teleology and Spontaneous Generation in Aristotle: A Discussion *Apeiron* 22.4:181–193.

Gotthelf, A. 2012. *Teleology, First principles, and Scientific Method in Aristotle's Biology*. Oxford: Oxford University Press.

Gotthelf, A. and Lennox, J., eds. 1987. *Philosophical Issues in Aristotle's Biology*. Cambridge: Cambridge University Press.

Graham, D.W. 1989. The Etymology of Entelecheia. *American Journal of Philology*, 110, 73–80.

Graham, D.W. 1995. The Development of Aristotle's Concept of Actuality: Comments on a Reconstruction by Stephen Menn. *Ancient Philosophy* 15:551–64.

Hagen, C. 1984. The ΕΝΕΡΓΕΙΑ-ΚΙΝΗΣΙΣ Distinction and Aristotle's Conception of ΠΡΑΙΞΙΣ. *Journal of the History of Philosophy* 3.22:263–280.

Hardie, W.P.R. 1968. *Aristotle's Ethical Theory*. Oxford: Oxford University Press.

Heidegger, M. 1995. *Aristotle's Metaphysics Θ 1–3: On the Essence and Actuality of Force*, tr. W. Brogan and P. Warnek. Bloomington: Indiana University Press.

Heidegger, M. 1998. "On the Essence and Concept of Φύσις in Aristotle's Physics B,1." In *Pathmarks*, tr. T. Sheehan and W. McNeill, 183–230. Cambridge: Cambridge University Press.

Hirst R.J. 1959. *The Problem of Perception*. New York: Macmillan.

Hoffman, W.M. 1976. Aristotle's Logic of Verb Tenses. *Journal of Critical Analysis* 6: 89–95.

Hull, D.L. 1968. The Conflict between Spontaneous Generation and Aristotle's Metaphysics, in *Proceedings of the Seventh Inter-American Congress of Philosophy*, Vol. II, 245–250. Quebec: Les Presses de l'Universite Laval.

Hussey, E., tr. 1993. *Aristotle's Physics Books III and IV*. Oxford: Clarendon Press.

Johnson, M.R. 2005. *Aristotle on Teleology*. Oxford University Press.

Kant, I. 1998 [1781]. *The Critique of Pure Reason*. tr. P. Guyer and A.W. Wood. Cambridge: Cambridge University Press.

Kelsey, S. 2003. Aristotle's Definition of Nature. *Oxford Studies in Ancient Philosophy* 25:59–87.

Kosman, A. 1969. Aristotle's Definition of Motion. *Phronesis* 14.1:40–62.

Kosman, A. 1984. Substance, Being, and Energeia. *Oxford Studies in Ancient Philosophy* 2:121–49.

Kosman, A. 1994. The Activity of Being in Aristotle's Metaphysics. In *Unity, Identity, and Explanation in Aristotle's Metaphysics*, eds. T. Scaltsas, D. Charles, and M.L. Gill, 195–213. Oxford: Clarendon Press.

Kosman, A. 2013. *The Activity of Being: An Essay on Aristotle's Ontology*. Cambridge: Harvard University Press.

Lennox, J. 1982. Teleology, Chance, and Aristotle's Theory of Spontaneous Generation. *Journal of the History of Philosophy* 20.3:219–238.

Makin, S., tr. 2006. *Aristotle, Metaphysics Book Θ*. Oxford: Oxford University Press.

Mamo, P.S. 1970. Energeia and Kinesis in Metaphysics Θ.6. *Apeiron* 4:24–34.

Mayr, E. 1974. Teleological and Teleonomic: A New Analysis. *Boston Studies in the Philosophy of Science* 14.1:91–117.

Menn, S. 1994. The Origins of Aristotle's Concept of Ἐνέργεια: Ἐνέργεια and Δύναμις. *Ancient Philosophy* 14:73–114.

Menn, S. Forthcoming. *The Aim and Argument of Aristotle's Metaphysics*. <https://www.philosophie.hu-berlin.de/de/lehrbereiche/antike/mitarbeiter/menn/contents>

Meyer, S.S. 1992. Aristotle, Teleology, and Reduction. *The Philosophical Review* 101.4:791–825.

Mirus, C. 2004. The Metaphysical Roots of Aristotle's Teleology. *The Review of Metaphysics* 57.4:699–724.

Mulhern, M.M. 1968. Types of Process According to Aristotle, *Monist* 52:237–51.

Panayides, C. 1999. Aristotle on the Priority of Actuality in Substance. *Ancient Philosophy* 19:327–344.

Panayides, C. 2013. Aristotle on Chance and Spontaneous Generation. A Discussion Note. *Filozofia* 68.2

Penner, T. 1970. Verbs and the Identity of Actions—A Philosophical Exercise in the Interpretation of Aristotle. In *Ryle: A Collection of Critical Essays* eds. O. Wood and G. Pitcher, 393–453. New York: Anchor Books.

Peramatzis, M. 2011. *Priority in Aristotle's Metaphysics*. Oxford: Oxford University Press.

Pickering, F.R. 1977. Aristotle on Walking. *Archiv für Geschichte der Philosophie* 59: 37–43.

Polansky, R. 1983. Energeia in Aristotle's Metaphysics IX. *Ancient Philosophy* 3:160–170.

Ross, W.D., ed. 1924. *Aristotle, Metaphysics: A Revised Text with Introduction and Commentary*. Oxford: Oxford University Press.

Ross, W.D., ed. 1936. *Aristotle, Physics: A Revised Text with Introduction and Commentary*. Oxford: Oxford University Press.

Ryle, G. 1954. *Dilemmas*. Cambridge: Cambridge University Press.

Sachs, J., tr. 1995. *Aristotle, Physics: A Guided Study*. New Brunswick: Rutgers University Press.

Sachs, J., tr. 1999. *Aristotle, Metaphysics*. Santa Fe: Green Lion Press.

Sentesy, M. 2018. Are Potency and Actuality Compatible in Aristotle? *Epoche* 22.2:239–270.

Sorabji, R. 1980. *Necessity, Cause, and Blame: Perspectives on Aristotle's Theory*. Chicago: University of Chicago Press.

Stavrianeas, S. 2008. Spontaneous Generation in Aristotle's Biology. *Rhizai. A Journal for Ancient Philosophy and Science* 2:303–338.

Tredennick, H., tr. 1933. *Loeb Classical Library, Aristotle XVII: Metaphysics I-IX*. Cambridge: Harvard University Press.

Vendler, Zeno. 1957. Times and Tenses *Philosophical Review* 66.2:143–160.

Vendler, Z. 1967. *Linguistics in Philosophy*. Ithaca: Cornell University Press.

Witt, C. 1989. Hylomorphism in Aristotle. *Apeiron* 22.4:141–158.

Witt, C. 1990. Charlton on the Uses of Actuality. *Boston Area Colloquium in Ancient Philosophy* 5:23–26.

Witt, C. 1994. The Priority of Actuality in Aristotle. In *Unity, Identity, and Explanation in Aristotle's* Metaphysics, eds. T. Scaltsas, D. Charles, and M.L. Gill, 215–228. Oxford: Oxford University Press.

Witt, C. 1995. Powers and Possibilities: Aristotle vs. the Megarians. *Proceedings of the Boston Area Colloquium in Ancient Philosophy, Vol. XI*, ed. J.J. Cleary and W. Wians, 249–273. University Press of America.

Witt, C. 1998. Teleology in Aristotelian Science and Metaphysics. In *Method in Ancient Philosophy*, ed. Jyl Gentzler, 253–269. Oxford University Press.

Witt, C. 2003. *Ways of Being: Potentiality and Actuality in Aristotle's Metaphysics*. Ithaca: Cornell University Press.

Yu, J. 1997. Two Conceptions of Hylomorphism in Metaphysics ZHΘ. *Oxford Studies in Ancient Philosophy* 15:119–145.

Yu, J. 2003. *The Structure of Being in Aristotle's Metaphysics*. Dordrecht: Kluwer Academic Publishers.

COLLOQUIUM 3

Language as *Technē* vs. Language as Technology: Plato's Critique of Sophistry

D.C. Schindler
The John Paul II Institute, Washington, DC

Abstract

This essay argues that the difference between philosophy and sophistical rhetoric that Plato presents in the *Gorgias* turns most fundamentally on different conceptions of the nature of language. After presenting some of the decisive moments in the debate between Socrates and Polus, Gorgias, and Callicles, this essay draws on the discussion of *technē* in *Republic* I to elucidate the "precise" sense of *technē*: namely, *technē* is ordered to the benefit of that over which it is set. The essay also draws on the discussion of names in the *Cratylus* to show that the (proto-)*technē* that is language, considered most precisely, is ordered to the manifestation of the truth of being more basically than to communication. Sophistry, by contrast, presumes what the essay calls a "technological" interpretation of language, which is essentially indifferent to being, and is ordered instead simply to communication, now understood principally in the mode of manipulative persuasion.

Keywords

Gorgias – rhetoric – language – technē – technology

If, according to Plato, the quarrel between philosophy and poetry is an ancient one, the quarrel between philosophy and sophistry is arguably more fundamental, and in any event, more pervasive in Plato's oeuvre.[1] The quarrel breaks

---

[1] See *Republic* x, 607b. One could argue that the quarrel between philosophy and poetry is ultimately the same thing as that between philosophy and sophistry under a different name: in the *Protagoras*, the sophist explains that his art is an ancient one, which has gone under the guise of poetry—as well as of mystery religions and sometimes even of athletics: *Prot.* 316b. The (distinctively Platonic) question concerning what it is that unites all these would warrant some reflection. It should be noted, moreover, that though Socrates is aiming his critique in

out around every corner in his dialogues, in the unlikeliest places, but reaches a peak, no doubt, in the *Gorgias*, a dialogue that sets the tone for the encounter between philosophy and sophistry with its first three words: "war and battle." Socrates is unusually pugnacious in this dialogue. Though his relentless pursuit of a particular line of inquiry is typical, the *Gorgias* finds him displaying an aggressive edge that one doesn't see elsewhere. One reason for this intensity is no doubt that he is outnumbered: not only is it three against one—the dialectical "war and battle" unfolds in three successive skirmishes, against Gorgias, Polus, and Callicles, each picking up the fight when his predecessor fails—but these well-known sophists also call the mass of humanity to their side, while Socrates finally has no one but himself with whom to enter into an alliance.[2] The deeper reason, however, is that what he shows to be at issue in this battle is nothing less than the ultimate existential question of Greek philosophy: How ought we to live? (500b–c), and the answer to this question, in turn, follows, as we will see, upon an even more fundamental metaphysical question concerning the nature of the cosmos as a whole in its relation to God.[3]

One of the astonishing things about the *Gorgias* is that these radical philosophical themes unfold from what seems at first to be a rather trivial question that Socrates raises right at the outset. As he, Chaerephon, and Callicles make their way to see the famous speaker, Socrates mentions that what he most wishes to ask him is "what is the power of the *technē*" (ἡ δύναμις τῆς τέχνης) that Gorgias claims to teach? Gorgias is a successful sophist, a professional teacher, who has students flocking to his lessons even at significant expense, and Socrates wants to ask Gorgias to clarify what he is giving them in exchange for their money. While Polus at first attempts to deflect the question and defend

---

the *Gorgias* at rhetoric rather than sophistry *per se*, he also says that these ultimately amount to the same: *Gorg*. 520a. We will take the terms as interchangeable for our present intents and purposes.

[2] Socrates admits to Polus that "nearly every Athenian and alien will take your side on the things you're saying, if it's witnesses you want to produce against me to show what I say isn't true," and confesses he stands alone: "Nevertheless, though I'm only one person, I don't agree with you" (*Gorg*. 471e ff. Translations are taken from the Cooper 1997 edition of Plato's *Complete Works*, unless otherwise noted. Unattributed parenthetic references are to the *Gorgias*). Socrates goes on to say and, indeed, to show, that Polus agrees with him in spite of himself (476a), but Polus refuses to concede any of it. In the end, Socrates is reduced to carrying on the conversation with himself alone (505d–e).

[3] As Marina McCoy puts it, "Socrates' questions in the *Gorgias* have an agonistic character because Socrates is engaged in a real battle over the nature of the good life" (McCoy 2008, 85). Towards the end of the dialogue, Socrates presents the theme of the good life in its cosmological dimensions, revealing that it is a participation in the order that is the friendship between the world and God, and that rejecting this participation implies a radical dis-order: 507e–508a.

his master (448a–b), Gorgias is willing to risk an answer. He tells Socrates that what he sells is ἡ ῥετορική, "oratory" or "rhetoric" (449a). The question driving the rest of the dialogue becomes, then, whether *rhetoric* can indeed be considered a *technē*, a term whose meaning we will be exploring, but which we may translate for the moment as "skill" or "art." Is rhetoric an art?

What I wish to do in this essay, through a closer look at some key passages in the *Gorgias*, is to try to understand what Plato means by this question, and why the nature of reality as a whole and our proper place within it is at stake in the answer one gives to it.[4] To accomplish this, we will have to draw on other dialogues to consider the precise meaning of *technē* as Plato intends the term, the nature of the medium implicated by rhetoric, namely, language, and the significance of language in human life. Each of these is of course an immense theme in itself, which would warrant more sustained attention than we can offer it here. But, leaving the deep exploration of these great philosophical questions for another occasion, I hope in this essay at least to point out what seems to me to be a clear and simple path through the ideas these themes present, a path that connects the basic question Plato raises at the beginning of the *Gorgias*, "Is rhetoric an art?" with the profound question that emerges by the dialogue's end: "How, then, are we to live?"

So, let us begin with Gorgias's attempt to define what rhetoric is in response to Socrates's initial request. As we have indicated, Gorgias believes that rhetoric is a *technē*, indeed, one of the greatest *technai* there is. If it is a *technē*, that would at least seem to make it a skill that can be acquired, and therefore taught, and therefore sold as a course of lessons. Socrates points out, in the face of Gorgias's grand claims, that every *technē* concerns some specific aspect of reality, "some one of the things that are" (τί τῶν ὄντων, 449d), and asks Gorgias therefore to delimit the field covered by the *technē* that he believes rhetoric to be from that of every other *technē*, which he ought to be able to do if rhetoric indeed qualifies as one. This delimitation proves to be much more difficult than one might have expected. Gorgias begins by distinguishing what we might call "manual" skills, such as painting or sculpture, from intellectual skills—*technai* that are exercised primarily or even exclusively in the sphere of *logos*, speech, or reason—and classifies rhetoric among the latter (450b–c). But more

---

4 David Roochnik observes that, at stake in this simple question, is a whole approach to life: is life something to be mastered by an acquirable expertise? See Roochnik 1994, 129–30; 153. Roochnik's characterization of the question in these terms, however, presupposes that a *technē* is a "mastery over," in the sense that would subjugate the object of the *technē* to the will and intentions of its practitioner. We intend to show, to the contrary, that such a presupposition fails to grasp the specifically *Platonic* sense of *technē* and takes for granted something much more like sophistical "technique" instead.

is needed to satisfy Socrates' question. As the philosopher points out, there are many *technai* that operate in the sphere of *logos*, each of which has a particular aspect of this sphere as its defining concern: arithmetic, for example, is a *technē* about number, and astronomy is a *technē* about heavenly motion. What is rhetoric about?

The answer to this question is astonishing and brings us to the essential point. In a word, what distinguishes rhetoric is that it is about specifically *nothing*. The preposition "about" is, in fact, inappropriate here to the extent that it designates some objective content. Rhetoric is not about some determinate matter, but instead concerns the *way* one speaks about *any given* subject matter. Gorgias initially says that rhetoric concerns *logoi*, speeches, about "the greatest and the best" human affairs (451d), but then admits, under Socrates' questioning, that any specific human affair would in fact fall under a specific *technē*. It is the absence of specificity or, in other words, the essential indeterminacy of the power of rhetoric that distinguishes it from the intellectual *technai* that are all ordered to some specifying object. For Gorgias, rhetoric's indeterminacy is just what makes it so valuable; as he puts it, rhetoric "encompasses and subordinates to itself just about everything that can be accomplished" (456a).[5] What he means by this claim is that, while a given art may be able to perform some discrete work, it remains ineffective unless it is accepted as such by other people. Even a competent doctor can do nothing unless people actually believe he is qualified and are willing to hire him. We trade in the various *technai* and their products through the medium of language, and so he who controls language in a sense controls everything else. The effective significance of things depends on speech, and the most effective speaker is therefore the one who finally determines what they mean. Because rhetoric is not limited in its scope like the other *technai* but can apply to any field at all, it may be said to represent a kind of universal power, at least in the sphere of actual human existence. It is a power that gives effective power to every other art.

Playing along with Gorgias here, Socrates observes, with a certain irony, that this makes rhetoric rather "demonic" (δαιμονία, 456a), or in other words makes it a power that goes beyond the realm of nature. The very thing that Gorgias touts as the value of rhetoric Socrates identifies as posing a problem. If rhetoric is indeterminate in the way that Gorgias describes, it cannot be a *technē*, since the *technai* are all specified by some particular function. They are

---

5   More literally, rhetoric gathers under itself the powers of all the other *technai*: ἁπάσας τὰς δυνάμεις συλλαβοῦσα ὑφ' αὑτῇ ἔχει.

all determinate by their very nature.⁶ But, insofar as the determinacy of the *technai* is what makes them a matter of knowledge, this implies that rhetoric is characterized specifically by the *absence* of knowledge. Socrates proposes to define rhetoric as a "producer of persuasion" (453a), significantly avoiding the word "*technē*."⁷ Even this definition, however, requires qualification, for each of the particular *technai* includes a power to persuade with respect to its specifying subject matter: a doctor, for example, has the capacity to persuade regarding medical matters. This is why the *absence* of knowledge is crucial in specifying rhetoric. If one masters rhetoric, as Gorgias understands it, one can speak well about any matter, whether or not one has knowledge about it; rhetoric is essentially indifferent to content. Moreover, as Socrates goes on to point out, one will be able to speak well about any matter only to those who are likewise ignorant about the matter at issue (459a ff.). While a rhetorician, ignorant of medicine, may speak persuasively about medical matters to an indiscriminating crowd, he will not be able to impress a real doctor. Rhetoric presupposes an absence of knowledge, not just in the speaker, but also in the audience.⁸

To put the point in different words: rhetoric is an approach to language that *abstracts* from any particular subject matter or reality—"one of the things that are"; it concerns the *form* of speaking, separated from the matter of any

---

6   In what is the most thorough book on Plato's notion of *technē*, David Roochnik points to determinacy as one of the most essential traits of a *technē*: see Roochnik 1996, 192–99. We will be suggesting that the lack of determinacy in sophistical rhetoric is a symptom of its most essential trait, namely, its essential abstraction and so indifference to reality.

7   πειθοῦς δημιουργός (453a). The word δημιουργός is typically associated with *technē*, but Plato clearly means to avoid the word "*technē*" here. The word δημιουργός itself simply means one who produces a work for public consumption. On the relation between the two words, see Balansard 2001, 95. See also Vernant 1983, 103: "in Homer and Hesiod this term [δημιουργός] did not originally refer to the artisan as such, as a 'worker' or 'producer.' It defined all activities pursued outside the framework of the οἶκος, for the benefit of a public, δῆμος."

8   One might raise an obvious objection here: given two competent doctors, wouldn't the one with rhetoric better be able to persuade? In other words, even if rhetoric does not require knowledge, isn't it compatible with having knowledge, so that it remains a skill worth having, as long as we supplement it with knowledge? There are three responses to this (which is effectively Gorgias's position: 456c–457c) that one can infer from Plato: (1) Plato appears to take for granted that one who knows the how and why of a thing is also one who can explain it. In this case, the better doctor, the one who understands the art more, would *also* be able to speak more persuasively to other doctors, which means that rhetoric, as an "additive," is irrelevant; (2) a doctor with rhetoric would be better, not at persuading simply, but only at persuading the ignorant many; (3) these things being said, it remains the case that Plato does finally have a place for what he calls "true rhetoric," which we will explain below.

particular speech.⁹ To be able to appreciate why Plato infers from this that it is not a *technē* requires us to be able to see beyond what is a common assumption in our own culture. One of the ways we use the word "skill" is to indicate something that turns out to mean something much more similar to Gorgias's rhetoric than to Plato's *technē*. According to this particular usage, a skill is an ability that is more or less free of content. It is something that we acquire through education, which we *subsequently* apply to a particular content, after our education is over, in one field or another, when we are "on the job." A skill, in this sense, is different, for example, from the sort of ability one would acquire in an apprenticeship, in which the ability arises in the actual *doing* of a particular work, and bears a natural relationship to that work.¹⁰ We prize such a "skill" for its general applicability, since this is what makes it especially "marketable," in contrast to the essential specificity of an apprenticeship; a liberal education, for example, is praised for its promise to teach students how to read, think, speak, and write, which are "skills they can use in any field." But it is just this that, for Plato, removes *technē*-status from a skill so described, and it is why we must be careful in translating Plato. It does not suffice simply to find the correct word; more fundamentally, we have to understand the word correctly, which means that translation is invariably also a philosophical act.¹¹

The need for understanding becomes evident, for example, in the choice of the word "technique," which would seem like an obvious translation for *technē*. But what we said above concerning "skill" might be said similarly of "technique."¹² We tend to think of a technique as a way of doing something that brings about some desired effect, a method that can be mastered in itself, regardless of

---

9   As Jörg Kube explains, the suffix "-ικη" in the word ῥετορικη, apparently coined by Plato (see Reames and Schiappa 2017, 1), indicates a relatively self-contained body of knowledge that can be separated from the person of the speaker (Kube 1969, 16). This is just what removes it from the sphere of *technē* for Plato.

10 "The apprentice has learned a more fitting and responsible (responsive to his or her context) focus, has become more attentive to the surrounding context, and has given up ambition to take the world by force.... . The apprentice becomes a master not by bending the world to his or her own will but by submitting to, and learning to work within, and developing an affection for the rich possibilities within the craft" Wirzba 2006, quoted in Baker and Bilbro 2017, 203n29. This theme is expounded brilliantly by Crawford 2009.

11 As R. Schaerer puts it, translating Greek is not just about finding a corresponding word in the relevant modern language, because "each notion possesses, beyond its proper meaning, a sort of atmosphere in which it bathes and which unites it with other notions, through ties of association, opposition, and unconscious evocation" (Schaerer 1930, VII).

12 C.S. Lewis uses the word in this way. Contrasting the "ancient" view of knowledge as a conforming of the soul to the real, Lewis says that "for magic and applied science alike the problem is how to subdue reality to the wishes of men: the solution is a 'technique'" (Lewis 2001, 77).

whether one knows how or why it works. In this case, a technique is, so to speak, a detachable form of operation, which, as detachable, presupposes for its use neither an in-formed subject nor an object, a reality, that would guide, and so inform, the operation. One can, for example, apply a memorized mathematical formula in physics and generate correct answers to problems without being able to explain why they are correct or, indeed, even what they mean. While the word "technique" is obviously derived from the Greek *technē*, understood in this way it betrays what Plato means by *technē*. Indeed, the term "technique," so meant, would more properly translate the words and expressions that Plato employs to *distinguish* rhetoric from genuine *technai*: rhetoric, he insists, is an ἐμπειρία, a "knack," or more generally a τριβή, a "routine" or "procedure," which are precisely opposed to *technē*; Plato qualifies the τριβή of rhetoric explicitly as ἄτεχνος (*Phaedrus* 260e; cf. *Laws* XI, 938a), an activity accomplished essentially *without technē*. In a manner similar to the description above of a mechanical application of formulae, Plato explains that an ἐμπειρία "has no account of the nature of whatever things it applies that would govern its application, so that it's unable to state the cause of each thing. And I refuse to call anything that lacks such an account a *technē*" (465a; translation modified).[13] Characterizing rhetoric thus as ἄτεχνος makes sense if we recognize that, for Plato, *technē* is a form of knowledge, and knowledge is always *of* something real; it is a grasp of being in some respect.[14] Because rhetoric is an abstract method, which can be indifferently applied to a variety of things, it may indeed be a "technique" in the typical modern sense, but it fails to qualify as a *technē*, an art or skill, as Plato understands the term. Rhetoric designates a kind of method that can be mastered in order to achieve some desired effect, whether or not one has an understanding of the substance of what one is speaking about: it is, as Socrates puts it, not a way of knowing, but a "producer of persuasion."[15]

---

13 Aristotle similarly characterizes one with *technē* as being able, not only to accomplish a work (which is something a person with ἐμπειρία can also do), but to explain the cause (*Metaphysics* A 1, I.1, 981a20–b10).

14 See *Rep.* V, 476e–477a, 478a: "Knowledge is set over what is, to know it as it is."

15 It should be pointed out, here, that what I am taking to be essential in Socrates' critique of sophistical rhetoric is the absence of a rational relation, a *"logos,"* to the *real nature* of things, their *"ousia"* or being. A sophist can certainly offer an explanation of what he is doing as a description of the device he uses to achieve a certain effect, and in this sense would be able to provide a kind of "account" (*"logos"*), which allows him to be able to teach his methods as a course of lessons, and so forth. But the key point is that the desired effect is to produce persuasion, not to illuminate the nature of some real thing. On the other hand, as Socrates shows in other contexts, a philosopher may be unable to give an exhaustive account of a thing, in the sense of capturing the truth of a reality in a

In order to illuminate this point, it seems to me helpful, albeit at the risk of anachronism, to contrast Platonic *technē* with technology. By "technology," in this context, I mean three things: the separation of means from real ends; the subsequent formalizing of the means, thus isolated, with an aim to make them "produce results" in an indeterminate sense ("optimized efficiency"); and, finally, the tendency to reify the means, thus formalized, as a relatively independent reality that can be made itself the object of other activities: for example, a commodity that can be bought and sold.[16] Given this description of technology, we may think of the contrast between Socrates and Gorgias, philosophy and sophistry,[17] as a contrast between language interpreted along the lines of *technē* and language interpreted as a "technology." As we have seen, Gorgias celebrates rhetoric as a skill that thus has a certain intelligibility already in itself, without reference to any particular end. While Socrates cannot answer the question, "What does it mean to speak *well*?" without asking in turn, "About *what*, exactly?" Gorgias takes this subsequent question to be effectively irrelevant. For him, one can learn to speak well prior to, and in abstraction from, any particular content, which can be "inserted" at a later moment into the perfected form. Language appears here as a formalized means, which the sophist strives to make as *effective* as possible. The more effective it is, the more indeterminate power it offers. It is just this potent instrument that Gorgias offers for sale.

---

    proposition, but this knowing transcendence of knowledge ("*docta ignorantia*") remains a rational relation to nature. For a fuller argument on this point, see Schindler 2008, 226–82. This is why there is no contradiction between Socrates' claim that he practices the *technē* of politics (521d), and his famous confession of ignorance (509a), although David Levy suggests there is: Levy 2005. Levy concludes that "Socrates' practice of philosophy cannot amount to a *technē* for precisely the same reason that Gorgias's practice of oratory does not" (Levy 2005, 213). I am proposing that philosophy and sophistry are not similar in this respect, but are perfectly opposed. We might consider in this context Plato's observation that there are two reasons one might have difficulty giving precise answers to questions: either too much darkness or too much light (*Rep.* VII 516e–517a; 518a-b).

16   This description of "technology" bears many similarities to Horkheimer and Adorno's characterization of the instrumentalizing of reason in Enlightenment thought and Max Weber's rationalizing of means in the "disenchantment" of modernity: see Horkheimer and Adorno 2007, Horkheimer 2013, and Weber 2002 and 2004. I prefer to use the word "technology," in part, because of the resonance with *technē* and also because of the broader cultural resonance the term has.

17   The principal subject of discussion in the dialogue is rhetoric, which Socrates at various points distinguishes from sophistry (cf. 465c, 519c, 520b). But, as I noted already in n1, above, he also insists that, in relation to the basic critique he is mounting, they amount to the same thing (see 520a).

I have just drawn a contrast between language as a *technē* and language as a technology. This contrast, however, presupposes the legitimacy of interpreting language along the lines of *technē*. The question is therefore raised: is it proper to think of language along these lines? To answer this question, we need to examine more closely what Plato means by *technē* and how he understands language. As we can glean already from our discussion thus far, *technē*, for Plato, is a kind of knowledge, which is distinguished from other kinds of knowledge in its being directly concerned with activity, generally, but not exclusively, activity of a productive sort.[18] Plato defines language in the *Cratylus* in just this sense: naming, giving words to things, is an action (*praxis*), and the carrying out of this action properly ends up producing something; in other words, language is a kind of *poiēsis* (*Crat.* 387b). Plato defines *poiēsis* as the causing of a transition from non-being to being, and he says that every *technē* represents a *poiēsis* in this sense.[19] We will leave aside for a moment the question whether and in what sense its poetic essence makes language a *technē*, or more precisely what it is that language, as a *poiēsis*, brings into being. But at this point we wish to attend simply to the fact that language, as Plato describes it, aims by its very nature at the accomplishment of some (yet to be determined) end, a "work" (*ergon*), which implies a standard by which it can be evaluated: if we know what one is trying to accomplish in speaking, we can judge in principle whether one is speaking well or poorly. For reasons we will explain shortly, to speak well, for Plato, is to *instruct* or *teach*, that is, to communicate knowledge.[20] If there is a standard by which it is possible to judge whether one is speaking well, it also means that one can cultivate the ability to speak well in

---

18   Philological studies generally agree that *technē* is first a kind of knowledge, which is to say that it is theoretical before being practical. For an account of the meaning of *technē* in Plato's thought, see Roochnik 1996, Balansard 2001, Kube 1969, and Schaerer 1930. In my judgment, the best "philosophical" presentation of the role of *technē* in Plato's philosophy generally is Kato 1986. Balansard criticizes interpretations that bind *technē* too closely to productivity (as does J.P. Vernant, from a different perspective: see Vernant 1983, 250–254), but this criticism applies only to a technological sense of productivity. In a broader sense, one can say that the exercise of *technē*, as a kind of *praxis*, aims to accomplish some end.

19   As he puts it in the *Symposium*, "everything that is responsible for creating something out of nothing is a kind of poetry; and so all the creations of every craft and profession are themselves a kind of poetry, and everyone who practices a craft is a poet" *Symp.* 205b–c. If everyone who practices a *technē* is a *poiētēs*, it is because every *technē* is a *poiēsis*.

20   Plato says that the "power" or the proper "good" (καλόν) of words is "to give instruction" (διδάσκειν): *Crat.* 435d. In the *Gorgias*, Socrates draws a fundamental distinction between having learned a thing and simply being persuaded, which would correspond to the distinction between teaching and simply exerting the power to persuade. In the *Cratylus*, Socrates defines words as "instruments of teaching" (*Crat.* 388b–c) and says that "names are spoken in order to give instruction" (*Crat.* 428e). We will discuss this further below.

reference to this standard, which is to say that one can *learn*, in some sense, to speak well.[21] Plato therefore identifies teaching, speaking well, as a *technē* (*Crat.* 428e). This notion of speaking well is evidently presupposed in the contrast he draws between Socrates and Gorgias: in one case, we have speaking considered as a *technē*, which aims at an actual and so determinate end, in the other speaking as the manipulation of an effective instrument, which can be used indifferently for any end whatever.

It thus seems clear that Plato thinks of the activity of speaking, the proper *use* of language, as a *technē*; but do we have grounds for making the stronger claim that language *itself* is a *technē*? In other words, we have been describing language in its *operation* as a *technē*; is it possible so to describe language in its *essence*? Is the very acquisition of language—not learning to speak *well* in one instance or another but learning to speak *at all*—the acquisition of a *technē*? Plato suggests as much in certain places. In the *Protagoras*, he presents the original articulating of sounds in speech as the *first* expression of human *technē*, prior to the invention of housing, clothes, and so forth: after manifesting through worship the likeness to the gods that the possession of *technē* confers, the first humans "then quickly articulated sounds and names by means of *technē*" (*Prot.* 322a, trans. modified).[22] This description, which admittedly comes from the mouth of a sophist, finds some confirmation in Plato's description in the *Cratylus* of the original name-givers exercising *technē* in their initial production of words (*Crat.* 389a).[23] Moreover, in that dialogue, Plato compares words to a weaver's shuttle, and weaving is a paradigmatic *technē* for Plato.[24]

However close he comes in these instances, it remains the case nevertheless that Plato does not simply present speech itself as a *technē* in so many words. This is significant. The difficulty of thinking of language itself simply as a *technē*, of course, is that language—i.e., *logos*, which for Plato is inseparably both speech and reason—is the very medium of knowledge, as Plato shows in

---

21 Strictly speaking, for Plato, the closer a thing is to knowledge, the less able it is to be *taught*, in the sophistic sense, which is the paradoxical conclusion of the *Protagoras*. True knowledge is not inserted into the soul from outside, but *recollected*; for this, one needs, not a (sophistic) teacher, but a "midwife." See *Rep.* VII, 518b–c and *Theaetetus* 149a ff., in which Socrates describes midwifery specifically as a *technē*.

22 As noted above, the translations of Plato's dialogues used in this essay are from the Cooper edition; in this case, the translation is by Stanley Lombardo and Karen Bell.

23 It is worth noting that the word Plato uses in the *Cratylus* for the original name-givers, νομοθέτης, is precisely the word he uses for the activity he opposes to sophistry (see *Gorg.* 465c). What is at stake in the question of sophistry and the status of rhetoric is the nature of language in its most original sense.

24 In the *Statesman*, for example, Plato describes at considerable length the noble *technē* of politics (see *Gorg.* 464b) according to the model of weaving: 279a ff.

the *Theaetetus*.[25] As such, it would appear to be too fundamental, so to speak, to represent a *determinate* body of knowledge, which is what a *technē* generally is. *Technē* is knowledge; but it does not seem quite right to say simply that knowing or knowledge is a *technē*.[26] Language would seem to run up against the same difficulty, since it appears to be presupposed already by every specific *technē*.[27] There are some scholars that infer from this fundamental status that language is therefore simply "non-technical,"[28] but this is deeply problematic.[29] Language may not be one particular *technē* over against others, but this does not mean it is simply ἄτεχνος in the way that rhetoric is ἄτεχνος. Instead, I want to suggest it is more appropriate to say that language is *analogous* to *technē*—or even more properly speaking, that the *technai* are all analogous to language, for reasons I will give below. If speech itself is not simply a *technē*, it is nevertheless a "proto-*technē*."

Let me clarify the distinction I intend here. By "proto-*technē*," I do not mean simply "something like a *technē*" or even simply that language represents the natural capacity to acquire *technē*, though this is closer.[30] Instead, I am proposing that language represents the "*Ur-technē*," the original relationship to reality that allows the determinate relations specified by the various *technai* to exist. Rather than being itself a particular *technē*, I am suggesting that it is, not "non-technical," as some scholars suggest,[31] but that it is "technicality" itself, as it were. It is the *root* of all *technē*—not the absence of *technē*, but its essential foundation. In this sense, language will exhibit in a specifically *analogous* way the features that generally belong to *technē*, which I have been describing here: *technē* is essentially a kind of knowing that aims at a kind of *poiēsis*, the achievement of an end outside of itself.

---

25   *Tht.* 189e–190a: thinking is "a talk which the soul has with itself about the objects under its consideration." Notice that, though this talk takes place "internally," so to speak, it nevertheless concerns objects "outside" the soul.

26   See *Tht.* 147b–c.

27   Plato affirms that every *technē* in some respect concerns *logoi*: *Gorg.* 450b. The difficulty of *specifying* what is *fundamental* arises often in Plato: see, e.g., Socrates' discussion with Polemarchus, *Rep.* I, 332d ff., and Charmides, *Charmides* 166b ff.

28   Although Roochnik 1996 is not speaking about language simply, but focuses more directly on the issue of morality, he essentially makes this argument, and ends up having difficulty drawing any real distinction in the end between philosophy and sophistry.

29   Kato provides the correct reply to this problematic inference: Kato 1986, 20.

30   Roochnik also uses the term "proto-*technē*," but in a different sense from the one we are proposing (see Roochnik 1996, 219). For Roochnik, the term means a natural ability to acquire *technē*, while we mean the term to express a fundamental relation to reality that makes specific knowledge, and so *technē*, possible.

31   In addition to Roochnik 1998, see, e.g., Levy 2005, 208–14 and Brickhouse and Smith 1994, 3–29.

We can accept this, however, only if it is possible to determine the end, and so we must ask another fundamental question: what exactly is the end of language—*per se* and not just of a particular speech act? What are words *for*? Plato says that language is a *poiēsis*: what does language *produce* or bring into being from nothing? Our first inclination might be to say that it effects *communication*, or in other words to affirm that communication is the purpose that defines language as such. We speak in order to communicate our thoughts to others. This seems to be Aristotle's understanding, at least as he is typically characterized.[32] Whether Aristotle means by this what one would mean by it in a contemporary setting—namely, the transfer of information regarding mental states from one individual to another—is not a question we can pursue here,[33] but in any event *communication* alone does not suffice to express Plato's view. Plato admits, of course, that language is a persuasive power and presents it as accomplishing any number of purposes. The question is, however, whether there is a particular end that is so essential to language as to *define* it, to capture its most basic nature and distinguish it from every other activity. What exactly do words *do*? It is crucial that we answer this question with the requisite precision.

To aid our efforts to do so, let us pause for a moment to consider Plato's discussion of *technē* in what he says is the most *precise* sense of the notion, before returning to the question of the defining end of language. In a well-known scene at the beginning of the *Republic*, Socrates contests the sophist Thrasymachus's claim that ruling is a *technē* undertaken for the benefit of the one who rules (*Rep.* I, 336b ff.). To challenge this claim, Socrates makes the same point about *technai* that we saw him make in the *Gorgias*, namely, that every *technē* is set over a particular reality, and it is this reality that defines it, distinguishing

---

32   According to Aristotle, "spoken words are the symbols of passions in the soul (τῶν ἐν τῇ ψυχῇ παθημάτων)," *De Interpretatione* 1, 16a. In a discussion of ancient theories of language, R.M. van der Berg contrasts Plato's view, which is that the purpose of language is to name *being* (as we will see below), somewhat simplistically with Aristotle's, which he says is simply the communication of thoughts: van der Berg 2008, 4.

33   The McKeon edition of Aristotle's *Basic Works* encourages this interpretation by translating Aristotle's sentence thus: "spoken words are symbols of mental experiences," which follows a modern tendency to "subjectivize" the soul. Aristotle did not have a "psychologistic" interpretation of the psyche. Παθήματα are the reception in the soul of something real, beyond the soul, which means that the παθήματα point ultimately to being, just as is the case with Plato. Aristotle is clear about this point in the sentences that follow the passage quoted from the *Int.* and confirms it with his reference to the relevant discussions in the *De Anima*. It may be the case that Aristotle was generally interpreted in the tradition as opposed to Plato on this matter (to the point of Proclus's complaint that the Peripatetics' method, in contrast to Plato's, was "stripped bare of things" [van der Berg 2008, 136]), but arguably this interpretation does not do justice to Aristotle's actual teaching.

it from other activities (*Rep.* I, 341c; 345e–346a).[34] But in *Republic* I, Socrates draws out a further implication, given the argument he is trying to articulate there. In response to Thrasymachus's affirmation that rulers seek to benefit themselves and are right to do so, he explains that every *technē* is in reality directed to something other than itself and aims to benefit that over which it is set, rather than the *technē* itself or the practitioner of the *technē* (*Rep.* I, 341d). A German scholar uses the word *"Fürsorge"* to describe this feature: every *technē* has some reality *for* which it *cares*.[35] Thus, medicine is the art of healing; it *cares for* the health of bodies, and this directedness is what defines it. The activity, of itself and independently of the practitioner's intentions, has the form of concern for its particular object. A doctor may benefit from his practice of the art; we presume that he is paid for his work. But this benefit is subsequent to the work, recompense for the work having been done. It is not what the work is *about*, in such a way that it would define work as what it is. Many kinds of work, after all, involve payment, and yet we recognize them as different kinds, which means that money-making does not constitute their identity (*Rep.* I, 346c). Socrates describes money-making as a distinct art in itself, which tends to accompany the practice of the other *technai*, and remarks that its doing so reinforces the point he made earlier, namely, that *technē* aims at the benefit of its object, rather than of its practitioner: this is why he demands money in return for the other-benefitting efforts the *technē* itself implies by its form (*Rep.* I, 346e–347a).

Thrasymachus's objection to Socrates' argument betrays a fundamental misunderstanding, which is illuminating with respect to our larger question, and so worth considering with some attention. Indeed, it is a simple point, but it is also subtle and thus easy to miss. Thrasymachus sneers that Socrates thinks that a shepherd tends sheep for the sheep's benefit, rather than recognizing the obvious fact that he is fattening them up for the butcher. Tellingly, Thrasymachus does not offer this interpretation with a desire to help Socrates clarify his meaning, but intends the charge to put an end to that part of the discussion, as he redirects their attention to a different topic. Socrates does not get a chance to defend his position at much length, though he does reiterate the point about what characterizes a shepherd precisely insofar as he is practicing the art of shepherding (*Rep.* I, 345c–d). The argument he would have given in response is nevertheless clear: to affirm that the end of shepherding is happy sheep is not just to indulge in romantic fantasies about the selfless nature of

---

34   Cf. *Gorg.* 449c–451d, in which Socrates reveals the various crafts as being concerned with some one of the things that are, i.e., some aspect of being, as we discussed above.
35   Kube 1969, 140; cf. Kato 1986, 24–27.

shepherds;[36] in other words, the point is not to deny that the end of this specific activity can, and normally will, be taken up in the service of further ends. It is nevertheless crucial to recognize the distinction between the proximate end that properly defines the activity and the higher order ends to which this activity, in its integrity, is subsequently ordered. The shepherd qua shepherd cares for the sheep before he delivers them to the butcher, and the shepherd must care for them well if the butcher is going to be able to carry out his *technē* properly in turn. If the shepherd believes his job is to cut sheep into pieces *instead of* making them whole as far as possible, he will make a serious mess of things. The art of the butcher, which just *is* the articulation of sheep, so to speak, is presupposed in turn by the art of the chef. And so on.

In light of this precise specification of the nature of *technē*, let us return to the question of the purpose of language, which we are seeking to interpret as a proto-*technē*. As we said above, language has the power to persuade and is generally a means of communication, but we said that these do not represent its most basic "*ergon*." The most precise definition of language to be found in the Platonic corpus occurs unsurprisingly in the *Cratylus*. In a passage that became a *locus classicus* for ancient hermeneutics, Plato explains that language is "a tool for giving instruction, that is to say, for dividing being" (*Crat.* 388b–c). Note that language *instructs*, rather than simply communicates, and it does so because it is directed *to being*: the καὶ in this definition is explicative rather than consecutive or additive, which is to say that the division of being, or the penetration of reality, clarifies just what is meant by "to instruct."[37] To be sure, Plato also admits the role of language in communicating one's "internal" experiences[38] and, even more generally, draws attention to the power inherent in language to lead souls and thus to persuade: the power of language, he says, is *psychogōgia*, the capacity to direct souls (*Phdr.* 271c). But—and this is the crucial point—Plato recognizes that it is not possible to lead souls without taking them somewhere; leading necessarily presupposes a destination, and that destination cannot in this case be finally anything other than being.[39] Words do

---

36   Julia Annas misses the point entirely when she judges that Socrates, here, is being "absurdly optimistic"; see Annas 1981, 49.

37   In this passage, Plato compares words to a weaver's shuttle: the shuttle "divides" by passing back and forth between the alternating threads on the loom, but instead of thereby *separating* them from each other, the thread guided by the shuttle binds the other threads together, producing an "intricate," meaningful whole.

38   In *Gorg.* 481c–d, Plato describes speaking as "communicating to another person the experiences (πάθημα) belonging to oneself," using the same word that Aristotle uses in *Int.*, and making a similar point with respect to the need for a common experience.

39   This does not mean, of course, that one cannot tell a lie or that deception in speech is not possible. One of the main thrusts of the *Sophist* is to show that the possibility of deception is rooted in *relative* (as distinct from *absolute*) non-being, since language can

not lead us simply to the thoughts, beliefs, or impressions of other souls, but, if they lead to these, they also lead *through* them always ultimately to reality itself. Thoughts and beliefs, after all, are not just *of* thoughts and beliefs, but are inevitably *about* something, as Plato makes clear in the *Parmenides*: "'Is each of the thoughts one, but a thought of nothing?' 'No, that's impossible,' he said. 'Of something, rather?' 'Yes.' 'Of something that is, or of something that is not?' 'Of something that is'" (*Parm.* 132b–c).[40] The *power* of words, according to Plato, does not come principally from the speaker, but from the reality spoken about, of which language is a more or less adequate image (see *Crat.* 393c–394a).[41] The most basic purpose of words, as Plato says repeatedly, is quite simply to "make clear the nature of the things that are,"[42] which is to say, to manifest being. If language is too fundamental to be a specific *technē*, it is not because it is simply without determination, but because the object that determines it, being itself, is literally everything.[43] What specifies language, in other words, is *everything* in a certain respect—namely, with regard to its being or essence. As he puts it in the *Cratylus*, speaking is proper to the extent that it corresponds to the *nature* (φύσις) of what it speaks about (*Crat.* 387b–c). It is precisely the being of things that comes to expression (δηλουμένη) in language, and governs its use (ἐγκρατής), which is to say that it presents a standard by which the language is measured. This is what Plato means in the *Cratylus* by the "correctness of names" (περί ὀνομάτων ὀρθότητος), which is that dialogue's principal theme.

---

    never be detached from being *simpliciter*. Even the relative non-being that allows deceptive appearances ultimately depends on the *things that are*.

40 Cf. a similar point in *Soph.* 262e.

41 To say that it is an image does not mean that there are any common features between it and the reality: *Crat.* 432c–d, but only that it recalls the reality in some way, makes it present (cf. *Phd.* 73c-74a).

42 *Crat.* 422d; cf. 393d, 428e, 436e; *Soph.* 263b; *Gorg.* 453a. See Kato 1986, 65.

43 This is the fundamental problem with Roochnik's argument in *Of Art and Wisdom*, which takes the *indeterminacy* of rhetoric to be the most basic reason for Plato's criticism. Because of this formulation of Plato's critique, Roochnik ends up conceding that there is ultimately no fundamental difference between philosophy and sophistry (and in fact offers this lack as a sort of psychological explanation for the acerbity of Socrates' attack) see Roochnik 1996, 179ff. But, as we have been suggesting, properly speaking the "indeterminacy" of philosophy and sophistry have a radically different cause: Philosophy is "indeterminate"—or, better, supra-determinate—because it is concerned with being, while sophistry is indeterminate because it lacks any real object. In this regard, they have nothing in common; sophistry is nothing but a deceptive image of philosophy (as Plato shows in the *Sophist*). This basic issue—that the difference between philosophy and sophistry concerns the nature of language—does not appear on McCoy's list of the various accounts that have been proposed to explain Plato's critique of sophistry (see McCoy 2008, 85–86), and this may be why she, too, ends up denying any significant difference between rhetoric and philosophy: ibid., 85–110.

Regarding the *Cratylus*, there is an ongoing debate about the role of convention in speaking, whether there is such a thing as a natural language, and even whether language can, in fact, adequately express being.[44] There is also a difficult question concerning what it would mean to apprehend being *beyond* language, which Plato affirms at the end of the dialogue.[45] But if we cannot enter into these debates and questions in the present context, it suffices for the argument we are making simply to note that, for Plato, language aspires to being, and this aspiration is what most properly defines it. There can be no doubt about *this*.[46] When we listen to speech, for Plato, the words are not the ultimate object of our perception, nor are the thoughts of the person speaking. Instead, the object of our perception is ultimately and inescapably the *being* of things that we hear always *through* the speaker's thoughts and words.[47]

The distinction we presented from *Republic I* can help us avoid confusion on this point. An activity is defined by its most proximate end; a *technē* is ordered to the benefit of that over which it is set. If we are correct that language, as Plato interprets it, is, if not a *technē* simply, in any event the "proto-*technē*," it must be interpreted in relation to its proximate end. It is clear, as we observed above, that there are always a host of purposes at work in every speech act. We inevitably mean to convey our opinion about things and desire to bring something about in response. We hope our words have some effect. We use language to influence people, and get things done. But *Republic I* helps us to see that we

---

44 See, for example, Soltes 2007; Riley 2005; Baxter 1992; Ademollo 2011; Palmer 1989; Barney 2001.

45 Socrates argues that the capacity to judge the correctness of names depends on the possibility of knowing things independently of names (*Crat.* 438e), but does not attempt to show this possibility in the *Cratylus*. Such a possibility does appear to be affirmed, however, in the *Seventh Letter* 342a–343d.

46 See Kube 1969, 210: "What Plato aims to show in the *Cratylus* is the rootedness of names in being." To say that language aspires to being does not exclude the possibility—which Professor May Sim helpfully proposed—that it also aspires beyond being to the good which is being's ultimate cause (and even that the aspiration to being is necessarily founded on the aspiration to the good). Although Plato does not make this claim explicitly, taking it seriously and unfolding its implications would seem to open up an illuminating way to account for the essentially self-transcending character of images, and therefore also of language (which is an image of being), in Plato's thought. For a general argument along these lines, see chapter five of Schindler 2008, 226–82.

47 This does not imply, of course, that we are ever aware of the being of things explicitly as such. Plato generally presents such an awareness as a rare and indeed rather heroic achievement. But it nevertheless remains the case that being lies at the foundation of *all* our awareness, even of our deception by appearances, as we mentioned above (n39). It is, finally, why Socrates is finally able to argue, with confidence, as he does in the *Gorgias*, that his interlocutors' disagreement with philosophy will ultimately be a disagreement with *themselves*, an *internal conflict*, regardless of how things may appear on the surface.

can only achieve these ends if we first do justice to the nature of language itself. As proto-*technē*, language is ordered to the benefit of that over which it is set. The principal object of language is the "being of things." Therefore, before benefitting its users, and indeed as a condition for benefitting them, language, let us say, cares for the good of being. What could this possibly mean? What good could we possibly do to being itself?

The answer to this question is, once again, fairly simple: if we speak properly, we make some reality clear, we make it manifest.[48] We might think here of Heidegger's insight that, for the Greeks, *technē* is understood generally as enabling the "showing forth" that constitutes *physis* (nature).[49] One would have to account for the more obviously creative and practical aspects of *technē* than perhaps Heidegger does,[50] but the basic point is a good one: these practical aspects are relative to what is absolute, namely, the showing forth. Speech, as a proto-*technē*, may be said to be a praxis that "amplifies" the *physis*, that is, recapitulates the nature of a given reality in the intelligible order. In other words, when we speak, we help things show themselves for what they are in truth. As Plato puts it, the purpose of a name lies in "expressing the nature of one of the things that are" (*Crat.* 422d). To say that, insofar as every *technē* is ordered to the benefit of that over which it is set, language, as a proto-*technē*, is analogously ordered to the benefit of being in a particular respect means not that we somehow improve things or make them happier by speaking about them.[51] Instead, it simply means that the defining purpose of language is just

---

48 Plato makes this point variously in various contexts: φανερόν, 505e; καταφανές, 457e; cf., δηλοῦν, *Crat.* 422d.

49 See Heidegger 1993, 318–19: "*Technē* belongs to bringing-forth, to *poiēsis*; it is something poetic .... *Technē* is a mode of *alētheuein* .... Thus what is decisive in *technē* does not at all lie in making and manipulating, nor in the using of means, but rather in the revealing mentioned before. It is as revealing, and not as manufacturing, that *technē* is a bringing-forth." All of this makes sense especially if we recognize language itself as the "primal *technē*," so to speak, which is the proposal we are making here. For further discussion of *technē* in ancient Greek thought, see Heidegger 1994.

50 Heidegger's account is indispensable, but one might reasonably object that in reaction to the modern "pragmatic" reduction of *technē*, he tends to downplay the way a *technē* transforms an object.

51 There may be some sense this is true, but it would require a certain development beyond Plato. The point would be that there is an analogy between "happiness" and internal perfection, and that the manifestness of things in language, as truth, is a perfection of them. Leibniz affirms an analogy between happiness and the perfection or completion that can belong to an inanimate object: see Spaemann 2015, 204–5. In this respect, one might say that, by making manifest the truth of their nature, naming things contributes to their *excellence*: Plato refers to the excellence of things as their internal perfection, correctness, craftsmanship (see *Gorg.* 506d–e).

truth, irrespective of whatever benefit the truth of things might subsequently confer. At the root of our speaking, regardless of whether or not we are conscious of it or deliberate about it, lies an aim to make something manifest and communicate this manifestness to others. This aim is, by its nature, a common good (κοινὸν ἀγαθόν, *Gorg.* 505e), as distinct from the private benefit sought in the perversion of *technē* championed by Thrasymachus.[52] Plato does indeed describe speaking as a *poiēsis*, a productive activity, as we saw above; we may now say that what it *produces* is the lighting up of truth, which makes it available to others.

Of course, this requires that we use the word "*poiēsis*" in an analogous sense, not as bringing into being something non-existent in the literal sense, since language is directed precisely *to* the being of things, but as effecting the manifestation of that being. One might object that being is already manifest in itself, which means that the only effect that language can bring about is manifesting it to others—that is, communication. In this case, it would seem that language does not benefit *being*, but only those seeking to perceive it, and so the directedness to being cannot define language as such. To this objection, we must reply, first of all, that it does not make sense to say that being is manifest *in itself*, since "manifest" means revealed, opened to an other who can perceive it. It is not possible in the present context to explore the sense in which being manifest to others is essential to being in itself or, in other words, the sense in which being is self-communicative as a matter of its very essence, in Plato, which would imply a relation to intelligence, and so *logos* as thought and speech, at the foundation of being. We can nevertheless affirm that, if speaking is always a communication of truth (so that a betrayal of truth is a betrayal of speech and not simply a bad use of an indifferently disposed instrument), and that speaking is thus a manifesting to others of what is so to speak "meant" to be so manifest, then for Plato the communicative dimension of speech rests on the more fundamental aspect of truth. In this sense, we can say that *logos* is directed both to being and to others, but it is *more basically* directed to being than to the perceivers of being. It therefore "benefits"—it is ordered to—being in a manner that is genuinely *analogous* to the way the shepherd is ordered to the flourishing of sheep *and also, but secondarily*, to the supplying of sheep for human consumption. Speech is "set over" being; it is ordered to the service of

---

52   In this particular passage of the *Gorgias*, Socrates is saying that the truth regarding the "matters we are discussing" is a common good, but since the matters being discussed are the need to speak the truth in public for the benefit of souls, as opposed to flattering for the sake of private gain, it appears to be warranted to suggest that Plato holds truth, simply, to be a common good.

truth, the manifesting *of being*, which by implication also means *to others*. And it is just this that constitutes it as the "proto-*technē*."

This point allows us to respond to a further, related objection. One might point out that we use language for all sorts of things, and not simply to express truth; thus, even if we intend to express truth, we almost always intend that its use is relative to some more basic purpose (to communicate ourselves, to persuade others, to enable the accomplishment of some task or other, and so forth), which is analogous to Thrasymachus's charge that Socrates stupidly fails to see that a shepherd feeds sheep only to fatten them for the butcher. It is, indeed, the case that language is always directed at some level to other people and that, when we speak, we always desire to introduce some notion into others' minds, and in this respect to persuade them of one thing or another.[53] "*Psychogōgia*," the leading of souls, is not an accidental feature of language, but belongs to it by nature. Plato does not at all deny the power of language in this respect and even affirms the "rhetorical" enhancement of that power: not only does he outline the various means of persuasion in some detail in the *Phaedrus* (266d–267d),[54] but in the *Menexenus* he also has Socrates present himself as a student of rhetoric, following regular lessons from Aspasia.[55] Nevertheless, the *power* of persuasion, for Plato, is always a determinate power; it is always ordered to some real end.[56] The true and good desire to persuade cannot be isolated from the more basic function of language, which is simply to display

---

[53] In their translation of the *Phaedrus*, Nehemas and Woodruff present speeches as things that are "applied to" the soul, as if the soul were the object of speech (*Phdr.* 270e), but in fact the Greek says that the *logoi* are "brought to" the soul: the object of language remains being.

[54] What is remarkable about this discussion is how quickly Socrates runs through these "techniques," as if they are obvious, once one grasps the essence of the matter.

[55] *Mene.* 235e–236a. It is likely that Socrates is being ironic, but his point is that, for all of his criticisms, he is no less capable of rhetorical flourish than other well-regarded speakers, which is a claim one could make even more strongly with respect to Plato. While some take this to be a sort of "performative contradiction," a case can be made that it is quite consistent with Plato's understanding of philosophy. For such a case, I refer again to the concluding chapter of Schindler 2008, 283–336.

[56] See Kato 1986, 29. In *Gorg.* 493a ff., Plato explains that the "part of our souls in which our appetites reside is actually the sort of thing to be open to persuasion," and suggests that the use of rhetorical techniques is addressed specifically to this part of the soul. There is no space to work out all the details here, but there is reason to think that, for Plato, the "moving" capacity of language corresponds to the body, or better, the embodied dimension of human existence, while the intelligible content concerns the *nous*, which always remains unmoved: in this case, *learning* is recollection, i.e., not simply the introduction of new ideas, but a re-cognition of them, a retrieval of what is already there, while *persuasion* is then the bringing of the lower parts of the soul into alignment with what is true.

the truth of things.[57] It is just this that Plato means by speaking of "true rhetoric" (517a; cf., *Phdr.* 269b).[58] To do justice to the nature of things, we must respect this most essential function, even as we take it up into more complex and higher-order activities. A disregard for this essential nature is a disorder, like the shepherd who thinks *he himself* is a butcher, but it is far more fundamental and pervasive in its effects insofar as it touches on what makes us human and, indeed, on the basic meaning of all things, which becomes manifest in a paradigmatic way in language.

Let us now turn back to Socrates' engagement with the sophists in the *Gorgias*. As we have seen, Gorgias thinks that learning to speak well means acquiring a method in abstraction from any content, a method that can then be applied indifferently to any particular subject matter. He takes language to be a sort of *neutral* instrument, a "technology," which is to say that it presents a *mere* means, detached from any given end: Gorgias himself *intends*, of course, that this instrument be used well, for the benefit of the people, but he cannot be held responsible for the bad use others may make of it (456d–457c). For Plato, however, the point is not in the first place what one intends in the use of language—it may turn out to be the case that Gorgias and all of his disciples seek to use their rhetorical skill *exclusively* for the betterment of society. It remains, even in this (admittedly not very likely) case, an *abuse* of language precisely to the extent that language is conceived as a mere instrument, which is in itself indifferent to reality.[59] To think of speaking as an abstract method, and thus *not* as a *technē* in Plato's sense of the term, is in fact not neutral at all: language in this case is defined in itself by the absence of reality. To put it in a more directly Platonic idiom, language in this case has the very form of ignorance.[60] If it happens to be used to express truth, not only is this an accident,

---

57 It is worth observing that the "truth of things" is not simply equivalent, for Plato, to "just the facts." The being to which language aspires is never, for Plato, reality in the positivistic and empirical sense, but in the sense of the essentially transcendent "really real reality," which, as Plato demonstrates in the *Phaedrus* among many other places, can often best be "captured" in the imagery of poetic expression better than in what may appear to be a more "technically correct" language.

58 For an account of "true rhetoric" in Plato, which aims to please the gods rather than men, see Black 1979, 171–221.

59 In the passage *Gorg.* 454e–455a, Plato explains that rhetoric produces belief but *does not teach*; it is, however, the very nature of words to teach, as we have seen. Thus, even if used for ostensibly good ends, sophistical rhetoric violates the nature of language.

60 By contrast, the very endeavor to discern the etymologies of words, such as we find in great abundance in the *Cratylus*, however successful or unsuccessful they may happen to be, presupposes that language has the form of knowledge: some insight into the nature of things, so to speak, is embedded in words, regardless of any particular user's intentions.

but in a certain respect it is actually a *violence,* insofar as this accidental contact with reality is an alien *intrusion* on its essence, a transgression of the boundaries that necessarily define a method that is specified precisely by its abstraction.

If language is not defined by the end of manifesting the being of things, then what is left to define it? To answer that we would be left with defining language by the end of the communication of thoughts only defers the question, since, as we pointed out above, thoughts are always *of* something, an attempt to correspond to some reality beyond themselves.[61] Since language is the power to lead souls to reality, then removing reality leaves us with the indeterminate power to lead souls literally "any which way." In other words, language as an abstract method is reduced to the sheer—and essentially empty—"power to persuade" (as Socrates says). It is not an accident that Socrates' discussion with Polus, which succeeds his discussion with Gorgias, turns so directly on the nature of power (466b ff.). Because we have already laid out the basic pattern, we do not have to enter into the details to get to the heart of the matter in this discussion. For Socrates, it is not possible to understand and genuinely evaluate power except in relation to an actual end, which ultimately and inescapably means in relation to the good as such (468a–b). As Plato regularly affirms, the good is what all desire in some respect in everything they do without exception.[62] The moment we think about power in a concrete and real way, we are compelled to inquire into the end that always-already defines it and so are led to the necessity of knowledge. Polus, by contrast, seeks power in an abstract sense, power simply as such, separated from any dative that would direct and therefore limit it. We could say that he conceives power "technologically," as we have described that term above. As abstract, this power appears to be unlimited, but it is not difficult for Socrates to show that, when seen in the light of reality, such an indifference to reality is actually indistinguishable from the absence of power.[63] If language, detached from reality, has the form of ignorance, power detached from reality has the form of impotence (ἐλάχιστον ... δύνασθαι, 466b). The point, for us, is simply to indicate a connection between

---

61 Even thoughts about thoughts are still directed to those thoughts as analogous to reality, to which they seek to correspond, and by which their adequacy may be measured.
62 See *Rep.* VI, 505e; *Symp.* 206a; *Gorg.* 468b.
63 An indeterminate will that does not order itself to the good, which it nevertheless cannot help but desire, cannot be said to do what it wants to do, which is another way of saying it is impotent. Regarding the violent whims of the "powerful" tyrant, who appears to be doing just anything he wants, Socrates asks: "And is he also doing what he wants if these things are actually bad? Why don't you answer?" Even Polus finally admits the logic of this point: "All right, I don't think he's doing what he wants" (*Gorg.* 468c–e).

the conception of rhetoric as a method and a preoccupation with power. If language is not understood as an image of reality, there will be an inexorable tendency to substitute it for reality, to reify the means that has no intrinsic relation to an end beyond itself. Plato emphasizes that, in striking contrast to Socrates, who never "reified" his thought in writing, the sophists love to "package" their courses and sell them, and strive to acquire power through the writing of speeches (see *Phdr.* 257d–258c).[64]

What is at stake in Plato's critique of the "technology" of language? It has become apparent that what is at stake is much more than simply the classification of a particular phenomenon, sophistry, and the "techniques" it professes to teach. We saw that Gorgias praised rhetoric as a "demonic" power, which summed up in itself the various powers of all the particular *technai*. It is indeed the case that one's interpretation of the nature of language bears in some sense on the entire spectrum of these human activities. Language as the proto-*technē* or, in other words, as the medium of knowledge and so of the human soul's relation to reality simply, lies at the root of all particular *technai*. If language is interpreted as a technology in the manner we have been describing, it means that all the *technai* will be conceived most basically as forms of power. In this case, the dimensions of reality for which the *technai*, by their own inner logic, have care and responsibility, will be transformed into mere means to be exploited in pursuit of self-serving projects. The sophistic reluctance to answer simple questions, to take an interest in the nature or essence of things, is not first a moral failing, but rather a natural result of the technological conception of language. Language, thus understood, is not naturally drawn to reality, so to speak, but is averse to it, as we suggested above, to such an extent that speaking truth does violence to language.

For Plato, by contrast, language has a natural attraction to, affinity for, the being of things. We might say that language has the form, the inner logic, of love of the real.[65] Because this is its form, to allow oneself to be led by language

---

64   Jacques Derrida significantly misreads this point in his well-known critique of Plato's suspicion of writing: Derrida 1989, 61–172. Plato criticizes the separation of the word from the speaker, not because of some anxiety about presence, which would imply a desire to retain control, but precisely because such a separation implies a "technology" that offers at least the illusion of control. For a defense of Plato on this point, see Pickstock 1998.

65   We are not using "form" here in the technical Platonic sense. Though Plato does not himself characterize language explicitly in terms of the love of the real, it arguably captures the proper spirit of his conception. Language, we have seen, is an *image* of the being of things; in *Phdr.* 75b, Plato describes the image as "reaching out toward" and "being eager for" the reality it represents: ὀρέγεται and προθύμεται. In the *Republic*, he describes the philosopher as driven by *eros* to attain the being or the nature of things, which is that at which the word aims (*Rep.* v, 490a-b). In the *Gorgias*, Socrates presents the words of

is to be guided *beyond it*, as Socrates concludes in the *Cratylus* (436a ff.). If language lies at the root of all *technai*, such a conception of language implies that *technē* itself will exhibit a natural inclination to the real. With this, we receive an insight into an important theme in Plato.[66] While *technē* is always a kind of knowledge ordered to activity, for the sake of some determinate *ergon*, it remains in the first place *a form of knowledge*, which is to say that its significance is never exhausted by its practical effects. To put this point more positively and more simply, the *technai*, which have the proto-*technē* of language at their root, are all a matter of *truth*, even as they concern the accomplishment of some *ergon*. For example, we build a house in order to display the excellence of what a house *is* and what it *ought to be, as well as* in order to have a place in which to live. And it will be a better place to live the more carefully we have attended to the truth of "house." This concern to display excellence, to show what is true, accompanies all human activities to the extent that they are human. To live in this properly human way, which Plato describes as being "devoted to truth" (526c), is to receive, to recapitulate, and so to reinforce the order that is inscribed in things and, indeed, in actions,[67] prior to their usefulness for human projects. It is to live in the harmony that Plato identifies as the ontological friendship that constitutes the cosmos, man's friendship with himself, with the world, and with the gods (507e–508a).

The possibility of this friendship turns on the nature of language. If we are brought into the being of things in our speaking, and in this way entrusted with their care, then the question of power will always be raised within a determinate context against the measure of the good; if by contrast language is nothing but a technology, there will be no measure but unmeasured power—in the form of competing private interests—for shaping human existence. We have here what Plato presents as one of the fundamental questions that faces each human soul, with respect to which it will be judged.[68] Do we acknowledge an order inherent in reality, to which we subordinate ourselves, or do we not? This eschatological contest, Plato writes, "I hold to be worth all the other contests in

---

philosophy as staying true to their beloved (in contrast to the sophist, whose words are as fickle as the sophist's beloved, namely, the crowd: 481d ff.). If we acknowledge a connection between *eros* and *logos*, we have a way of resolving the classic problem of the unity of the *Phaedrus*, which seems to fall into two unrelated parts on love and on rhetoric, but of course *how* this is so cannot be a question we pursue here.

66 To be sure, we have to make a distinction between *technē* in the properly philosophical sense that we have been elaborating, and *technē* in its more common "banausic" sense, which Plato occasionally contrasts with theoretical practices: see *Gorg.* 512b–c; *Rep.* VII, 522b, 590c; *Phdr.* 248c (texts cited in Kato 1986, 15).
67 *Crat.* 387a–c.
68 See Kube 1969, 6.

life" (526e). At the beginning of the *Gorgias*, Socrates asked the sophist about the power of his *technē*, and then dueled with his disciple, Polus, over the nature and scope of power simply. By the end, in taking on the third opponent, Callicles, Socrates says, with urgency and indeed some exasperation, "For you see, don't you, that our discussion's about this—and what would even a man of little intelligence take more seriously than this?—about the way we're supposed to live" (500c). The reason the discussion was about this all along is that to view and thus to use speech as an abstract method, which can be learned independently from one's engagement with the real, is to exile the human soul from communion with the world. If there is no natural friendship, we might say, between the word and being, there can be no friendship in the end between man and the gods.

The force of this insight from Plato seems to me not to have faded over the centuries, but quite to the contrary to have intensified and deepened by many orders of magnitude. How can we, in the 21st century, make sense of real, "cosmic" friendship as the context from within which to consider the so-called problem of technology, when technology is becoming the very medium of friendship? Freedom from this self-enclosed and ever-constricting circle can be found if we learn from Plato once again to ask, and to care about, simple questions: What is a word? Is rhetoric an art?[69]

---

[69] This paper was originally delivered as a lecture at Boston College, on October 26, 2017. I would like to thank all the participants at the lecture for their questions, and especially Prof. May Sim and Fr. Gary Gurtler, SJ, for their work in organizing the event—and their improvisational skills when the fire alarm sent us all out into the rain. I am grateful in a particular way to Prof. Max Latona, who gave a thoughtful and incisive paper in response to mine. Finally, an anonymous reviewer offered substantial questions and exceptional comments on an earlier draft of this essay, which allowed me to rethink some of the claims and clarify many parts of the argument.

COLLOQUIUM 3

Commentary on Schindler

Max J. Latona
Saint Anselm College

Abstract

This essay responds to D.C. Schindler's "Language as *Technē* vs. Language as Technology," which argues that, for Plato, language is a craft that has for its subject matter being itself. While Schindler's thesis is consistent with what we know as the Platonic philosophical project, it raises several questions. First, does being, as the subject matter of language, constitute a determinate subject matter, such as is required by all crafts? Second, does the ordinary language user meet the epistemic bar of a true craftsman, who possesses a rigorous knowledge of his or her subject matter? And third, in as much as Plato himself expresses doubt about our ability to master reality through language (given the propensity for language to deceive), is it feasible to see linguistic competence as a form of technical mastery?

Keywords

Plato – language – art – craft – being

1   Introduction

In his paper "Language as *Technē* vs Language as Technology," Schindler makes the remarkable claim that for Plato, language—that is, the system of signs itself and not merely the spoken expression of a given language (what elsewhere Saussure refers to as *langue* as opposed to *parole*)—bears fundamental similarities to art or craft (Gr. τέχνη), and is arguably the original human art, or proto-*technē*.[1] In so doing, Schindler intends to highlight several otherwise

---

[1] The expression proto-*technē* first appears in this context in Roochnik (1996, 218). In his discussion of Protagoras' speech in the *Protagoras*, Roochnik notes that Prometheus gives to human beings technical intelligence (τὴν ἔντεχνον σοφίαν) (*Prot.* 321d1), which Roochnik refers to as proto-*technē* inasmuch as it is the original capacity from which all specific skills emerge. Schindler argues that for Plato it is language that plays this role. It is worth noting that Plato

overlooked features of language: first, like all other *technai*, language has a determinate subject matter; second, it accomplishes something that is of benefit for that subject matter; and third, in providing this benefit, language establishes the basic human orientation that makes possible all other *technai*, as well as a life lived well. In what follows I will briefly review his analysis, and then raise a few possible concerns for consideration.

11   Summary of Schindler's Argument

Schindler's analysis takes its point of departure from the dispute over rhetoric in Plato's *Gorgias,* a dispute which is unusually pitched because, according to Schindler, what is at stake is not simply the status of rhetoric as art, but the nature of language and the good life.[2] Two sides emerge on these issues. On the one side are those who, like Gorgias, Polus, and Callicles, see rhetoric as a genuine *technē* because it employs language with great skill and power in persuading all manners of people on all manners of topics. At work here, says Schindler, is a particular view of human language whereby words are simply tools that can be skillfully adapted to one purpose or another depending on the devices and stratagems of their user. Such is the "technological" view of language and, according to Schindler's reading of Plato, it contributes to a view of human life as oriented towards power and gratification. Against this stands Socrates, who vehemently denies rhetoric the status of *technē* for at least three reasons. First, true craft is always about something (περί τινός): cobbling is concerned with shoes, and weaving with clothes, but rhetoric's very adaptability to all subjects makes it a craft about nothing in particular, and therefore not a real craft.[3] Second, and because it lacks a specific subject matter, rhetoric is characterized by an *absence* of knowledge of anything, and therefore its know-how is not a *technē* but an empirical knack (ἐμπειρία) or routine (τριβή). Third, all crafts produce some good for their subject matter—physicians produce health for bodies, and bakers bake bread for food—but the orator and sophist provide

---

would not be the first among the ancient Greeks to associate language and craft. Aeschylus refers to writing as *technē* (*Prometheus Bound*, 441–506), and Sophocles lists speech (*logos*) as among the *technai* that make man the most wondrous and terrible (δεινότατον) of creatures (*Antigone,* 335).

2   Cf. McCoy 2008, 85.

3   To claim, as Gorgias does, that rhetoric is about speeches is to obscure the problem, for cobblers can give good speeches about shoes, and weavers about clothes. What does rhetoric give speeches about? Of course, Gorgias counters that it is precisely its adaptability to any subject matter that gives rhetoric its power—the orator can speak effectively and convincingly about any topic, making it the most powerful of all kinds of *technē*.

nothing but empty speeches that fail to instruct, but only gratify their audience as they manipulate its emotions for purposes of persuasion.

According to Schindler, at work here in Socrates' emphatic refusal to confer the title of *technē* on rhetoric is the perception that rhetoric fundamentally misuses language—treating it as a mere instrument when in fact it is an art in its own right. As an art, it is structurally oriented towards a specific subject matter and a certain good, such that it can in fact be improperly deployed, if directed in such a manner by the practitioner. To draw a loose analogy, if the medical art can be misused when it is utilized to harm and not to heal, so too language can be misused when it is made simply to enhance the speaker's power over his or her listener.[4] As Socrates declares in the *Cratylus*, words are naturally employed as "a tool for giving instruction, that is to say, for dividing being" (*Crat.* 388b10–11). This suggests that, whatever else language might be doing in a performative sense, it has its primary function to instruct, and such instruction happens if and only if words display things, particularly how things are different from one another in their natures.[5] From this Schindler concludes that the subject matter of language is none other than being and that the benefit that words provide to being is (drawing language from Heidegger) that they make being manifest, they bring it to light. And this means that the creature who is fundamentally characterized by *logos*, namely the human being, is by nature set over the subject matter of being: being is in our keeping and care, one might say, just as a patient is in the keeping and care of a doctor, or a friend in the keeping of a friend. Human life then, properly lived with *logos*, becomes a life lived in communion with reality, abiding in an ontological friendship with being.[6] In stark contrast, the orator and sophist untether words from things, and in so doing unmoor human life itself.[7] Without the discipline and purpose of serving reality with our words, the rhetorician becomes aimless and subject to his own desires for gratification, power, and self-aggrandizement.

---

4 This claim stands in contrast to Roochnik, who claims that *technē* is value neutral in the Platonic dialogues. Medicine, for example, can produce *both* disease or health: "it is in the use of the *technē*, and not the *technē* itself, that ethical value resides" (Roochnik 1996, 31).

5 As Socrates remarks to Cratylus: "the correctness of names consists in displaying the nature of the thing it names" (*Crat.* 428e). Thus, language has as its ultimate referent and subject matter not thoughts or meanings, but things themselves.

6 This resembles the language of the Neo-Thomists who suggest such a "friendship" with being. Indeed, Maritain characterizes the relationship between mind and being as a nuptial one (Maritain 1946, 8). See also W. Norris Clarke (2001, 139).

7 As McCoy (2008, 90–91) points out, this is consistent with Gorgias's view as articulated in his work, *On Being*. There, Gorgias argues that perception is divorced from things, and that *logoi* are divorced from perceptions.

Broadly speaking, Schindler's conclusions here seem consistent with the principles and commitments of what we know as the Platonic philosophical project, commitments to truthful speech, the pursuit of knowledge, the virtuous life, etc.—all of which Plato was at pains to articulate in distinguishing the philosopher from the orator and sophist. However, Schindler's analysis generates several concerns, specifically around the identification of language as a *technē*. These concerns are, in turn, metaphysical, epistemological, and ethical.

III   The Problem of the Unity of Being

My first concern is generated by the requirements of *technē*: does being, which is the subject matter of language on Schindler's reading of Plato, constitute a determinate subject matter, such as is required by all *technai*? We have said that words are about things, so that the subject matter of language is—at least in principle, and given its expansive power—everything. However, recall that one of the main reasons for rhetoric's disqualification from the status of *technē* is that it too claims to be about everything. So, we must ask: what is the difference between the "everything" of Schindler's language and the "everything" of the orator's and sophist's rhetoric, such that the former qualifies as a determinate subject matter of *technē*, and the latter an indeterminacy that dooms its governing practice to a mere knack? According to Schindler, it is a matter of how the everything is approached, for he remarks that "what *specifies* language ... is everything *in a certain respect*—namely with regard to its being or essence. "[8] In other words, rhetoric's "everything" is in fact nothing because rhetoric contains no concern for the natures of things about which it speaks, but for Plato, in contrast, words make clear the natures of things that are. So the subject matter of language appears to be the indefinite number of essences or natures that exist. Here we must ask: is this subject matter many or one? If many, then many *technai* would seem to be required to cultivate them, each devoted to a specific essence. If one, then how do things retain their essential differences, differences which it is the very purpose of language to set forth? In short, if language is to count as *technē* in Plato, what is required is some formal unity of all of the individual essences so that together they comprise a determinate subject matter, a unity that does not destroy the differences which give words their variety of meaning. Of course, Aristotle offers a possible solution to this problem of the unity of being (and even does so by drawing an analogy

---

8   Italics are mine.

with the same medical art), but it would perhaps need further work to show that it is not an anachronism to attribute such a thesis to Plato.

IV   The Problem of Linguistic Competence as Rigorous Knowledge

My second concern approaches the same problem but from the perspective of human knowledge: does ordinary language meet the epistemic bar of a *technē*? Socrates remarks to Gorgias and Polus that rhetoric "isn't a craft, but a knack, because it has no account (*logos*) of the nature of whatever things it applies by which it applies them, so that it's unable to state the cause (αἴτιον) of each thing" (*Gorg.* 465a). I take this to mean that a true craft must know what it is about in a rigorous way, having precision (ἀκρίβεια) in its applied methods, its materials, and its tools, all of which flow from an accurate knowledge of its subject matter. When it comes to being itself in Plato's work, it is the practice of *philosophia* (later, metaphysics or ontology) and not ordinary language that begins to emerge as the discipline for cultivating a precise and rigorous knowledge of being, giving an account of the causes and principles. So if we are seeking a *technē* of being, would not metaphysics or ontology be a more appropriate candidate than ordinary language? Again, if we assert that it is individual essences that we are concerned with, and not τὸ ὄν *per se*, then it is the individual sciences and crafts that know their subject matter best—and not ordinary language.[9] Now to be fair, Schindler himself admits that it is awkward to speak of language as *technē*, because language is too fundamental to represent a determinate body of knowledge, and in fact makes possible all determinate bodies of knowledge, including *technai*. Again, following Heidegger, Schindler describes language as a "lighting up" of things whereby things are made manifest and can become objects of knowledge in the first place. Now we may be fairly sympathetic to this view of language, but I am not sure that it is Plato's. Towards the end of the *Cratylus*, as Schindler himself acknowledges, Socrates declares that in order to ascertain whether words correctly name something, we must go beyond language altogether: he remarks that "it seems it must be possible to learn about the things that are, independently of names" (*Crat.*

---

9   Again, if Socrates can argue that each craftsman is the appropriate expert in giving speeches about its subject matter—the physician about health, the sculptor about sculpting, etc.—he could say the same about language: the expert in language about health is not the average language user, but the language user who is a physician, and the expert in language about sculpting is the sculptor, etc. In short, language itself is not a form of rigorous knowledge, but retains the capacity to reflect such rigorous knowledge when it is present in the practitioner.

438e). This, I take it, is a direct knowledge of the Forms, unmediated by language.

v   The Impossibility of a Technical Mastery of Being through Language

This doubt about the trustworthiness of language leads to a final concern about Schindler's thesis, which is ultimately in some sense an ethical one. There is a deep and admirable optimism about *technē* and language at work here in Schindler's thought, one that expresses a confidence in the possibility of human mastery of craft and, by extension, of language and reality. But this optimism, this confidence, is not necessarily matched by Plato. For although it is true that Plato seems to extol *technē* as a model of moral knowledge in the so-called early dialogues, he seems to have soured on that notion, and on the admirableness of craft altogether, in the middle and late dialogues. This is explicit at *Phaedrus* 248e where, far from praising the craftsman, Plato ranks the craftsman *below* the poet, and just ahead of the sophist and tyrant. In fact, in several dialogues Plato classifies *technē* as a form of fabrication (ποίησις), and the craftsman (τεχνήτωρ, δημιουργός) as a kind of poet (ποιητής).[10] Given Plato's views of poetry, this is not wholesome company that *technē* is keeping, which suggests that, whatever its merits, *technē* has a dark side. That darker side is revealed in *Republic* 10, where the craftsman, artist, and poet alike are portrayed as engaged in imitation (μίμησις) of the Forms, but an imitation that necessarily entails distortion and remove from the truth. If, to use Plato's example, the Idea is 'Bed itself,' the carpenter's bed is at the second remove from the Idea, and the painter's bed is a third remove from Bed itself (insofar as it modeled not on the Idea, but on the carpenter's bed). While the poet is likened to the painter here, what is important to note is that even the activity of imitation at a second-remove from the Idea, that is, the carpenter's bed, is flawed. As Socrates remarks there: "Let us not wonder if this [the carpenter's bed], too, happens to be somewhat faint in comparison with reality."[11] In other words, no matter how skillfully imitation is performed, such an activity is doomed to a degree of failure insofar as the result invariably renders something perfect into something imperfect. For this reason, the activity of imitation is never a matter of sheer duplication, but always entails interpolation: reproduction always

---

10   See *Symp.* 205b–c.
11   Μηδὲν ἄρα θαυμάζωμεν εἰ καὶ τοῦτο ἀμυδρόν τι τυγχάνει ὂν πρὸς ἀλήθειαν (*Rep.* 597a10–11).

involves production or fabrication (ποίησις). Plato is well-attuned to the connotations of this term, ποίησις. In the *Symposium,* Diotima remarks:

> Well, you know, for example, that 'poetry' (ποίησις) has a very wide range. After all, everything that is responsible for creating something out of nothing is a kind of poetry (ποίησις); and so all the creations of every craft (*technai*) and profession are themselves a kind of poetry, and everyone who practices a craft is a poet. (*Symp.* 205b–c)[12]

It seems that the craftsman and poet alike are engaged in fabrication, a distorted imitation whereby they simply "make things up," as it were.

This problem with poetry and the crafts points to a deeper problem with language, since language is itself described as imitation (μίμησις) (*Crat.* 423c ff; 430a ff.). Like other forms of imitation, Plato was aware of the possibility for slippage in language—that words can fail to name properly, and thereby not reveal but cover over and conceal. As Socrates remarks: "But don't you see, Cratylus, that anyone who investigates things by taking names as his guides and looking into their meanings runs no small risk of being deceived?" (*Crat.* 436a–b). It seems here that language too can engage in fabrication (ποίησις), a bringing into existence what was not there before, despite even the best efforts of the original name-givers (literally rule-setters, νομοθέτοι). It is because of this possibility of "making things up" with language that Socrates advances an extra-linguistic eidetic insight at the end of the *Cratylus.* And it is for this reason, perhaps, that Plato suggests in the *Seventh Letter* that the true doctrine cannot be put into words; instead, it will be born in the soul "like light flashing forth when a fire is kindled" (*Epist.* 341c–d). In conclusion, Schindler eloquently remarks on the moral danger of failing to see language as an image of reality; yet I think Plato's cautionary words here point to another danger of trusting our mastery over language (and being) as we might think we have mastered a craft. Language may mirror reality, but it may do so badly, and rhetoric and sophistry are excellent examples of this.

---

12 As Schindler himself notes, according to Plato the ποιητής calls something into existence that was not there before. If language does so as well, this is not on my reading a credit to language, but a sign that it is capable of distortion.

COLLOQUIUM 3

Schindler/Latona Bibliography

Ademollo, F. 2011. *The Cratylus of Plato: A Commentary*. Cambridge: Cambridge University Press.

Annas, J. 1981. *An Introduction to Plato's Republic*. Oxford: Oxford University Press.

Baker, J. and Bilbro, J., eds. 2017. *Wendell Berry and Higher Education: Cultivating Virtues of Place*. Lexington: University Press of Kentucky.

Balansard, A. 2001. *Technè dans les dialogues de Platon*. Sankt Augustin: Academia Verlag.

Barney, R. 2001. *Names and Nature in Plato's Cratylus*. Abingdon: Routledge.

Baxter, T. 1992. *The Cratylus: Plato's Critique of Naming*. Boston: Brill.

van der Berg, R.M. 2008. *Proclus' Commentary on the Cratylus in Context: Ancient Theories of Language and Naming*. Boston: Brill.

Black, E. 1979. Plato's View of Rhetoric. In *Plato: True and Sophistic Rhetoric*, ed. K. v. Erickson, 171–221. Amsterdam: Rodopi.

Brickhouse, T. and Smith, N. 1994. *Plato's Socrates*. Oxford: Oxford University Press.

Clarke, N.W. *The One and the Many: A Contemporary Thomistic Metaphysics*. Notre Dame: University of Notre Dame Press.

Cooper, J., ed. 1997. *Plato, Complete Works*. Indianapolis: Hackett.

Crawford, M. 2009. *Shop Class as Soulcraft*. New York: Penguin.

Derrida, J. 1989. Plato's Pharmacy. In *Dissemination*, 61–172. Chicago: University of Chicago Press.

Heidegger, M. 1993. The Question Concerning Technology. In *Basic Writings*, ed. D. Krell, 311–41. San Francisco: Harper.

Heidegger, M. 1994. *Basic Questions of Philosophy*. Bloomington: Indiana University Press.

Horkheimer, M. and Adorno, T. 2007. *Dialectic of the Enlightenment*. Stanford: Stanford University Press.

Horkheimer, M. 2013. *Critique of Instrumental Reason*. New York: Verso.

Kato, M. 1986. *Techne und Philosophie bei Platon*. Frankfurt: Peter Lang.

Kube, J. 1969. *ΤΕΧΝΗ und ΑΡΕΤΗ: Sophistisches und platonisches Tugendwissen*. Berlin: De Gruyter.

Levy, D. 2005. Technē and the Problem of Socratic Philosophy in the *Gorgias*. *Apeiron* 38.4: 185–228.

Lewis, C.S. 2001. *Abolition of Man*. San Francisco: Harper.

Maritain, J. 1946. *Distinguish to Unite or The Degrees of Knowledge,* trans. from the 4th French edition under the supervision of Gerald B. Phelan, 1995. Notre Dame, IN: University of Notre Dame Press.

McCoy, M. 2008. *Plato on the Rhetoric of Philosophers and Sophists.* Cambridge: Cambridge University Press.

McKeon, R., ed. 1941. *Basic Works of Aristotle.* New York: Random House.

Palmer, M. 1989. *Names, References, and Correctness in Plato's Cratylus.* Bern: P. Lang.

Pickstock, C. 1998. *After Writing.* Oxford: Blackwell.

Reames, R. and E. Schiappa. 2017. *Logos Without Rhetoric: The Arts of Language before Plato.* Columbia, SC: University of South Carolina Press.

Riley, M. 2005. *Plato's Cratylus: Argument, Form, and Structure.* Amsterdam: Rodopi.

Roochnik, D. 1994. Is Rhetoric an Art? In *Rhetorica: A Journal of the History of Rhetoric* 12.2: 127–54.

Roochnik, D. 1996. *Of Art and Wisdom: Plato's Understanding of Technē.* University Park, PA: Penn State University Press.

Schaerer, R. 1930. *Etudes sur les notions de connaissance et d'art d'Homère à Platon.* Macon: Protat Freres.

Schindler, D.C. 2008. *Plato's Critique of Impure Reason.* Washington, DC: Catholic University of America Press.

Soltes, O. 2007. *The Problem of Plato's Cratylus: The Relation of Language to Truth in the History of Philosophy.* Lewiston, NY: Edwin Mellen Press.

Spaemann, R. 2015. What does it Mean to Say that 'Art Imitates Nature'? In *The Robert Spaemann Reader,* eds. D.C. Schindler and J. Schindler, 192–210. Oxford: Oxford University Press.

Vernant, J.P. 1983. Work and Nature in Ancient Greece. In *Myth and Thought in Ancient Greece,* 248–70. New York: Routledge.

Weber, M. 2002. *The Protestant Ethic and the Spirit of Capitalism.* New York: Penguin.

Weber, M. 2004. Science as Vocation. In *The Vocation Lectures,* ed. David Owen and Tracy Strong, 1–31. Indianapolis: Hackett.

Wirzba, N. 2006. *Living the Sabbath.* Grand Rapids, Mich.: Brazos Press.

Zeyl, D.J., tr. 1987. *Plato: Gorgias.* Indianapolis: Hackett Publishing Co.

COLLOQUIUM 4

Epicureans on Pity, Slavery, and Autonomy

Kelly E. Arenson
Duquesne University

Abstract

Diogenes Laertius reports that the Epicurean sage will pity slaves rather than punish them. This paper considers why a hedonistic egoist (such as an Epicurean) would feel pity for her subordinates, given that pity can cause psychological pain. I argue that Epicureans feel bad for those who lack the natural good of security, and that Epicureans' concern for others is entirely consistent with their hedonistic egoism: they will endure the pain of pity in order to achieve the greater pleasure of social cohesion and to avoid the greater pain of social conflict. According to Epicureans, our feelings for fellow humans prevent us from becoming savages, unable to enter into trustworthy compacts to promote our safety.

Keywords

Epicurus – Epicureans – pity – autonomy – security

1   Introduction

In his doxography of Epicurus, Diogenes Laertius reports that the Epicurean sage will refrain from a number of activities, including falling in love, participating in politics, and worrying about funeral rites. Among Diogenes' list of the Epicurean sage's personal prohibitions, just after one about mingling with women in a way forbidden by law, is a proscription that seems uncharacteristic for a hedonistic egoist: "neither will he [the sage] punish household slaves; however, he will pity them and pardon one who has good qualities" (X.118).[1] Adding nothing more about Epicurean attitudes toward slaves, Diogenes

---

[1] οὐδὲ κολάσειν οἰκέτας, ἐλεήσειν μέντοι καὶ συγγνώμην τινὶ ἕξειν τῶν σπουδαίων. The subject of the sentence is ὁ σοφός. Unless otherwise noted, translations in this paper are mine. The Greek

continues on with his list of the many activities the Epicurean sage avoids, among them making fine speeches, making less than fine speeches when intoxicated, begging, and "turning Cynic." It's unfortunate that Diogenes' customary practice is merely to compile, rather than to explain, the data on his subject, since his record of the Epicurean sage's comportment toward slaves is sorely in need of clarification: why would someone whose goal in life is her own pleasure feel pity for her subordinates, given that pity can be a source of psychological pain?

It is tempting to answer that an Epicurean's pity for her slaves is merely the product of her cold-hearted calculation to maximize her own pleasure: if the property-managing sage appears to care for the well-being of her slaves, she may make them more obedient and efficient, resulting in less work for the manager herself. Motivating this sort of interpretation may be the theory that an Epicurean's pity for slaves manifests as a behavioral response rather than an emotional one. In other words, an Epicurean's pity takes the form of 'showing mercy toward' or 'taking pity on,' which may mean that an Epicurean is lenient and refrains from harshly punishing her slaves but has no emotional stake in their plight. According to such an interpretation, the sage's pity takes the form of an action that she pursues in order to benefit herself. Although I think such an interpretation cannot be entirely ruled out, this paper argues that Epicureans feel genuine concern for others in certain circumstances—their pity entails compassion for those who suffer certain misfortunes—and that such concern is consistent with hedonistic egoism.

Diogenes Laertius reports that Epicurus himself held several slaves, one of whom, Mys, is said to have been educated in the Epicurean school (DL X.3, X.10). Mys and three other slaves were manumitted in Epicurus's will (DL X.21), but beyond that not much is known about Epicurus's relationship with his subordinates. We know more about Epicurean attitudes toward slavery from Philodemus, an Epicurean from the first-century BCE, whose remarks suggest he was interested in his slaves mainly for their potential to increase their master's pleasure. In *On Property Management* (*De oeconomia*), a polemical text aimed at the household-supervision strategies proposed by Xenophon and Theophrastus, it's clear Philodemus expects that an Epicurean manager will have slaves, whose labor is useful for making a profit and providing the manager with leisure time to spend with friends (XXIII.11–18).[2] At times

---

text of Epicurus's works and accounts from Diogenes Laertius that I cite here is from Arrighetti 1973, unless otherwise noted.

2 Translations from *On Property Management* are Voula Tsouna's (2013). The Greek text is from her edition as well.

Philodemus fits the bill of a cold-hearted, egoistic calculator, such as when he discounts Theophrastus's advice "to make auspicious sacrifices and to provide enjoyments for the sake of servants rather than for the sake of free men" (X.21–5), noting that such advice "does more violence to our convictions" (X.25–6). Although Philodemus does not explain his reasoning, he makes this remark in the course of describing the many behaviors that harm or at least do not promote the manager's well-being, including "watching over everything oneself" and waking up before and going to sleep after one's slaves (XI.25–38). These activities, he claims, are "wretched and unfitting for the philosopher" (XI.30–1). The Epicurean manager should not be overly concerned about his servants (or about anything else), Philodemus argues, since excellence at managing one's property is stressful, time-consuming, and detrimental to one's character.

Although it makes sense that a hedonistic egoist (such as an Epicurean) will use pity toward her subordinates as a behavioral tool to maximize her own pleasure, this paper argues that Epicureans will nevertheless have genuine feelings of concern for people, such as slaves, who are deprived of the natural good of security and the autonomy to behave in ways necessary to avoid pain. As I aim to show, Epicureans believe insecurity is worthy of pity, and achieving confidence in one's security requires the freedom to change not only one's beliefs but also, and more importantly, one's behavior. I contend further that Epicureans will endure the psychological pain of pity for the sake of social cohesion, the pleasure of which outweighs the pain of feeling bad for others. More broadly speaking, my paper aims to shed light on the perennial problem of interpersonal relations in the lives of hedonistic egoists, and to challenge the standard scholarly view that Epicurean happiness is something achievable by anyone with correct beliefs.

II   Pity and Security

There is evidence that Epicureans believe confidence in security is a natural good, the lack of which is worthy of pity. In *Kyriai Doxai* (*KD*) 7, Epicurus considers the common belief that fame will bring security, one of the many false assumptions held by those who are ignorant of the true nature of human needs and desires. As Epicurus explains, if the famous fail to ensure their safety, they lose a good that humans desire by nature:

> Some desire to be honored and admired by everyone, believing that in this way they will preserve their security against other people. If their life is secure, they receive the natural good; but if it is not secure, they do not

have that for the sake of which they have striven from the beginning according to what is naturally one's own.[3] (*KD* 7)

Although it's unclear whether Epicurus is denying that fame can sometimes ensure one's security,[4] it's not unclear that he believes security is a good, toward which we are naturally inclined.

Similar ideas are found in *KD* 6, where Epicurus relates security to the means of acquiring it: "For the sake of acquiring good courage from other people, anything from which this can be procured is a natural good" (*KD* 6).[5] As Emily Austin argues, if any means of acquiring confidence in one's security is a natural good, then security itself is a natural good.[6] Elsewhere, Epicurus doubts that many common methods of acquiring security will succeed, particularly the pursuit of public admiration, great wealth, and political authority.[7] Such supposed means to security would not be natural goods, according to *KD* 6, if they should fail to provide the end for which they are sought. According to *KD* 40, those who achieve security "live most pleasantly," no doubt because they avoid bodily harm from other humans and suffer no anxiety about staying safe. Safe people achieve physical as well as psychological pleasure, the twin pillars of Epicurean hedonism.[8]

The rest of *KD* 40 is rather important too, since it contains the only instance of some form of ἔλεος ('pity') in Epicurus' own extant works. *KD* 40 describes the appropriate (that is, Epicurean) emotional response toward the death of

---

3 Ἔνδοξοι καὶ περίβλεπτοί τινες ἐβουλήθησαν γενέσθαι, τὴν ἐξ ἀνθρώπων ἀσφάλειαν οὕτω νομίζοντες περιποιήσεσθαι ὥστε, εἰ μὲν ἀσφαλὴς ὁ τῶν τοιούτων βίος, ἀπέλαβον τὸ τῆς φύσεως ἀγαθόν· εἰ δὲ μὴ ἀσφαλής, οὐκ ἔχουσιν οὗ ἕνεκα ἐξ ἀρχῆς κατὰ τὸ τῆς φύσεως οἰκεῖον ὠρέχθησαν.
4 Other evidence suggests that Epicurus disapproves of the pursuit of fame. See *Vatican Sayings* (*VS*) 81 and the scholium to *KD* 29.
5 My translation of *Kyriai Doxai* (*KD, Principal Doctrines*) is based on Usener's text (1887), which excludes the material in brackets: Ἕνεκα τοῦ θαρρεῖν ἐξ ἀνθρώπων ἦν κατὰ φύσιν [ἀρχῆς καὶ βασιλείας] ἀγαθόν, ἐξ ὧν ἄν ποτε τοῦτο οἷός τ' ἦ παρασκευάζεσθαι. Hicks (1925) and Austin (2012) also follow Usener's text. Arrighetti (1973) includes the bracketed text, as do Inwood and Gerson (1994), which results in a problematic translation: "The natural good of public office and kingship is for the sake of getting confidence from [other] men, [at least] from those from whom one *is* able to provide this" (Inwood and Gerson). It's unlikely that Epicureans consider public office and kingship to be natural goods, given their aversion to politics and public life (see *VS* 58; *VS* 81; *KD* 14; Lucretius, *De Rerum Natura* (*DRN*) V.1130; DL 10.10; DL 10.119; Cicero, *ad Atticum*, XIV.20 [8U]; and Plutarch, *Adversus Colotem* 1127e). In addition, the second clause of Inwood and Gerson's translation seems nonsensical: it has Epicurus say that confidence can be acquired from those from whom one can acquire it.
6 See Austin 2012, 113–14.
7 See *VS* 25, 67, and 81, as well as Philodemus's *On Choices and Avoidances*, col. v.2.
8 See *Letter to Menoeceus* (*Ad Men.*) 128 and 131.

those who, while alive, enjoyed the security that comes from living among friends:

> As many as had the power of procuring for themselves good courage especially from their neighbors, they also lived with each other most pleasantly, having the firmest guarantee. And since they received the fullest intimacy, they did not mourn as though it were a piteous thing the premature end of one who had died. (KD 40)[9]

Those who experience the pleasure of a close-knit community enjoy the greatest confidence in their security; if they die living this good life, their passing, even if premature, is not grievous. One assumes that those who die prematurely in a secure community succumb to something natural and unpreventable; they were not victims of human violence, their fear of which was eliminated in their safe environment. From an Epicurean standpoint, there is nothing sad about the death of one who died enjoying the safety of her community. What KD 40 may mean, though, is that what *is* worthy of pity is the painful life (and, presumably, death) of those who, lacking the protection of a friendly community, have no confidence in their security. Such people suffer the psychological pain of anxiety about their present and future safety, and physical pain too if their fears of bodily harm are realized. KD 40 suggests that an unsafe life is worthy of pity because such a life fails spectacularly to achieve what the Epicureans believe is necessary for human happiness.

However, by interpreting KD 40 differently one might object that Epicurus is claiming that individuals in secure communities come to realize that death is *not* worthy of pity; pity is felt by those with *no* security, who are more likely to fear their own death and that of others, and for whom death might be more emotionally wrenching and terrifying than it is for those whose only vital threats are natural causes. As Austin writes regarding KD 40, "friendship within a stable political community enables an individual to acquire the appropriate attitudes toward death, as manifested in a tendency not to pity those who die" (2012, 115). Epicurean friends might reinforce each other's belief that death is nothing and, thus, that the dead should not be pitied. Indeed, at the end of the *Letter to Menoeceus* Epicurus recommends practicing the Epicurean lifestyle not just by yourself but also "with someone similar to you," the result of which will be your living "as a god among men" (*Ad Men.* 135). Cyril Bailey also claims

---

9 Ὅσοι τὴν δύναμιν ἔσχον τοῦ τὸ θαρρεῖν μάλιστα ἐκ τῶν ὁμορρούντων παρασκευάσασθαι, οὗτοι καὶ ἐβίωσαν μετ' ἀλλήλων ἥδιστα τὸ βεβαιότατον πίστωμα ἔχοντες, καὶ πληρεστάτην οἰκειότητα ἀπολαβόντες οὐκ ὠδύραντο ὡς πρὸς ἔλεον τὴν τοῦ τελευτήσαντος προκαταστροφήν.

that KD 40 expresses the fundamental Epicurean tenet that death is not worthy of pity because it is not a bad state: Epicureans may "mourn their own loss," Bailey claims, but not the non-existent pains of the deceased (1926, 373–4). In other words, this objection might go, the Epicureans pity no one, which means that KD 40 is obviously not about whom they will pity; rather, KD 40 is about the differences between the emotional states of endangered loners and sheltered friends.

Although it may be true that Epicureans in secure communities acquire the belief that the death of a friend is not worthy of pity, this does not rule out their pitying other people, such as those in unsafe communities. Epicureans in safe environments may learn that an easy, natural death that follows an easy, secure life is not a sad thing, but this doesn't mean they refuse to consider what a sad thing would be. Although sheltered friends will probably experience pity very rarely—sheltered friends spend most of their time among their sheltered friends, whose easy lives and deaths are not worthy of pity—Epicurus gives us no sense that he believes pity should be eliminated altogether. And nothing says that Epicureans themselves cannot be the endangered loners, among whom pity may be a common experience in violent environments. An Epicurean may find herself among the endangered if she is unable to find like-minded friends or if such friends are not particularly adept at defending themselves and others. In addition, *pace* Bailey, it seems unlikely that the overall message of KD 40 is that death is not worthy of pity if it is nothing to us. If this is what Epicurus means, it's unclear why he specifies premature deaths as not worth pitying. If *no* deaths deserve pity, then it should go without saying that no *premature* deaths deserve pity. Better sense is made of the passage if we understand Epicurus to be saying that premature deaths in particular are not pitiable if the prematurely deceased have spent their lives in the safe company of friends. This implies that if a premature death *is* pitiable, the death occurred outside of the community of "fullest intimacy" that Epicurus describes so positively in KD 40.

Further evidence that Epicureans link pity with insecurity is found in Lucretius's description of the development of human civilization in Book V of *De Rerum Natura* (DRN). Once primitive humans began to "lose their toughness" by living in huts, making fires, and starting families, they required assurances from each other that the weakest among them would be protected. Lucretius claims that everyone was compelled to feel pity for those who were unable to ensure their own security, the social consequences of which were extremely positive:

It was then, too, that neighbors, in their eagerness neither to harm nor be harmed, began to form mutual pacts of friendship, and claimed protection for their children and women, indicating by means of inarticulate cries and gestures that it is just for everyone to pity the weak (*imbecillorum esse aequum misererier omnis*). Although it was not possible for concord to be achieved universally, the great majority kept their compacts loyally. Otherwise the human race would have been entirely extinguished at that early stage and could not have propagated and preserved itself to the present day. (*DRN* V.1019–27)[10]

Note that in Lucretius's account, unlike in *KD* 40, the pitied are *alive*, and interpersonal emotions play a crucial role in keeping them that way. The passage shows that how you live, and not just how you die, can be a thing worth pitying according to an Epicurean.

If Epicureans pity those deprived of the pleasure of a trustworthy belief in their security, it stands to reason that Epicureans will pity slaves, whether their own or someone else's. Although much of our evidence concerning the treatment of slaves in antiquity is anecdotal, and there is very little documentation from the perspective of slaves themselves, there is sufficient evidence of the legal and economic realities of ancient chattel slavery to conclude that personal security eluded many members of the slave class. Although there was some legal protection for slaves in ancient Athens, they nevertheless could not initiate litigation, and testimony in most Athenian court cases was admissible from slaves only if they had been tortured.[11] Furthermore, mistreatment of slaves was not automatically prosecuted: either the master or some third-party was required to bring suit against the alleged perpetrator, and suits were rare when the perpetrator was the master himself. For Athenian slaves hoping to escape persecution, they could either run away or plead for asylum at a few sacred places around the city. The latter option did not guarantee a reprieve: it merely gave the slave the opportunity to be sold to a different master. Slaves in ancient Athens could not own property, and they required permission before spending their own money.[12] In Rome, the situation was worse in many respects: in the slave society of Philodemus's Rome, the law permitted owners to execute slaves for any reason.[13] In addition, slaves were often separated from their families, a practice that must not have been too uncommon by

---

10   Trans. Smith 2001, with modifications. The Latin text is from Bailey 1922.
11   See Garlan 1988, 42; Cuffel 1966, 334; and Sternberg 2006, 146–63.
12   For a good account of the legal rights of slaves and the laws regarding slavery in Ancient Greece, see Garlan 1988, 41–45.
13   See Harris 2002, 321, and Westermann 1955, 75–6.

Philodemus's time, since he mentions a recommendation by Xenophon that masters should raise the children of good slaves but not those of bad ones, advice which Philodemus abhors (*De oec.* x.18–21). Although slaves could be manumitted in both ancient Greece and Rome, freed slaves often continued to struggle to maintain their security and community.[14] All of this suggests that many slaves in antiquity had trouble maintaining confidence in their security and were therefore deprived of the Epicurean highest good of freedom from bodily and mental pain.

III Behavioral Autonomy and Epicurean Happiness

So far I have argued that people who are deprived of confidence in their security are unable to achieve Epicurean happiness, but someone might contend that Epicurus thinks people who fear for their safety can be happy as long as they have correct beliefs about matters that are essential to living well, particularly the gods, death, and the limits of human desire. In other words, unsafe people might be unhappy not because they lack security, but because they lack true beliefs about, say, the harms of death or the realities of pain. One might add that the Epicureans make statements that seem rather useful for combatting fears for security, such as the infamous Epicurean mantra that severe pains will be short-lived and chronic ones will be mild,[15] and the argument that death is nothing to us. Why wouldn't an Epicurean therapist simply explain to her patients who are alone and fearful of being harmed that they can dissolve their worries by realizing that pain will not last long and death is not a bad thing? If Epicureans believe that someone who lacks confidence in security can become happy simply by correcting her cognitive errors, then it seems they have little reason to pity her.

Such an objection relies on the standard scholarly view that Epicureans believe harmful emotions and painful desires are caused by errors in judgment,[16] and that people can exercise autonomy over their psychological responses by

---

14 Manumitted slaves in ancient Greece frequently remained obligated to their master or his family as specified in a legal agreement called παραμονή, according to which manumission could be revoked and slaves could be tortured if they failed to meet their master's demands. Παραμονή was more or less another form of slavery, and it made it even more difficult for slaves to build security among their families: as part of the agreement, slaves could be required to trade the freedom of their children for their own liberty.

15 For this advice, see *KD* 4 as well as Cicero's ridicule of it at *De Finibus* (*De Fin.*) II.93.

16 See, e.g., Annas 1989, 154n21; Warren 2004, 1–16; Konstan 2006, 202; and Sanders 2011, 212–13.

remaining free of false beliefs. Since any rational person is capable of obtaining correct beliefs, any rational person is capable of becoming happy. According to this view, people who internalize correct beliefs are psychologically autonomous, meaning that they are able to remain independent of harmful fears and wants, and their cognitive functioning is not enslaved to things outside their control. There are numerous descriptions of this sort of independence (αὐτάρκεια) in the Epicurean corpus, the best examples of which appear in the Epicurean *Vatican Sayings* (vs). *Vatican Sayings* 44, for instance, describes the sage's freedom from unruly desires: "When he considers the necessities of life, the wise man especially knows how to share rather than take, so great a store of independence (αὐταρκείας) has he found."[17] And vs 45 attributes the sage's independent state of mind to the study of nature, which according to Epicureans results in correct beliefs:

> Natural philosophy (φυσιολογία) does not produce bombasts, or loud talkers, or those who display the culture that is a matter of contention among the many, but people who are fearless and self-sufficient (αὐτάρκεις) and who take pride in their own good qualities rather than the goods that occur as a result of external affairs. (vs 45)

In addition, Epicurus explains in a fragment from a letter reported by Stobaeus that the goal of his ethics is freedom from worry, not asceticism: "We have striven for independence (αὐτάρκειαν) not so that we may use cheap and simple things all the time, but rather so that we may be confident about them."[18]

Many scholars who support the standard interpretation also argue that Epicurean therapeutic methods are largely cognitive: Epicurean therapists employ rational arguments to remove false beliefs about sources of anxiety, and sometimes therapists make use of non-rational but nevertheless psychological faculties, such as the imagination, memory, and emotions.[19] Whether the therapy appeals to patients' intellects in order to replace false beliefs with true ones, or whether the therapy is more broadly cognitive and makes use of the

---

17 Ὁ σοφὸς εἰς τὰ ἀναγκαῖα συγκριθεὶς μᾶλλον ἐπίσταται μεταδιδόναι ἢ μεταλαμβάνειν· τηλικοῦτον αὐταρκείας εὗρε θησαυρόν.
18 ἐζηλώσαμεν τὴν αὐτάρκειαν οὐχ ὅπως τοῖς εὐτελέσι καὶ λιτοῖς πάντως χρώμεθα, ἀλλ' ὅπως θαρρῶμεν πρὸς αὐτά (58A).
19 Nussbaum, for instance, writes, "And since belief is the root of the illness, the cure must work through a treatment of belief. The curative art must therefore be an art that is equipped to challenge and conquer false belief" (1986, 36). Tsouna also notes, "all Epicurean techniques are cognitive in a broad sense, while many of them are strictly intellectualist, and, indeed, judgmental" (2009, 252). She makes this point about Epicurean techniques in general and about Philodemus's in particular. See also Tsouna 2007, 75–6.

mind's rational as well as non-rational faculties, the consensus is that Epicurean treatments are not *non*-cognitive: since they engage the mind in some way or another, they are not strictly behavioral. As Voula Tsouna notes, the prescriptions of Epicurean therapy do not resemble the dietary restrictions advised by Posidonius and Galen.[20]

Although there is no disputing that Epicurean therapy is primarily cognitive and its main tools are rational arguments, I think the role of psychological autonomy in Epicurean ethics has been overplayed. Epicureans acknowledge that psychological autonomy is not always sufficient for happiness: several texts show that independence from false beliefs is of limited value in avoiding and treating pains whose causes are non-cognitive. Even people with correct beliefs can suffer psychological pain that is remediable only by behavioral changes.[21] Without the behavioral autonomy to avoid pain, people whose pain is not caused by an error in judgment and who are dealing with exceptionally harmful people, situations, and desires will be unable to achieve happiness and will therefore become objects of pity.

Behavioral autonomy is most necessary, according to Epicureans, when dealing with the most recalcitrant of human fears, chief among them the fear of being harmed or killed by others. In order to eliminate this fear and enjoy confidence in one's security, one must be at liberty to make behavioral as well as cognitive changes, as several Epicurean texts show. For instance, KD 14 advocates a quiet life, removed from the troubles of society: "Although some security against other people arises by means of the power to resist and by means of prosperity, the purest security comes from quietude and withdrawal from the many."[22] In addition, KD 39 endorses avoidance tactics to treat a broad range of disturbances, including the fear of violence, advising us to steer clear of bothersome things if they become unmanageable:

> The one who best stands against the lack of courage about external threats has made the attainable things akin to himself, and has at least made the unattainable things not alien to himself. But those things for

---

20 See Tsouna 2007, 75–6, and Tsouna 2009, 252.
21 Cognitive therapy (i.e., modifications of belief) might of course result in behavioral changes (e.g., changes in belief about what is healthy to desire may change one's eating habits), but my point is that there are times when cognitive therapy alone is ineffective—because of the nature of the disturbance, for instance—in which case behavioral changes must be undertaken in the absence of cognitive changes.
22 Τῆς ἀσφαλείας τῆς ἐξ ἀνθρώπων γενομένης μέχρι τινὸς δυνάμει τε ἐξερειστικῇ καὶ εὐπορίᾳ, εἰλικρινεστάτη γίνεται ἡ ἐκ τῆς ἡσυχίας καὶ ἐκχωρήσεως τῶν πολλῶν ἀσφάλεια.

which it was not possible (τὰ δὲ μὴ δυνατά) for him to do even this he avoided and got rid of, in as much as it was profitable to do so. (*KD* 39)[23]

Although it's unclear in the second sentence of *KD* 39 whether Epicurus is talking about unmanageable *things* or unmanageable *people*—the text reads τὰ δυνατά, which could go either way but probably refers to people since humans are the most common "external threats" Epicurus mentions—the point is the same: sometimes the only way to deal with a fear or other psychological problem is to distance oneself physically from the cause of disturbance.

In addition, Epicureans claim that the best way to ensure one's security and remain confident about it is to be part of a friendly community, the formation of which requires behavioral autonomy. *KD* 28, for instance, stresses the importance of making friends for security:

> One and the same judgment brings about confidence that nothing fearful is eternal or long lasting, and sees that security (ἀσφάλειαν) from these limited fearful things is brought about most of all through friendship (φιλίας). (*KD* 28)[24]

Vatican Sayings 56–57 explains that the wise person will not betray his friends, since without them "his whole life will be confounded and overthrown on account of distrust (δι' ἀπιστίαν)." Other texts show that it is the activity of friendship, rather than some belief about it, that ensures the happy life: *KD* 40, again, reads, "As many as had the power of procuring for themselves good courage especially from their neighbors, they also lived with each other most pleasantly, having the firmest guarantee." It seems that the best advice an Epicurean therapist could offer a person who fears being killed by others is to go out and make some friends. It is likely the therapist would also suggest several practical tips for pursuing friendships, such as that one should be choosy in one's selection of friends but not so choosy that one ends up alone. Such advice comes right from *VS* 28: "One must not approve of those who are most available for friendship nor those who are reluctant; but, one must take some risks for the sake of friendship."[25] Although Epicurean therapists may need to employ cognitive techniques to convince a misanthropic patient that friendships are

---

23 Ὁ <τὰ ἑαυτοῦ πρός> τὸ μὴ θαρροῦν ἀπὸ τῶν ἔξωθεν ἄριστα συστησάμενος, οὗτος τὰ μὲν δυνατὰ ὁμόφυλα κατεσκευάσατο, τὰ δὲ μὴ δυνατὰ οὐκ ἀλλόφυλά γε· ὅσα δὲ μηδὲ τοῦτο δυνατὸς ἦν, ἀνεπίμεικτος ἐγένετο καὶ ἐξηρείσατο ὅσα <πρὸς> τοῦτ' ἐλυσιτέλει πράττειν.
24 See also Epicurus's ebullient praise of friendship in *VS* 52 and *KD* 27.
25 Οὔτε τοὺς προχείρους εἰς φιλίαν οὔτε τοὺς ὀκνηροὺς δοκιμαστέον· δεῖ δὲ καὶ παρακινδυνεῦσαι χάριν φιλίας.

essential to her happiness because they will increase her confidence in her security, the main technique will have to be behavioral: no amount of true beliefs about the value of friendship will make friendless people feel safe. Rather, the remedy lies in the activity of socializing with others and forming lasting communities of trustworthy individuals.

Although Epicureans do employ behavioral therapeutic techniques to treat fears regarding security, we might wonder why they would need to: how would Epicureans explain cognitive therapy's failure to cure some fears for one's safety? As Austin (2012) has persuasively argued, cognitive therapy fails to treat the fear of being killed by others because the underlying fear of death that leads one to pursue safety among friends is beyond the reach of rational persuasion: the fear of death at the hands of others is not necessarily based on false beliefs, and the desire that generates this fear is 'brute.' As I argued earlier, Epicurus considers security to be a natural good in itself, and it would seem to be required for all three of the goods mentioned in the *Letter to Menoeceus* that can be attained by necessary desires, namely, happiness, freedom from bodily troubles, and life itself (*Ad Men.* 127). The desire for security is natural and necessary, which means it will inevitably lead to pain if unfulfilled; it is ineradicable, just like all other natural, necessary desires.[26] I can no more eliminate my desire for safety than I can my desire for life-sustaining food and water, and my fear that I will lack these things cannot be diminished by means of rational arguments. It is for this reason that the steps one must take to ameliorate—though not dissolve—one's fear of death at the hands of others must be largely behavioral rather than cognitive. Granted, this doesn't render cognitive therapies altogether useless for treating the fear of death: other varieties of this fear can be targeted successfully by the Epicureans' dicta regarding the nature of pain and death. The fear of natural death, for instance, can be dissolved by cognitive therapy alone. Nevertheless, the fear of unnatural death, such as death at the hands of others, cannot.

Further evidence that Epicureans employed behavioral techniques to treat psychological problems, though not necessarily those regarding security, is found in *vs* 18, which concerns the treatment for the sickness of love, one of the more intractable and harmful desires according to Epicureans. The saying reads, "If you take away seeing and conversing and being in contact [with the beloved], the emotion of erotic love is let go."[27] Evidently, the treatment for lovesickness consists not in being rationally persuaded that one's beliefs about love are false, but in physical avoidance, which, of course, requires behavioral

---

26 See *KD* 30.
27 Ἀφαιρουμένης προσόψεως καὶ ὁμιλίας καὶ συναναστροφῆς ἐκλύεται τὸ ἐρωτικὸν πάθος.

autonomy. But perhaps it's the case that although the behavioral therapy "lets go" the emotions of love—the jealousy, the rage, and the anxiety—it does not also eliminate the false beliefs on which love is based, which would be the job of cognitive therapy. Nevertheless, the possession of true beliefs is not itself the goal of Epicurean ethics, as shown in a passage from an unknown Epicurean text, quoted by Porphyry:

> Empty is that philosopher's reasoning by which no human affliction is cured. For just as there is no benefit in the medical art if it does not cure the diseases of bodies, so there is no benefit in philosophy if it does not drive affliction out of the soul.[28]

The goal of Epicurean therapy is to feel better, and Epicureans evidently believe that some behavioral techniques are conducive to this goal.

There is therefore good reason to believe that Epicureans use behavioral strategies to treat the most serious threats to mental and bodily health—our most recalcitrant desires and most harmful fears—such as the ineradicable dread of being killed or harmed by others, one of the main fears experienced by people with few ways to guarantee their safety. It seems to be the case that the more severe the psychological disturbance, the more likely it is that cognitive therapy will fail or will need to be supplemented by behavioral tactics, such as making trustworthy friends or removing oneself from the source of pain. Since behavioral changes are not an option for everyone, and since Epicureans believe such changes are sometimes necessary in order to achieve or maintain happiness, it is not the case that the Epicurean best life is achievable by any rational person.[29]

IV   Savagery, Social Cohesion, and Pleasure at Others' Misfortune

Although Epicureans may acknowledge that slaves are deprived of key features of the Epicurean good life, why would they allow themselves to experience an

---

28   Porphyry, *To Marcella* 31 (221U, 247A). κενὸς ἐκείνου φιλοσόφου λόγος ὑφ᾽ οὗ μηδὲν πάθος ἀνθρώπου θεραπεύεται. ὥσπερ γὰρ ἰατρικῆς οὐδὲν ὄφελος εἰ μὴ τὰς νόσους τῶν σωμάτων θεραπεύει, οὕτως οὐδὲ φιλοσοφίας εἰ μὴ τὸ τῆς ψυχῆς ἐκβάλλει πάθος.

29   The Epicureans also acknowledge that chance can affect one's happiness (*Ad Men.* 133). Although the good Epicurean will know how to minimize the negative effects of bad fortune—e.g., getting used to having very little so as not to be disappointed in times of scarcity—Epicureans nevertheless acknowledge that one's happiness is not completely in one's control.

emotion that is likely to be psychologically disturbing? Surely a hedonistic egoist would be better off avoiding the pain of feeling sorry for others. It's one thing to acknowledge that someone's situation is unfortunate; it's quite another thing to feel compassion for another's suffering. I might believe that, say, living in a jail cell is unfortunate, but at the same time I might not feel bad for prisoners. If this is what Epicureans believe, then why will they feel bad for anyone?

I will argue two points in response, the first based on the fundamental Epicurean tenet that pains should be endured if doing so will yield greater pleasure, and the second based on the Epicurean habit of reflecting on the relative hedonic superiority of one's own situation. As Epicurus explains in the *Letter to Menoeceus*, "every pleasure is good on account of having a nature akin to us (πᾶσα οὖν ἡδονὴ διὰ τὸ φύσιν ἔχειν οἰκείαν ἀγαθόν)," but a pain is more choiceworthy when its benefits outweigh its harms (*Ad Men.* 129). Epicurus goes on to suggest that we should decide on all our choices and avoidances by "comparative measure (συμμετρήσει)," weighing the hedonic pros and cons of our options (*Ad Men.* 130). According to this reasoning, it makes hedonic sense to feel bad for others if there are sensible grounds for believing that enduring the pain of pity will yield greater pleasure later. But when is pity worth it?

There is good reason to believe that Epicureans will bear the psychological discomfort of pitying others in order to achieve the greater pleasure of social cohesion and to avoid the greater pain of social conflict. According to several texts, Epicureans believe pity is necessary for fostering solidarity among fellow humans, and solidarity is important for warding off fears for one's safety, as I discussed earlier. As we saw from *De Rerum Natura*, Lucretius claims that pity lays the foundation for human compacts for security, and without such compacts the human race would have died out completely (*DRN* v.1019–27). Evidently, the pleasure of security is worth the pain of pity and any other pains that might arise from agreeing to protect other people. Other texts suggest that Epicureans believe that feelings for other humans keep us from becoming heartless savages; some emotion is better than none at all. Plutarch reports, with subtle mockery, that Epicurus makes claims along such lines:

> I think I will take from them first the following, that they quarrel with those who do away with grief and tears and groaning about the death of friends, and they say that the absence of grief, which renders us inhuman, arises from another, greater evil, namely, the most raw savagery or an untempered and raging thirst for fame. As a result, they think it is better to be affected somewhat and to be distressed and for the eyes to glisten and melt with tears. Because of what they have written concerning how they

feel, some think they are tender and friendly. For this is what Epicurus has said in many other places, including in his writings about the death of Hegesianax to the father, Dositheus, and the brother, Pyrson, of the deceased. By chance I recently went through his letters. (*Non Posse* 1101a-b)[30]

According to Plutarch's account of the Epicurean position, one who attempts to eliminate emotional pains, particularly those concerning other people, is inhuman and cruel. And we already know from Lucretius that inhumanity is connected with friendlessness: without feelings for others, people fail to form reliable social bonds and end up leading solitary, endangered lives.

Plutarch also suggests in this passage, although not very clearly, that the Epicureans believe emotional apathy stems from a desire for fame, which elsewhere they classify as both unnatural and unnecessary and rank among the most noxious desires: fame, like love, always leads to pain and should never be pursued.[31] Are the Epicureans disparaging some unnamed people who hope to earn a reputation for remaining unemotional in the face of great distress? If so, the target is most likely the Stoics and the Megarians, whom the Epicureans criticize for being overly phlegmatic. Seneca reports the following concerning this disagreement between the schools:

> You want to know whether Epicurus is right to criticize, as he does in one letter, those who say that a wise man is self-sufficient and so does not need a friend. Epicurus makes this objection against Stilpo and those [i.e., the Stoics] who held that the highest good is a soul free of passions.[32]

The Epicurean criticism reported by Plutarch and Seneca seems to be that the basic human need to connect with other humans is facilitated by our feelings for one another, and there are only bad reasons to suppress such feelings: an affectless person is either an utter brute or consumed by an unhealthy desire for notoriety. That the Epicureans have no desire to eliminate their feelings toward others is confirmed by Diogenes Laertius's account of the views of the

---

30   My translation follows Usener's Greek text (120U): τοῖς ἀναιροῦσι λύπας καὶ δάκρυα καὶ στεναγμοὺς ἐπὶ ταῖς τῶν φίλων τελευταῖς μάχονται καὶ λέγουσι τὴν εἰς τὸ ἀπαθὲς καθεστῶσαν ἀλυπίαν ἀφ' ἑτέρου κακοῦ μείζονος ὑπάρχειν, ὠμότητος ἢ δοξοκοπίας ἀκράτου καὶ λύσσης, διὸ πάσχειν τι βέλτιον εἶναι καὶ λυπεῖσθαι καὶ νὴ Δία λιπαίνειν τοὺς ὀφθαλμοὺς καὶ τήκεσθαι, καὶ ὅσα δὴ παθαινόμενοι καὶ γράφοντες ὑγροί τινες εἶναι καὶ φιλικοὶ δοκοῦσι.

31   See DL 10.10; *KD* 7; the scholium to *KD* 29; Plutarch, Λάθε βιώσας, 1128b ff. See also my earlier note about the Epicureans' withdrawal from public life.

32   Seneca, *Letters on Ethics*, 9.1 (174U), trans. Inwood and Gerson 1994.

Epicurean sage, who Diogenes claims "will pour forth more with emotions, but it will not hinder his wisdom" (DL X.117).[33] Indeed, the wise course of action may just be to "pour forth with emotions," given that the sage stands to reap hedonic benefits in the long term by allowing herself to have feelings.

One might object, however, that an Epicurean can achieve social harmony and avoid social conflict by merely pretending to experience pity: if she *appears* to have genuine feelings, she may succeed in forming beneficial bonds with others. A sociopathic Epicurean could, for instance, act solicitously or utter sympathetic statements to struggling friends, all the while experiencing no genuine feelings of concern, or even antipathy or contempt. As long as an Epicurean displays the outward signs of compassion, an unsuspecting friend may never know the difference. An objector might add that we seem to get a whiff of this problem in the passage from Plutarch I quoted above: when Plutarch reports that the Epicureans consider it appropriate "for the eyes to glisten and melt with tears," it's almost as if he suspects there is something fake or exaggerated about the outward manifestation of the Epicureans' emotions. One might conclude that an Epicurean who poses as a genuinely concerned citizen may be using pity merely as a tool to reap some benefit from others.

Although it is possible that some people will attempt to fake their emotions in order to win friends and influence people, it's doubtful that Epicureans will go this route. For starters, it's arguably more work to fake an emotion than it is to feel it genuinely: it is a struggle to impersonate someone with genuine feelings, and even more trouble to do so convincingly. Faking will hardly be worth the trouble when the social benefits of pretending to feel pity can be achieved with less inconvenience by feeling the real thing. In addition, there is always a chance the faker's duplicity will be discovered, the consequences of which are likely to be devastating. According to Epicureans, the fear of being caught is a major deterrent to bad behavior,[34] and fakers will be wise to fear the repercussions of conning others: if exposed, fakers risk losing people's trust, which Epicureans believe is essential for security. One who is unwilling or unable to experience genuine pity for others may be seen as a threat to social cohesion: if, as Epicureans believe, pity and other interpersonal emotions bind humans to each other, a person without such emotions should not be relied upon to maintain the sort of lasting relationships that foster security and happiness. In tough times, the faker might not *feel* the emotions that compel humans to protect and support each other, resulting in less social stability.

---

33   πάθεσί <τισι> μᾶλλον συσχεθήσεσθαι, <ὃ> οὐκ ἂν ἐμποδίσαι πρὸς τὴν σοφίαν.
34   See *VS* 7 and 70; *KD* 34 and 35; and Plutarch, *Non Posse*, 1090d.

But why is it important for an Epicurean to feel genuine pity for her *slaves*, whose trust she might not care about maintaining? One might argue that an Epicurean should reserve her genuine feelings of pity for her friends, from whom she stands to achieve security, and show false pity for her slaves, relationships with whom may be of little consequence to her. In response to this worry we should note that the fear of being caught will still be a deterrent: even if the faker has little reason to worry that her duplicity will disrupt her relationship with her slaves, she should still worry that her fakery, if exposed, will lead her friends to suspect she's pretending with them too.[35] Furthermore, it's not a foregone conclusion that a master need not worry about the quality of her relationships with her slaves: Philodemus reports in *On Anger* (*De ir.*) that slave owners should fear that their mistreatment of slaves will lead to serious trouble for the owners themselves:

> And as for what comes from slaves, not just failures in services performed, but difficulties and all sorts of misfortunes result, because of their (i.e., the masters') rages, abuse, threats, and unmotivated, continual, and excessive punishments of their slaves, who are incited to everything (imaginable), and if they can kill their masters, do it with great pleasure; if they find they cannot, their children and spouses; or if not even those, burn down their houses or destroy the rest of their property. (*De ir.* XXIV.17–36)[36]

Although we saw earlier that Philodemus believes the ideal property manager should not show too much concern for her slaves, it's clear from *On Anger* that he also believes that a property manager's comportment toward her slaves does indeed bear on her security (and also, Philodemus suggests, on her profit). It thus makes no hedonic sense for slave owners to discount their subordinates' feelings or to risk the consequences of being caught faking their emotions.

In addition, Epicureans will endure the pain of pitying others when doing so allows them to derive pleasure from reflecting on the relative hedonic superiority of their own situation. In a famous and poetic passage from *De Rerum*

---

35 A similar issue is raised by Matt Evans (2004, 407–24) concerning an Epicurean friend's reasons for continuing to support another who can longer reciprocate her support: one who leaves a friend in such a circumstance may give others the impression that she herself is unreliable, thus jeopardizing her chances of acquiring new friends.

36 Forthcoming translation of *De ira* by Michael McOsker and David Armstrong. I thank them for their willingness to share their translation with me.

Natura, Lucretius describes the contentment one achieves by comparing one's tranquility with the distress of others:

> It is comforting, when winds are whipping up the waters of the vast sea, to watch from land the severe trials of another person: not that anyone's distress is a cause of agreeable pleasure (*iucunda voluptas*); but it is comforting to see from what troubles you yourself are exempt. (*DRN* II.1–4)[37]

Epicureans apparently do derive pleasure from comparing their circumstances to that of others, but, as Lucretius clarifies, they are not sadists: they take pleasure in their own relative painlessness, not in another's pain *per se*. Granted, one can be pleased by the relative happiness of one's own situation without pitying disadvantaged others, but pity tends to heighten one's sense of another's misfortune, which may heighten an Epicurean's sense of her own relative advantage. And, of course, only *genuine* pity will result in a heightened sense of one's hedonic advantage; the Epicurean has nothing to gain in this case from faking her feelings for others.

In the end, Epicureans will endure the psychological pain of pity in order to increase their own pleasure and minimize their own pain: pitying others strengthens interpersonal bonds, which in turn increases security, and pity allows Epicureans to achieve what may appear to some as a rather perverse pleasure from considering how much better off they are than others. Although my argument has given us no reason to believe that Epicureans' feelings for others will compel them to act altruistically or against their own interest, it nevertheless shows that their egoistic hedonism will not prevent them from genuinely feeling bad for others. This has interesting consequences for our understanding of the difference between Epicureans and Stoics on the role of the passions in the good life, though there is not sufficient space to do justice to this topic here. The Stoics claim that passions (πάθη), pity included, should be completely eliminated because they are always excessive and stem from false judgments. The Epicureans, as we have seen, believe that some passions are necessary for forming beneficial relations with other humans and avoiding isolation and unhappiness. The emotion of pity, painful though it might be, is therefore a means to a greater pleasure.[38]

---

37   Trans. Smith 2001. See also Cicero, *De Fin.* 1.62.
38   Many thanks to the audience members at St. Anselm College for their input on this paper. I would especially like to thank my commentator, Susan Stark, as well as the anonymous referee for the *Proceedings* for their thoughts and recommendations.

COLLOQUIUM 4

Commentary on Arenson

Susan A. Stark
Bates College

Abstract

This commentary raises questions about the moral value of feeling pity. Whereas Professor Arenson asks whether an Epicurean hedonist can rightly feel pity given that feeling pity may be unpleasant, I ask whether feeling pity may be morally problematic for other reasons. In particular, I argue that feeling pity involves an endorsement of a morally problematic hierarchy between pitier and pitied. Because of this, I believe that we should draw a little-made distinction between compassion and pity and that individuals should cultivate compassion rather than pity. I suggest one possible way to draw the distinction between compassion and pity.

Keywords

Epicurus – pity – moral psychology – Aristotle – compassion

1   Introduction

The subject of Professor Arenson's paper—pity and its appropriateness for an Epicurean hedonist—is timely.[1] There has recently been much interest in emotions in both philosophy and psychology, and there is a vibrant literature on pity itself. Professor Arenson's question concerns whether feeling pity detracts from the pleasantness of one's life. One example that occupies the Epicureans, and which Arenson discusses, is the question of whether it is appropriate for Epicurus to feel pity for a slave. Arenson asks, "Why would someone whose

---

[1] I am grateful to Kelly Arenson for her excellent paper. Many thanks also to Frank Chessa and Paul Schofield who gave me comments on versions of this commentary. Finally, thank you to May Sim for inviting me to BACAP, to the very hospitable philosophy department and the BACAP audience at St. Anselm College, and to an anonymous reviewer at the *Proceedings of the Boston Area Colloquium in Ancient Philosophy*. I am grateful to everyone for their feedback.

goal in life is her own pleasure feel pity for her subordinates, given that pity can be a source of psychological pain?" (Arenson 2019, 120). Whether or not we are modern-day hedonists, Arenson's paper addresses one worry that we might have about the value of feeling pity: that feeling it is unpleasant. Arenson shows that, initial appearances to the contrary, the unpleasantness of pity is not sufficient to cast doubt on its appropriateness: thus, there are good reasons to include pity in our emotional repertoire.

In what follows, I want to raise a different concern about pity: pity seems to require a hierarchy between pitied and pitier. This hierarchy is evident in the relationship between a free person and an enslaved person. But, I suggest, this hierarchy infuses other relationships of pitier to pitied. In all cases, I believe, where one person pities another, pity includes a value judgment that the pitied is beneath or below the pitier; I argue that we should understand pity as an emotion where the pitier endorses the lower status of the pitied and that this endorsement is partly constitutive of pity. This problematic hierarchy may point toward an unjust relationship between the two, or it may point to injustice within institutional structures, as it does in a society that allows and condones slavery. In short, where pity is felt, there may be endemic injustices in the relationship between pitier and pitied. Although I agree with Arenson that the unpleasantness of pity does not preclude the happiness of the pitier, the hierarchy between pitied and pitier and endorsed by the pitier is sufficient to cast serious doubt on the moral value of feeling pity. Instead, I argue that the goods potentially achieved by pity can be achieved by compassion. So even if feeling pity is warranted when the pity–compassion distinction is not drawn, it would be better to transform that pity into compassion, because, I argue, compassion does not include an endorsement of a hierarchy between pitier and pitied. Finally, though I have space only to gesture at this claim, I believe that the systemic injustices that exist where pity is felt will diminish the happiness of all members of society, pitied and pitier alike.

II Two Epicurean Arguments for Feeling Pity

The Epicureans acknowledge that the lives of slaves involve many hardships: lack of freedom, lack of security, little intimacy with loved ones, severe bodily harms, etc. Clearly, the life conditions of slaves are antithetical to flourishing. This is not a new idea, and the Epicureans can and do acknowledge this. But should this acknowledgment be contained in a belief about slaves and their poor life circumstances, or should it be contained in a potentially unpleasant emotion, pity?

Arenson argues that the Epicurean has two argumentative routes to support feeling pity at the poor life conditions of another: first,

> pains should be endured if doing so will yield greater pleasure, and ... second [pains should be endured according to] the Epicurean habit of reflecting on the relative hedonic superiority of one's own situation. (Arenson 2019, 132)

On the first argument, pity may foster solidarity among humans. Feeling pity keeps us from becoming "heartless savages," or "inhuman"; as Plutarch says, "it is better to be affected somewhat and to be distressed and for the eyes to glisten and melt with tears" (Plutarch, quoted by Arenson 2019, 132). On this view, feeling pity is humanizing and connects us with others in our society. And for these reasons, it would seem that feeling pity is valuable.

According to the second argument, Epicureans can feel pleasure at their own relative superiority or good fortune in their situation. As Lucretius puts it:

> It is comforting, when winds are whipping up the waters of the vast sea, to watch from land the severe trials of another person: not that anyone's distress is a cause of agreeable pleasure; but it is comforting to see from what troubles you yourself are exempt. (*De Rerum Natura* II.1–4, quoted in Arenson 2019, 136)

Arenson is quick to emphasize that this is not a sadistic pleasure at the misfortune of others, but rather pleasure at one's own freedom from the unpleasant situation. In contemporary terms, we might understand this as gratitude at our good fortune. I will return to this point below, but for the moment it suffices to say that this too seems valuable: feeling pity appears to include an accurate assessment of the absolute and relative well-being of members of a society, and that awareness contained in the emotion pity appears valuable.

In her exposition of the first argument, Arenson argues that Epicureans hold that it is appropriate to feel pity for those who experience insecurity in their everyday lives. In particular, Arenson says, "Lucretius claims that everyone was compelled to feel pity for those who were unable to ensure their own security" (Arenson 2019, 124). She then quotes Lucretius who says, "it is just for everyone to pity the weak" (125). Lucretius, like many others, does not distinguish pity from compassion. Many contemporary philosophers collapse this distinction as well. For instance, Martha Nussbaum writes:

> When I use the words 'pity' and 'compassion,' I am really speaking about a single emotion … . On the whole the philosophical tradition is in such vigorous conversation that the terms are frequently heard as translations of one another." (Nussbaum 1996, 28)

If Nussbaum is correct, it seems that many thinkers avoid drawing a distinction between pity and compassion. I shall argue, however, that this is a mistake.[2]

III Aristotle's Definition of Pity

To understand why, let us begin with an understanding of pity. Ἔλεος is variously translated 'pity,' or 'compassion,' or even sometimes 'mercy.' Arenson herself holds that the Epicureans feel genuine concern for others, and in certain contexts this concern is or includes pity or compassion. To understand pity further, we might turn to Aristotle. Aristotle holds that pity is "a feeling of pain caused by the sight of some evil… which befalls one who does not deserve it, and which we might expect to befall ourselves… soon" (Aristotle, *Rhetoric* II.8). Aristotle is commonly interpreted to identify three conditions for feeling pity, each of which is necessary and together are sufficient for pity. We feel pity: (1) for those who have suffered a significant harm or evil; (2) for those to whom harm has undeservedly befallen; and (3) for those with whom we identify.[3] Regarding the first condition, we feel pity for those who have suffered a great harm but not for those who have experienced a minor setback or upset. It would not be justified to feel pity for someone who got a paper cut, whereas it might be appropriate to feel pity for a guitar player who loses an arm in war. According to Aristotle, the harm must be substantial for pity to be appropriate. Second, Aristotle holds that the harm must be undeserved. Though this view has been questioned of late (Weber 2004), Aristotle reasonably holds that it is appropriate to pity those who are harmed not as a result of their negligence. The guitar player who loses an arm in war is not (absent contravening information) negligent for losing her arm in war. But a reckless driver who loses a limb in a car accident is. On Aristotle's view, it would not be appropriate to pity the reckless driver. Finally, Aristotle holds that we feel pity for those with whom we identify: we feel pity, in part, because we recognize that but for luck or

---

[2] Brian Carr (1999) also criticizes Nussbaum for failing to draw this distinction.
[3] Nussbaum interprets Aristotle as advancing these three conditions (Nussbaum 1996 and Nussbaum 1994). Carr (1999), though he criticizes Nussbaum's endorsement of these three conditions, does take them as a reasonable starting point for an account of pity.

circumstance, we might have been in the situation of the pitied. This makes sense. One of the social functions of pity is to link the well-being of two differently situated people: linking one who is suffering with one who is not, but might have been or might be in the future. Recall that Plutarch emphasizes this social function of pity. Pity contains the caring of one who is relatively well-off for one who is relatively not. Adam Smith also seems to hold this view. He holds that one of the advantages of both pity and sympathy are that they link the good of one person to the good of another (Smith 2009, 1.1). When someone feels sympathy or pity for another, the sympathizer or pitier takes on an unpleasant emotion that justifiably dissipates only when the circumstances of the object improve. In this way, their fates are linked, and furthermore, the one feeling pity or sympathy has a motive for helping improve the position of the other.

Unlike Aristotle and Smith, who hold that it is valuable to feel pity, many philosophers doubt the value of feeling pity. According to Nussbaum, both Nietzsche and the Roman Stoics (Seneca in particular) regard pity as an acknowledgement of weakness and insufficiency in both pitied and pitier (Nussbaum 1994, 150–152). For the pitier, to feel pity is to admit softness toward others and allow oneself to be negatively affected by the fate of the other. Nietzsche defends a Stoic rejection of the softness of pity, in favor of a cultivation of hardness, power, and creativity. Nietzsche also argues that it is inappropriate to be the object of pity, because pity falsely attributes value to worldly goods. That is, on Nietzsche's view, it is inappropriate to pity one in poor circumstances because despite appearances to the contrary, the poor circumstances do not in reality affect that person's well-being. To assume that the poor circumstances matter for well-being is to hold a false view of what is important for well-being. Nietzsche's view represents his adoption of a Stoic endorsement of the self-sufficiency of happiness.

IV   Hierarchy as a Conceptual Part of Pity

Though I am skeptical of this Stoic-Nietzschean view of pity, with its emphasis on hardness and self-sufficiency, I agree that pity is problematic. I want, therefore, to suggest another reason to worry about pity. The Stoic-Nietzschean view appears to begin with the common intuition that many of us prefer not to be the object of pity. As the 17th century philosopher, Spinoza puts it: "A [person] who lives by the dictates of reason strives... not to be touched by pity" (LeBuffe 2015). This starting point seems to me correct. Indeed, there may be two reasons why we desire not to be pitied. First, we naturally desire not to find ourselves in pitiable circumstances. If we never find ourselves in terrible circumstances, we would never be pitied. But even if we are in poor circumstances, still many of us do not wish to be pitied. This may be because the object of pity is seen to be demeaned or lower than the pitier; the one pitied might be regarded as having less dignity, and might be the object of condescension, or even perhaps contempt, as a result. The pitied may themselves feel less dignified. The pitiers take themselves to be above or better than the pitied. And even if the pitiers recognize that this is merely a matter of luck, or admit the possibility that their own life circumstances may change, or that they may be affected by evils, still the pitiers take themselves to be better off than the pitied. The pitiers may feel that were they in these terrible circumstances, they, unlike the pitied, would respond better; the pitiers may believe that they are inherently more dignified than the pitied. In sum, at the extreme, the pitied are seen to be undignified individuals, driven to this lowest point by their bad circumstances, but not necessarily so driven—the pitiers might believe that the person in poor circumstances might not have responded quite so badly to these terrible circumstances. Pity, on this view, necessarily or conceptually, involves hierarchy: the pitiers takes themselves to be above or better than the pitied.

We can see that when Epicurus pities a slave, this conceptually includes the belief that Epicurus is better than the slave. This is unproblematically true in the sense that Epicurus, having freedom, security, etc., is in a better situation than the slave. But pity seems to involve more than simply this belief in the relative well-being of the pitiers. Because otherwise, Epicurus's emotion could be characterized as gratitude: feeling happy for one's relative good fortune. By contrast, it makes sense to understand pity to involve the pitiers' endorsement of the lower status of the pitied.

Now this claim, that pity involves an endorsement of the lower status of the pitied, will strike some people as puzzling, or even as false. Indeed, pity involves a concern for the pitied on the part of the pitiers; so, it might seem strange to say that this concern also includes an endorsement of their lower status. Let me explain this claim. I believe that pity includes an acceptance of the situation that gives rise to the evil. When Epicurus pities a slave, the pity contains an acceptance of the social relationships constituted by slavery and an acceptance that these social relationships are, for now at least, here to stay. Contrast this with a different Epicurean, Epicurus*, who, instead of feeling pity for the slave, feels outrage for the conditions experienced by enslaved people and for the institutions that have led to these terrible life prospects for this enslaved person. Epicurus* may feel compassion or concern for the slave but also feels outrage for the slave and that outrage contains Epicurus*'s rejection of the institution of slavery and its injustices. But pity is different: it includes a complacency about these social relations and institutions. It includes an acceptance of the institution of slavery, an endorsement of that social relationship, and some complacency with regard to those social relationships and injustices.

A skeptic of my view might be willing to acknowledge that this account makes sense in the context of a relationship of slave-owner and enslaved-person, but does it make sense of the feeling of pity toward one whose long-time spouse has died? Even here, I do think that pity involves an endorsement of some form of hierarchy between the pitied and the pitiers. In the case of the spouse who has died, the pitiers look upon the pitied as someone who has suffered a terrible loss; at the same time, the pitiers recognize that they themselves have not suffered that loss (though they could suffer it). Feeling pity involves acknowledging the bad circumstances of the other and involves the recognition of the diminished status that results from being in these circumstances. Pity may also include an assessment of the response of the pitied to these bad circumstances: the pitiers may see the pitied as responding in a way that is undignified. And in so judging, the pitiers takes themselves to be better than the pitied.

One might further wonder how my account, with its emphasis on the endorsement of hierarchy between pitied and pitiers, would address self-pity, given that with self-pity the pitied and the pitier are the same individual. In particular, how would two selves or two aspects of an individual differ in status, one maintaining a higher status than the other and that one endorsing the lower status of the other? This is a big topic, and so I can indicate just a bit of how my view would handle this issue. I do think we sometimes hold bifurcated views of ourselves in which one part or aspect of the self takes a particular stance toward another part or aspect. For instance, one might look back at one's action taken and find that it was petty or unkind. It is only this sort of distance, which we often take toward ourselves in self-reflection, that is needed to achieve the two aspects of pity: the individual in a moment of self-reflection says, "I am pitiable both due to my poor circumstances and due to the way I am responding to them." Contrast this with another individual, also in poor circumstances, but who instead says, "I am in poor circumstances, but I am responding to them in the best way possible, in a dignified and honorable way." The latter does not feel self-pity, but the former does. And all that is needed to understand self-pity are these two perspectives, which are common to everyday examples of self-reflection.

V Objections to Extirpating Pity

It would seem that my view can make sense of both pity and self-pity. On both views, I have argued that an endorsement of hierarchy is a conceptual part of pity. But does this hierarchy mean that pity is sufficiently morally problematic that we should avoid cultivating it and work to extirpate it? As Arenson shows, feeling pity has some advantages. It connects us emotionally to the good of another: as the pitied is faring badly, so the pitier takes on a negative emotion. Nussbaum also argues that pity is important because it contains an acknowledgment of the fragility of our happiness and the extent to which our flourishing is subject to luck: according to Nussbaum, the one who eschews pity, as Nietzsche and the Stoics do, "doesn't see what the life of a beggar is, what it is really like to lose your only child, what it is really like to love someone with all your heart and be betrayed" (Nussbaum 1996, 161).

I agree that pity is not without its advantages. Moreover, I believe that it is important to preserve the system of value that acknowledges the fragility of these goods. But we do not need to cultivate pity to do this. Rather, I believe we must draw a distinction between pity and compassion, and that we should cultivate compassion rather than pity. Pity, we should understand as feeling sadness at the fate of another, where that includes the cognition that the pitied lacks dignity or is lower in status than the pitier. Compassion, by contrast, involves sadness at the fate of the other, without this belief about status. Indeed, one might even suppose that feeling compassion involves a kind of humility, a recognition that were circumstances different, the compassionate one would need compassion. To put it differently, whereas pity emphasizes the way circumstances or evils diminish the pitied, compassion instead emphasizes the evils or the bad circumstances themselves and the possibility that we all might face these circumstances one day. These evils are not seen as diminishing the agency or the dignity of compassion's object. Instead, compassion emphasizes the connection between the one who feels it for another and the other toward whom one feels it.

Returning to the third of Aristotle's three requirements for pity (that the pitier must identify with the pitied), I want to suggest two ways in which this identification might occur and thus further distinguish pity from compassion. I believe that in both pity and compassion the subject of the emotion must identify with the object. But in the case of pity, the emotional identification by the pitiers also involves a fear of falling into similar bad circumstances or a fear of losing one's dignity. As a result of this fear, the pitiers' emotions include some contempt for, or condescension toward, the pitied. The endorsement of their difference in status (contained in the contempt or condescension) serves to distance the pitied from the pitier and may enable the pitiers to psychically protect themselves from their fears. In feeling compassion, by contrast, the subject recognizes the ill fate of the other and feels sympathy without fear. Feeling compassion, rather than erecting a barrier between the two, connects the two in humble recognition of the precariousness of happiness. If this is correct, I believe it makes sense for individuals to cultivate compassion, rather than pity.

Before I close, I would like to make one further point about pity. One might think that it would be appropriate to cultivate pity, precisely because pity is tuned in to hierarchy. Feeling pity tracks the existence of a hierarchy between pitied and pitier. This can alert the pitiers to injustice and motivate them to work to eradicate it. While I have argued that pity does reliably indicate such an unjust hierarchy, still I doubt that this reason is sufficient to justify cultivating pity: pity not only tracks the existence of an unjust hierarchy, I have argued that the pitier, through feeling pity, endorses this hierarchy. And because pity endorses hierarchical relations among moral equals, pity is itself morally tainted by the unjust hierarchy. The awareness of injustice and the motivation to end it can instead be contained in compassion without the attendant endorsement of the hierarchy or of the diminished dignity of the pitied.

VI   Conclusion

Professor Arenson ends her thought-provoking and tightly argued paper by pointing out that there are important differences between the Stoic and Epicurean views of emotions: the Stoics regard nearly all emotions as important to eliminate for flourishing to be possible. Arenson has shown that this is not the Epicurean view: on the Epicurean view, feeling pity for a slave is appropriate and can be a motivation for altruistic action. Indeed, in feeling pity, Epicurus may be motivated to help the slave, including perhaps working to end the institution of slavery. While this is valuable, I have argued that these ends are better achieved by compassion.

Despite these clear differences, there also appears to be common ground between the Stoics and Epicureans, and even Aristotle: all of these ancient philosophers urge us to ask whether experiencing emotions is conducive to happiness. Arenson has shown that one aspect of feeling pity (its unpleasantness) does not preclude happiness. But I have argued that because of its conceptual link with hierarchy, pity is morally problematic. Pity conceptually involves an endorsement of hierarchy, whereas compassion does not. In response, we should distinguish these two emotions and work to cultivate compassion, rather than pity. Finally, I have barely hinted at the idea that a hierarchical relationship or society in which some are appropriately pitied involves a deep and fundamental injustice. And though I do not have the space to argue for this here, I believe that due to this injustice, no one in such a society can flourish: obviously not the pitied, but also not the pitier.

COLLOQUIUM 4

Arenson/Stark Bibliography

Annas, J. 1989. Epicurean Emotions. *Greek, Roman and Byzantine Studies* 30.2: 145–64.
Arrighetti, G., ed. 1973. *Epicuro, Opere*. 2nd ed. Turin: Giulio Einaudi Editore.
Austin, E. 2012. Epicurus and the Politics of Fearing Death. *Apeiron* 45.2: 113–14.
Bailey, C., ed. 1922. *Lucreti De Rerum Natura: Libri Sex*. 2nd ed. Oxford: Oxford University Press.
Bailey, C., ed. 1926. *Epicurus: The Extant Remains*. Oxford: Clarendon Press.
Ben-Zeev, A. 1990. Why Did Psammenitus Not Pity His Son? *Analysis*, 50.2: 118–126.
Callan, E. 1988. The Moral Status of Pity. *Canadian Journal of Philosophy*, 18.1: 1–12.
Carr, B. 1999. Pity and Compassion as Social Virtues. *Philosophy*, 74.289: 411–429.
Cuffel, v. 1966. The Classical Greek Concept of Slavery. *The Journal of the History of Ideas*. 27.3: 334.
Evans, M. 2004. Can Epicureans Be Friends? *Ancient Philosophy* 24.2: 407–24.
Garlan, Y. 1988. *Slavery in Ancient Greece*, tr. J. Lloyd. Ithaca: Cornell University Press.
Harris, W. 2002. *Restraining Rage: The Ideology of Anger Control in Classical Antiquity*. Cambridge, MA: Harvard University Press.
Hicks, R.D., tr. 1925. *Diogenes Laertius, The Lives of Eminent Philosophers* (2 vols). Cambridge, MA: Harvard University Press.
Inwood, B. and L. Gerson, ed. and tr. 1994. *The Epicurus Reader: Selected Writings and Testimonia*. Indianapolis: Hackett.
Konstan, D. 2006. Epicurean 'Passions' and the Good Life. *The Virtuous Life in Greek Ethics*, ed. B. Reis, 194–205. Cambridge: Cambridge University Press.
LeBuffe, M. 2015. *Spinoza's Psychological Theory*. Retrieved from Stanford Encyclopedia of Philosophy, January 28, 2018.
Nussbaum, M. 1986. Therapeutic Arguments: Epicurus and Aristotle. In M. Schofield and G. Striker, eds, *The Norms of Nature*, 31–74. Cambridge: Cambridge University Press.
Nussbaum, M. 1994. Pity and Mercy: Nietzsche's Stoicism. In R. Schacht, *Nietzsche, Genealogy, Morality*, 139–167. Berkeley: University of California Press.
Nussbaum, M. 1996. Compassion: The Basic Social Emotion. *Social Philosophy and Policy*, 13.1: 27–58.
Nuyen, A. 1999. Pity. *The Southern Journal of Philosophy*, 37.1: 77–87.
Roberts, W.R., tr. 1954. *Aristotle's Rhetoric*. New York: Modern Library.
Sanders, K. 2011. Philodemus and the Fear of Premature Death. *Epicurus and the Epicurean Tradition*, ed. J. Fish and K. Sanders, 211–34. Cambridge: Cambridge University Press.

Smith, A. 2009. *Theory of Moral Sentiments*. Classic House Books.
Smith, M.F., tr. 2001. *Lucretius, On the Nature of Things*. Indianapolis: Hackett.
Snow, N. 1991. Compassion. *American Philosophical Quarterly*, 28.3: 195–205.
Sternberg, R.H. 2006. *Tragedy Offstage: Suffering and Sympathy in Ancient Athens*. Austin: University of Texas Press.
Tsouna, V. 2009. Epicurean therapeutic strategies. *The Cambridge Companion to Epicureanism*, ed. J. Warren, 249–65. Cambridge: Cambridge University Press.
Tsouna, V. 2007. *The Ethics of Philodemus*. Oxford: Oxford University Press.
Usener, H. ed. 1887. *Epicurea*. Rome: L'Erma di Bretschneider.
Warren, J. 2004. *Facing Death: Epicurus and His Critics*. Oxford: Oxford University Press.
Weber, M. 2004. Compassion and Pity: An evaluation of Nussbaum's analysis and defense. *Ethical Theory and Moral Practice*, 7.5: 487–511.
Westermann, W. 1955. *The Slave Systems of Greek and Roman Antiquity*. Philadelphia: American Philosophical Society.

COLLOQUIUM 5

Aristotle on What to Praise and What to Prize: An Interpretation of *Nicomachean Ethics* I.12

Jan Szaif
University of California, Davis

Abstract

This essay offers an analysis and interpretation of the rarely commented-on chapter I.12 of the *Nicomachean Ethics*. Aristotle's goal in this chapter is to prove that human happiness belongs to the class of prized goods, also characterized as divine goods, whereas virtue ranks lower, being a merely praiseworthy good. It is not easy to see why this chapter is placed at the end of Aristotle's general discussion of the highest human good in Book I or why he included it at all. My goal is to show that it does make a contribution to the architecture of the *Nicomachean Ethics* as a whole by helping to prepare the ground for one of the main argumentative strategies in the treatise X.6–8 on scientific contemplation as the key component of supreme happiness. To this end, I analyze each step of the argumentation in I.12, drawing also on relevant material from other Aristotelian texts, and then demonstrate the connection with some of the arguments in X.6–8.

Keywords

Aristotle – happiness – virtue – praise – intrinsic worth

The literature on Aristotle's *Nicomachean Ethics* (*EN*) usually has very little to say about chapter 12 of Book I. The chapter's declared goal is to prove that human happiness (*eudaimonia*) falls into the class of prized or venerable goods (τίμια), whose status as *divine* goods is then also emphasized. It does not promise yet another proof that *eudaimonia* is the highest human good, but uses this assumption as a starting-point; and while it is true that it provides further support for the Aristotelian tenet that virtue, as a quality and disposition, cannot constitute the highest human good, this point has been established before, and more convincingly so than here. Within the framework of Book I, it is not clear that these results add anything relevant to the author's overall argument. I take it that this is the reason why this chapter has been neglected by students of the *Nicomachean Ethics*.[1] Yet I.12 is also placed at the end of Aristotle's general discussion of the highest human good in the *Nicomachean Ethics*, since I.13 serves as an introduction to the treatment of *virtue* in Books II–VI. If its argument is really as marginal as it is usually thought to be, we should regard I.12 as an appended minor supplementary argument, perhaps a piece of *ad hominem* reasoning targeting some follower or followers of Plato, who tended to identify *eudaimonia* with virtue but also viewed it as an approximation to a divine condition. While this might have been the original context in which this kind of argumentation was conceived, I don't think it is the best explanation for its current location. This essay is going to argue that I.12, being more than just an appendix, makes a noteworthy contribution to the architecture of the *Nicomachean Ethics* as a whole. My guiding hypothesis is that it features as the final chapter of the general account of the highest human good because it helps to prepare the ground for one of the main argumentative strategies in the Book X treatise on scientific contemplation as the key component of supreme *eudaimonia* (*EN* X.6–8). It thus serves as a link to this later discussion. To corroborate my hypothesis, I am going to provide first an internal analysis of the argument of I.12 and then explore its conceptual affinity to some of the arguments of X.6–8.[2]

I

The guiding question of *Nicomachean Ethics* I.12 is presented right at the beginning:

Part 1 Now that we have clarified these questions,[3] let us investigate with respect to *eudaimonia*[4] whether it belongs to the [class of] things praised

---

1 Grant (1885, I, 470) provides an early but telling example for the widespread dismissive attitude toward I.12: "The question which occupies this chapter ... is one that appears of little ethical interest, to have no important scientific bearing; in short, to degenerate into a sort of trifling. Aristotle, however, ... appears to have thought it worth a passing consideration."
2 While I think that the result of my investigation, if successful, could lend additional support to some version of a "dominant end" interpretation of Aristotle's theory of *eudaimonia*, this is not my primary concern here, nor do I claim that the interpretation of I.12 will help to resolve any of the known problems associated with the "dominant end" theory.
3 This clause implies that Aristotle is not trying to prove all over again that *eudaimonia* is the highest human good. This topic is among those that have been settled.
4 Throughout this essay, I will mostly use the Greek term *eudaimonia* rather than the traditional translation "happiness," since the English term has misleading connotations. The highest hu-

(ἐπαινετά) or, rather, to the [class of] things that are prized/honored (τίμια); for surely it does not belong to the [class of] powers (δυνάμεις). (1101b10–12)

We can infer from this opening that the argument of this chapter presupposes the following threefold division:

TED   Good things can be divided into
(i) things that are prized/held in honor (τίμια),
(ii) things that are praised (ἐπαινετά), and
(iii) powers (δυνάμεις).

Aristotle does not introduce TED as a classification of *what is good*, but we know from later sources that this is how this division was intended, and it also agrees with how he uses it in this chapter. The task Aristotle sets for himself is to show to which of these classes *eudaimonia* belongs. The desired conclusion (the QED) is that it belongs to class (i). Since the candidate "powers" is dismissed right away, the task narrows down to a choice between the first two classes in the list. Accordingly, if it should turn out that *eudaimonia* is not among the things praised, the only option left is that it is something we prize, or hold in honor.

The origin of this division is uncertain. In Aristotle's extant works, TED is mentioned only in *Nicomachean Ethics* I.12, but without any explanation or justification. Aristotle obviously expects that his audience is familiar with it and will accept it at least as an ἔνδοξον (a "reputable" view). It is therefore likely that this division was first introduced in Socratic circles or in the Old Academy, although it can also not be excluded that Aristotle himself was the first to introduce it in one of his exoteric writings now lost to us. The chapter cites Eudoxus, and it is at least a possibility that Eudoxus used a similar argument by elimination that also relied on TED, yet with a different goal, namely, to demonstrate the higher rank of pleasure compared to virtue, as part of his defense of hedonism (cf. *EN* X.2).

Later Peripatetic sources don't shed light on the question of the origin of this division, but provide some valuable information about its meaning. The sources in question are an excerpt by Alexander of Aphrodisias from a *Division*

---

man good Aristotle is talking about is not an episodic mood, but the excellent quality of a life as a whole. If one wants to connect this philosophical topic with contemporary concerns, one may point to the question as to what makes for a really good human life and what factors prevent such human flourishing.

of Goods attributed to Aristotle, and passages in the *Magna Moralia* (MM), in Aspasius's commentary on the *Nicomachean Ethics*, and in the excerpts from a doxographical work on Aristotelian ethics usually attributed to Arius Didymus.[5] Of these sources, the *Division of Goods* and the *Magna Moralia* are presumably the oldest.[6]

These sources are particularly helpful in allowing us to understand the mysterious class of "powers" (δυνάμεις). They all agree that these powers include things like health, good looks, wealth, and in general the so-called somatic and external goods (as opposed to goods of the soul). They add, moreover, that such "empowering" assets can be put to good or bad use, depending on whether the person equipped with them is good or bad.[7] While having certain Platonic or early Academic antecedents,[8] this specific use of the term δύναμις is quite alien to Aristotle. It has no direct connection with the extensive discussions on δύναμις (capacity, potential) in his theoretical philosophy or with the notion of δύναμις as natural capacity for some type of emotional reaction, familiar from *Nicomachean Ethics* II.5 and *Eudemian Ethics* II.2.

According to the Peripatetic sources, the division is even fourfold (TEDO), with a fourth class labeled (somewhat misleadingly) as "useful things" (ὠφέλιμα). It contains actions or things whose utility relates specifically to how they help preserve or restore the *powers*; for instance, medical treatment restoring one's health.[9] For the purposes of this essay, we can neglect this additional element. It is not mentioned in *Nicomachean Ethics* I.12 and could be a later addition.

The adjective τίμιον is derived from the noun τιμή, which can cover a relatively broad spectrum of applications ranging from "honor/respectability," as a

---

5 Alexander of Aphrodisias, *In Top.*, 242.4–8 Wallies; MM I.2, 1183b19–37; Aspasius, *In EN*, 32.9–18 Heylbut; Stobaeus, *Anthologium* II.7, 134.20–25 Wachsmuth.
6 It is possible that the *Division of Goods* was produced already in Aristotle's lifetime, as one of the many collections done or supervised by Aristotle. It must have been a collection of the various ways in which philosophers had divided between kinds of goods, or meanings of "good," presumably without attribution of sources, not unlike the collections of definitions of ἀγαθόν (good) and καλόν (fine/beautiful) that we find in his *Rhetoric*. The *Magna Moralia* are now viewed by most scholars as a work produced in the Peripatos.
7 The anonymous reviewer has pointed to an apparent inconsistency. In the passage quoted as Part II below (cf. 1101b16), strength seems to figure as a praiseworthy quality, whereas it is a δύναμις (as one of the somatic goods) according to division TED as reported by the Peripatetic sources. My take on this is that Aristotle uses certain qualities associated with athletic prowess as an example since people typically praise them. Yet, according to his own considered view, strength is not something praiseworthy like a moral or intellectual virtue, but a mere δύναμις that can be used badly if the person lacks virtue.
8 Cf. especially Xenocrates quoted by Clement of Alexandria in *Stromata* II.21, 133.5–6.
9 Cf. Szaif 2012, 212–25 on the notion of "powers" in TEDO and their relation to the ὠφέλιμα.

social status, to monetary value. Another derivative of this noun is the verb τιμάω with the meaning "to value, to honor, to revere, etc." Accordingly, depending on the context, a τίμιον is a thing *valued, prized, honored, revered,* or a thing *worthy* of such valuing, honoring, etc. In the context of TED (or TEDO), the category τίμιον must designate something that is valued or prized *for its own sake*, in contrast with the second-ranked category of praised things that qualify as good only on account of their relation to a higher good. If τίμιον is applied to a god or a person of exceptional merit, it may be translated as "venerable" or "worthy of reverence."[10] The connection with the notion of the divine plays, in fact, an important role in the argument of I.12.

As for the translation of ἐπαινετόν, this word form (derived from ἐπαίνω, "to praise") means either *something praised* or *something to be praised*. A convenient translation is "praiseworthy," but note that the notion of "worth" is not an explicit component of the Greek term. There is a significant discrepancy in the information our Peripatetic sources offer regarding the class of praised things (ἐπαινετά). According to the excerpt from the *Division of Goods*, this class includes virtues and *virtuous activities*. Aspasius uses an almost identical formulation.[11] The *Magna Moralia*, on the other hand, mentions only the virtues as ἐπαινετά, and the same is true of the very condensed report in Arius Didymus. Moreover, both the *Division of Goods* and Aspasius, but not the *Magna Moralia* and Didymus, label the class of praised things also as καλά (fine, beautiful, noble things). We will see that in Aristotle's application of TED it is important that only virtues and virtuous people, but not virtuous activities, or fine/noble things (καλά) accomplished through virtue, be classified as things praised (ἐπαινετά), whereas in a Eudoxan version of the argument from TED (if indeed he used TED) virtuous actions would have to belong to the class of things praised. Those discrepancies in the tradition might, hence, reflect the existence of different versions of TED (or TEDO) at the time of the Old Academy and Old Peripatos.

II

We can divide the argument of I.12 into five parts. Part I has been quoted above. The translations for the other parts will be quoted subsequently. Part I sets the stage by introducing the guiding question and narrowing the choice down to

---

10   Cf. Liddell-Scott-Jones *Greek-English Lexicon* s.v. τιμάω (see also *EE* 1216a1, 1242b19*f*).
11   Alexander of Aphrodisias in *Top.*, 242.6 Wallies: τὰς ἀρετὰς καὶ τὰς κατ'αὐτὰς ἐνεργείας; cf. Aspasius in *EN*, 32.12 Heylbut.

two candidates. Since it begins by eliminating the class of *powers*,[12] we expect an *argument by elimination*; and this agrees also with what we find in Part II, which argues that objects of praise are only *relational* goods. Yet Aristotle does not close the argument by elimination at this point, as he could have done by reminding the reader that *eudaimonia*, as a highest-ranking or ultimate good, cannot be classed together with relational goods and must, hence, be a prized thing (τίμιον). Instead, he introduces an argument that identifies the type of speech act appropriate for addressing a higher, *divine* kind of good (Part III). Since this argument includes *eudaimonia* among goods of this kind, it establishes an explicit conceptual link between *eudaimonia* and the notion of a divine good. Part IV is the statement of the overall QED that *eudaimonia* is a τίμιον, while Part V adds a brief argument that purports to prove directly that *eudaimonia*, on account of its function as a principle (ἀρχή), is a τίμιον.

Let's now look more closely at Part II. It contains a main argument and an additional subordinate argument, which is here printed with indentation.

Part II (1) Now, it seems that every praised thing is praised because it is qualified in a certain way (ποιόν τι εἶναι) and relates to something in a certain way (πρός τι πῶς ἔχειν);

(2) For we praise the just man, the courageous man, and, generally speaking, both the good man and [his] virtue on account of his actions (πράξεις) and achievements (ἔργα),

(3) and [we praise] the strong man, the fast runner, and so on, because they are naturally qualified in a certain way (ποιόν τινα πεφυκέναι)[13] and relate in a certain way (ἔχειν πως πρός) to something good (ἀγαθόν) and valuable (σπουδαῖον).

---

12   The reason why *eudaimonia* can obviously not be counted among powers is that the latter "empower" the person to achieve some higher, overarching goal and thus clearly are subservient goods, whereas *eudaimonia* is an ultimate goal. Cf. *Top.* IV.5, 126b4–6.

13   The verb πεφυκέναι could just be a variant for εἶναι, "to be." But the close parallelism with *Cat.* 8, 9a14–27, which uses the fast runner (δρομικός) as an example for a quality based on a natural capability, makes it more likely that Aristotle uses πεφυκέναι here because he thinks of the examples in (3) as natural capabilities that receive praise (cf. Stewart 1892, 153–155). In other contexts, to be sure, Aristotle is wont to emphasize that the voluntary character of an action is a precondition for its praiseworthiness (e.g., *EN* III.1, 1109b30–32). However, the argument in I.12 uses a different notion of ἔπαινος (taken from rhetorical practice) according to which not actions, but people with certain qualities, or their qualities, are praised.

(4) This is clear also from the praises regarding the gods. For they [*i.e., the praises*][14] are manifestly ridiculous since they are given with reference to us; and this comes to pass (συμβαίνει) since praises [*in general*] require reference [*i.e., to some good*] (γίνεσθαι τοὺς ἐπαίνους δι' ἀναφορᾶς), as we have said.[15]

(5) If (as is the case) praise is directed at[16] things of this kind, then clearly *there is no praise of best things* [**Conclusion A**],

but something more significant and valuable [is directed at them] [**Conclusion B**]. (1101b12–23)

The argument of Part II ends with Conclusion A, which states that praise is not directed at best things or, what amounts to the same, that praiseworthy things are not among the best things. This is *nota bene* only an interim conclusion, not yet the intended QED that *eudaimonia* is something prized (τίμιον). This interim conclusion is supplemented with the additional inference that there must be some "more significant and valuable" form of speech adequate for addressing the "best things." This second inference (B) will receive further support by the argument in Part III. The move from A to B presupposes, of course, some unexpressed premise; roughly, that there has to be some adequate form of speech for addressing the highest good human beings can aspire to. But this seems unproblematic at least as a working hypothesis. Let's look more closely at how Conclusion A is reached.

While the formulation in segment (1) of Part II still leaves open what the thing is to which the thing praised, qua praised, stands in a *relation*, segment (3) specifies that it is "something good and valuable." Thus we learn, from the two segments combined, that a thing is praised for two connected reasons: *because it is qualified in a certain way* and *because it relates to a certain good in a certain way*. We can distinguish four components in these formulations and need to ascertain how they are linked: *first*, the *object* of praise; *second*, the quality that renders it praiseworthy; *third*, the good to which the praised

---

14 The implied "they" in the Greek text could refer back to "the praises" or to "the gods." I agree with Aspasius (*In EN*, 33.1 & 6–7 Heylbut), Irwin, Rowe, and Reeve — against Stewart, Burnet, and Gauthier/Jolif — that it takes up "praises."

15 The translation and interpretation of (4) are uncertain because of the unclear Greek wording. Aristotle may hold that gods should be praised for other reasons than that they benefit us, or that they should not be praised at all, only felicitated, since there is nothing about them that could be correctly viewed as subservient to some higher good. Cf. Broadie and Rowe 2002, 290 f.

16 Literally, "is of" (objective genitive).

object, qua praised, stands in a relation (its *relatum*);[17] and *fourth*, the nature of this relation.

There is a certain ambiguity in Aristotle's remarks regarding the *object* of praise and the *quality* it has. The examples in segments (2) and (3) suggest that *people* with certain positive (moral or athletic) qualities are praised.[18] But (2) adds that both the virtuous person and the virtue he has are praised. In Part III, praise is said to be directed at virtue (literally, "to be of virtue," 1101b31*f*). Thus it seems that a virtuous quality is not only a *reason*, but also an *object* of praise.[19] I surmise that when Aristotle speaks of the *quality* as the thing praised, he has in mind the virtue a specific person has, not this virtue in general; and when he speaks of a person as being praised, he thinks of a person praised for his or her virtue. Accordingly, praise will be directed either at, say, Jane in view of her courage, or at Jane's courage. I submit that Aristotle does not bother to draw a sharp distinction between these formulations since they don't make a difference in practical terms for our acts of praising. However, the abstract formulation "(praised) because it is qualified in a certain way" in (1) is best understood as relating to a person being praised in light of a characteristic virtue.[20]

While segment (1) does not yet specify the nature of the *relatum*, (3) refers to it as "something good and valuable," and (2) suggests that it is some kind of *action* and/or *achievement*. Actions and achievements are, hence, the good relative to which a person and his or her virtue or prowess are praised. In the case of a just person, the action could, for instance, be an act of corrective

---

17   For this conceptual framework to remain consistent it is essential that the *relatum* be not itself an *object* of praise, just something that *informs* our praise. (See also my comments on *Rhet.* 1367b28 at the beginning of section III below.) This is where I part ways with Aufderheide, who claims that virtuous actions are here included among the set of praised things (2015, 43). Aufderheide's more general objections (see 2015, 44–49) against counting virtuous actions as genuine final goods will, in my view, fail to impress the inclusivist who maintains that an unobstructed joyful virtuous action does count as a form of *praxis* choiceworthy in its own right and with all the perfections needed to make it a eudaimonic type of action. Aristotle's πρᾶξις/ποίησις distinction in *EN* VI helps to strengthen this point.

18   The list of examples of positive qualities is certainly not meant to be exhaustive. There is no reason to believe that Aristotle would not also include good intellectual qualities among the reasons for praise (contrary to what the author of the *Magna Moralia* seems to believe; *MM* I.5, 1185b3–11, cf. Stewart 1892, I, 154). In *EN* I.13, 1103a8–9, Aristotle states explicitly that the intellectual virtue of σοφία is also an object of praise.

19   Aristotle characterizes virtues as "praiseworthy (ἐπαινεταί) dispositions" also in *EN* I.13 (1103a9*f*, cf. *EE* 1223a9*f*) and throughout his ethical treatises.

20   Since the characterization of the ἐπαινετόν in (1) is formulated in the neuter case, it could also apply to domestic animals and tools in light of their excellent quality (ἀρετή). However, this application plays no role in the argument of *EN* I.12.

justice, and the achievement the rectification of an unjust situation. In the case of a fast runner, we may think of an outstanding athletic performance resulting in victory. This gives us a clue also regarding the *nature* of the relation. The specific way in which the person praised relates to a desirable activity and outcome is that that the virtue or athletic prowess *predisposes* the person to perform certain desirable actions or bring about certain desirable outcomes. In light of these observations, we can now also see how the first of the two formal reasons for praiseworthiness (the thing's quality or form of excellence) hangs together with the second (the praised object's relation to some good): a person is praiseworthy on account of his or her form of excellence (say, justice) in light of the desirable actions and outcomes (say, just actions and outcomes) made possible by this form of excellence.[21]

When trying to reconstruct the argument contained (1), (2), (3), and (5), we need to bear in mind that TED is a distinction of ways in which something can be good. While it is, of course, granted that the objects of praise are also good things, the argument aims to show that they are not "best things." In other words, we are dealing here with a hierarchization of goods. This requires that we acknowledge the following implicit assumption in the argument: *If some x is good because it relates to some other good y, then y is a higher-ranking good than x, and x cannot be a highest-ranking good.* Such hierarchization of goods is a commonly held view and also agrees with how Aristotle has discussed means-end relations in Book I. The brief supportive argument in (4) uses the technical term δι' ἀναφορᾶς, "through reference [to some good]," to distinguish between *relational* and *absolute* goods. The "best things" mentioned in the conclusion are such absolute goods.

On this basis, we can paraphrase the gist of the argument in Part II as follows. Premise (i) corresponds to what we have extracted from segments (1) through (3), while premise (ii) is the implicit assumption just mentioned:

(i) If *x* is a praised thing, then the goodness of x is due to the fact that [it has a quality thanks to which] it relates in a certain way to some other good *y*.

---

21   It was suggested to me during the discussion that the first of the two characterizations acknowledges that virtue has intrinsic value, while the second speaks of its consequentialist or relational value. This is a possible reading (cf. I.7, 1097b2–5 and VI.12, 1144a1–6), yet it would obscure the main point of the argument in Part II, which is to emphasize the relational character of praiseworthiness *in order to infer* that virtue, *qua praiseworthy thing*, cannot be a highest-ranking good. That is why I read the two characterizations of praiseworthiness as connected such that the quality in question is good on account of how it enables good outcomes (actions and achievements).

(ii) If the goodness of x is due to the fact that it relates in a certain way to some other good *y*, then y is a higher-ranking good, and x is not a highest-ranking good.

(*Conclusion* A) If x is a praised thing, then x is not a highest ranking good.

One might wonder how the thought expressed in premise (ii) compares to Aristotle's analysis of the teleology of human goods in *EN* I.7, 1097a24–b6 (cf. I.6, 1096b7–26). There, Aristotle argues that certain good things can be choiceworthy both as final goals and in light of how they contribute to *eudaimonia*. Virtuous action is a case in point. A just person chooses to perform just actions because they are just, but also knows that they contribute to realizing his or her overarching goal of leading a life of excellence.[22] In I.12, Aristotle relies on a simplified model of the teleology of human action, which distinguishes only between highest-ranking goods and relational goods, without mentioning an intermediate level of goods that are both absolute (i.e., intrinsic) goods worth pursuing in their own right and relational goods worth pursuing in light of a certain outcome. We will encounter a similar issue with the brief appended argument in Part V (1102a1–3). It is, however, not uncommon for Aristotle to simplify when an acknowledgement of the full complexity of the subject-matter is not necessary for the purposes of the argument at hand. All that matters to him at this point is that *eudaimonia* is a highest ranking or ultimate good (ἄριστον), whereas virtue, or being a virtuous person, cannot be an ultimate good since its relational value implies that there is a higher good.[23]

Segment (4) of Part II contains an additional argument in support of the claim that the objects of praise are relational goods: The (alleged) laughableness[24] of praises granted to a god "with reference to us" is an indication that

---

[22] Cf. *EN* II.4, 1105a26–b5 (on how virtuous action is motivated by the virtuous quality of the action) and the frequent use of the phrase τοῦ καλοῦ ἕνεκα ("for the sake of what is fine/noble") in descriptions of the motivating factor of virtuous action. Recall also his analysis of other-regarding concern in the case of genuine, virtue-based friendship; cf. VIII.3, 1156a6–19, b7–10 (cf. 1155b31, 1157b31–32) and XI.4, 1166a29–32; 9, 1170b5–7; 12, 1171b32–34. On the question of the consistency of Aristotle's complex teleology of virtuous action, which also includes other-regarding concerns, cf. Szaif 2006, 167–193.

[23] Compare the notion of *eudaimonia* as a ἁπλῶς τέλειον [τέλος] (I.7, 1097a33), i.e., an unqualifiedly final goal whose value includes no relational component.

[24] This alleged laughableness reflects an endoxic view that is not held by the many but only by (some) respectable philosophers (cf. *EN* I.8, 1098b9–11, 27–29; VII.1, 1145b2–7 together with *Top.* I.1, 100b21–23; *EE* I.6, 1216b26–35; cf. Barnes 1980, 490–511), since the "ridiculous" practice of praising the gods for their gifts to humanity was very common and anchored in tradition, and only philosophically more advanced people would come to believe that this practice is based on wrong ideas about the nature of the gods and their relation to humans.

praise involves reference to some other good served by the object praised. Aristotle does not spell out what kind of "reference to us" he has in mind. Aspasius in his paraphrase of this chapter offers plausible examples taken from Greek folk religion.[25] The Greeks were wont to praise Dionysus for the gift of wine and Demeter for the gift of grain, gifts that benefit us humans. Why is it ridiculous to praise a god for this kind of reason? Because it would mean putting our own well-being above the goodness of a god in the hierarchy of goods.

The argument in Part II does not identify *eudaimonia* as the higher-ranking item in view of which praise is duly granted to a virtuous human. Rather, it points to certain actions and achievements as the higher goods enabled by praiseworthy dispositions. We know, of course, that Aristotle holds that *eudaimonia* is constituted by excellent modes of action. But at this stage of the argument, at least, the connection between virtuous activity and *eudaimonia* is not made explicit. It is also not needed to reach Conclusion A.

From Conclusion A, Aristotle could move directly to his intended QED by reminding us that *eudaimonia* is the highest ranking or ultimate practical good, as the previous chapters of Book One have already established, and that it can hence not be a relational good of the praiseworthy kind. The argument by elimination (AE) could take roughly the following form:

AE (i) [TED:] All goods fall into one of the following three classes: *things prized/honored, things praised*, and *powers*.
(ii) [self-evident premise:] *Eudaimonia* is not a power.
(iii) [Conclusion A:] No object of praise is an ultimate good.
(iv) [premise established previously:] *Eudaimonia* is an ultimate good.
(v) [from iii and iv:] *Eudaimonia* is not an object of praise.
(CON) [from i, ii, and v, by elimination:] *Eudaimonia* is *something prized or honored*.

However, Aristotle postpones completion of his argument and adds instead another piece of reasoning, Part III, which specifies the higher form of speech that corresponds to the things that are "best." Since the overall goal is to prove that *eudaimonia* is something to be prized (a τίμιον), we would expect reference to a type of speech that expresses how we honor or prize something. But Aristotle's argument takes a more complicated path.

---

25   Cf. Aspasius, in *EN*, 32.33–33.12 Heylbut.

III

The most conspicuous feature of Part III of *Nicomachean Ethics* I.12 is its reliance on a new kind of threefold division, MEE, which does not distinguish between classes of goods but between types of laudatory or celebratory speech. We find it also in a passage of the *Eudemian Ethics* (cited below as T-1) and in the received text of Aristotle's *Rhetoric* (I.9, 1367b28–36).[26] I'll comment on this division first, before I analyze the argument of Part III.

MEE (i) Felicitation (μακαρισμός, εὐδαιμονισμός): a kind of speech that celebrates the happy or blessed condition of a person's life;
(ii) Praise (ἔπαινος): a laudatory type of speech used for praising a person and his or her virtues;
(iii) *Encomium*: another laudatory type of speech, serving to praise and celebrate certain individual actions or exploits.

Owing to its likely origin in rhetorical studies, MEE commits to a rather specific and technical sense of ἔπαινος as a *form of speech*. Chapter I.9 of Aristotle's *Rhetoric* defines praise (ἔπαινος) as a "speech that highlights the greatness of [a person's] virtue/excellence (ἀρετή)" (1367b28). Such praise is based on the actions of a person (1367b22, cf. *EE* 1219b8 *f*) since actions are the "signs of a person's disposition (ἕξις)" (1367b32 *f*). In other words, actions serve as evidence for the person's character, but it is the character that is praised. Whereas praise (ἔπαινος) is, hence, a form of eulogy of a person's character, the *encomium* celebrates a particular achievement such as winning in the Olympic games or winning the first prize in a theatrical contest.

The terms μακαρισμός and εὐδαιμονισμός can be used interchangeably in this context (cf. *Rhet.* I.9, 1367b33–4). They correspond to the nouns μακαριότης and *eudaimonia*, of which the former suggests a blessed life and is often applied specifically to the lives of gods, while *eudaimonia* denotes the condition of a life that "has a good δαίμων" and thus *turns out exceedingly well*. In philosophical debates, this term came to be used as a generic label for an excellent or

---

26 The received text of *Rhet.* I.9, 1367b26–8a10 incorporates MEE, but the most recent editor (Kassel 1976) not only considers this whole segment a gloss by Aristotle, but also excises from this gloss the sentences in 1367b26–8a10 that distinguish ἔπαινος from *encomium* and εὐδαιμονισμός/μακαρισμός. The *Revised Oxford Translation* (Barnes 1984) follows Kassel (against Ross's edition of 1959). While there are certainly problems with the consistency and argumentative structure of the received text, completely excising MEE from *Rhet.* I.9 is a rather radical step. Cf. Rapp 2002, II, 423–7 for further discussion of this issue. For the purposes of this essay, we don't need to rely on *Rhet.* I.9 as evidence for MEE.

optimal mode of living. As to the celebratory speech act that attributes μακαριότης or *eudaimonia*, we may refer to it as "felicitation" for want of a better translation.

There is only a partial correlation between divisions MEE and TED. The speech act of *praise* relates to the class of praised things, but there is no parallel correlation between the class of *powers* and the speech type *encomium*; and while there is an overlap between the class of objects of felicitation and the class of things prized (τίμια), the extent of this overlap remains undetermined and also does not matter for the argument. In *Eudemian Ethics* II.1, MEE is used for an argument in support of the Aristotelian tenet that virtue as such (unlike virtuous *activity*) does not yet constitute the fulfillment of the highest human goal:

T-1   (1) Furthermore, why is *eudaimonia* not praised? Because on account of it the other things [receive praises or *encomia*],[27] either because they are referred back (ἀναφέρεσθαι) to it [i.e., to *eudaimonia*] or because they are parts of it.
(2) Thus felicitation (εὐδαιμονισμός), praise, and *encomium* differ:
The *encomium* is a speech about a particular achievement;
praise [is a speech about] someone who is such a kind of person in general;
and felicitation [is a speech that relates to a life's] goal (τέλος). (*EE* 1219b11–16)

A detailed interpretation of this quotation from the *Eudemian Ethics* lies outside the scope of this essay. We need to retain, however, that T-1 is committed to the idea that a virtuous character is praised in light of how it supports *eudaimonia*. Statement (1) of T-1 includes a distinction between two ways in which the objects of *encomia* and praises can contribute to the realization of *eudaimonia*: either as "parts" of it or as means that are "referred back" to *eudaimonia* as their end (τέλος). Aristotle does not spell out how exactly these two formulations apply to the objects of praises and *encomia* respectively, but given his general approach in the *Eudemian Ethics*, he probably has in mind that the

---

27   The immediately preceding argument 1219b8–11 distinguishes between praises and *encomia*. It is not certain but at least likely that the τἆλλα in the elliptical clause ὅτι διὰ ταύτην τἆλλα (b12) refers back to the objects of these two forms of speech, contrasting them with *eudaimonia*. If one chooses to follow the English translations by Solomon, Woods, Inwood/Woolf, and Kenny, which supplement the verb "to praise," the meaning of "to praise" ought to be taken broadly so as to encompass both ἔπαινος and ἐγκώμιον in the narrower technical sense of these words.

virtuous activities (the objects of *encomia*) are constitutive parts of a eudaimonic life-performance (the object of felicitation, μακαρισμός),[28] whereas the virtues (the objects of praise) are subservient to the realization of *eudaimonia* by way of enabling virtuous activity. They, hence, refer back to *eudaimonia* as their end (τέλος).

Note also that Aristotle is commenting here on the contribution that virtue and virtuous actions make to the agent's own *eudaimonia*. The agent's relation to the well-being of the community or to "other selves" is not a topic in this part of the *Eudemian Ethics*. A telling piece of evidence regarding how Aristotle views the connection between *eudaimonia* and praiseworthiness from the first-person perspective can be found at the end of his chapter on self-love in the *Nicomachean Ethics* IX.8. Referring to actions worthy of a good friend, like helping a friend in need, or ceding to a friend an opportunity to excel (which is a praiseworthy act of forgoing), the chapter concludes with the following statement:

T-2   Indeed, it seems that in all matters concerning praiseworthy things, the virtuous person (ὁ σπουδαῖος) allocates himself a greater share of what is fine (καλόν). This is how one ought to be selfish, as we have said; but one should not be selfish in the manner of the many. (1169a34–b2)

This passage applies the notion of praiseworthiness to *actions* and uses it, hence, in a broader application than chapter I.12.[29] Yet it nevertheless allows us to extrapolate how Aristotle understands the relation between social virtues and a person's own pursuit of happiness: The correct way to be "selfish"—or, rather, to pursue *eudaimonia* in a sensible manner of self-love—is to develop virtue so as to excel in virtuous acts, including acts that benefit others. While the desire to excel in praiseworthiness is not only compatible with, but even conducive to the common good, it is also inseparable from the virtuous agent's pursuit of *eudaimonia*—his or her own *eudaimonia*—through forms of excellent activity.

But would we really praise *another person*, say Jane, on account of how her excellent character helps her attain a good and happy life for herself? Is this a

---

[28] On the notion of "parts" of "*eudaimonia*" or "living well" cf. *EE* 1214b11–27, 1216a38–40. The view that *eudaimonia* is a mode of *activity* of complete virtue and that, hence, virtuous action, but not yet virtue as such, constitutes the good life is vigorously argued for in the immediate context of T-3; cf. 1219a8–39, 1219b1–3, b8–11, b16–20.

[29] For this broader application encompassing virtuous actions, see, e.g., *EN* III.1, 1109b30–32; *EE* VIII.3, 1248b18–23.

plausible way of praising someone's justice or bravery? Wouldn't it be more appropriate to praise someone's justice on account of how it supports the common good, or someone's bravery in warfare on account of how it helps to protect the community? We have some good evidence that ἔπαινος (praise), in the Greek context and as an element of oratory, quite typically highlighted the rewards that bravery and justice held for the praised person himself. Thus funeral orations for fallen warriors, a typical locus of praise, strove to demonstrate the virtue or valor (ἀρετή) of the fallen, but also highlighted the everlasting rewards for the fallen in the form of undying glory and remembrance.[30] Adeimantus in Plato's *Republic* (362e–363e) complains that justice is praised by the poets on account of the immense rewards that good reputation among one's fellow-citizens and recognition by the gods can bring to the just person. Glory, wealth, public honors—these are goods commonly associated with the pre-philosophical notion of *eudaimonia*. This might be the cultural background to Aristotle's statement in T-1 that praise (ἔπαινος), as a form of speech, includes reference to a person's overarching goal of *eudaimonia*.

IV

Part III of *Nicomachean Ethics* I.12 contains an incomplete report of an argument by Eudoxus in support of hedonism. The unclear demarcation of this testimonium poses one of the main challenges to the interpretation of this segment. While we can see where the text of Aristotle's explicit testimony begins, it is not easy to decide where it ends. For reasons that I will lay out shortly, I believe it ends at line b31. Since it is not an essential part of the argument but rather a kind of gloss, I'll print it with indentation. I am also including the ending of Part II to preserve the transition.

Part III ..., there is no praise of best things [= **Conclusion A**],
    (1) but something more significant and valuable [is directed at them (*i.e., at the best things*)] [= **Conclusion B**],[31] as is also manifest [for the following reasons]:

---

[30] Compare, for instance, Lysias's *Funeral Oration*: the ἀρετή (virtue, valor) of the fallen as the topic of praise (11.1 *et passim*); "immortal glory and *eudaimonia* as the reward of their ἀρετή" (11.23 f, 77–81, with the concluding μακαρισμός in 11.81).

[31] The elliptic phrase ἀλλὰ μεῖζόν τι καὶ βέλτιον requires the supplement ἔστι αὐτῶν.

(2) We felicitate (μακαρίζομεν) and pronounce happy (εὐδαιμονίζομεν) both the gods and the most divine among men, and likewise [the most divine] among the goods,[32]

(3) for nobody praises *happiness* (*eudaimonia*) as [one praises] what is just, but *felicitates* (μακαρίζει) it, since it is something better and more divine [than justice].

(4) It seems, indeed, that Eudoxus was a good advocate on behalf of pleasure in its fight for the first prize.[33] He held that the fact that [pleasure] is not praised, although it is one of the goods, indicated that it is superior (κρεῖττον) to what is praised, and that the god and *the good* are of such a [superior] kind, since the other things are referred back (ἀναφέρεσθαι) to them.

(5) For praise is directed at[34] *virtue/excellence*, since we perform fine/noble deeds (τὰ καλά) thanks to it, while the *encomia* are directed equally at physical and mental achievements (ἔργα)—but to elaborate on this matter seems a more fitting task for those who study *encomia*. (1101b22–35)

After stating the conclusion of the argument in Part II, namely, that the "best things" are not an object of praise, Aristotle seizes on the fact that *praise* is a form of speech, pointing out that if praise is not directed at ultimate goods, there has to be some other, more elevated, form of speech suitable for ultimate goods. The argument of Part III identifies "felicitation" as this type of speech. It reconfirms that praise is not directed at "the best things" and establishes a connection between the status of *eudaimonia* as an ultimate good for us and the notion of a *divine good*.

---

32   I am following Ramsauer 1878 and Burnet 1900 in reading ὁμοίως δὲ καὶ τῶν ἀγαθῶν as an elliptic phrase that mirrors the construction of the immediately preceding clause, with a partitive genitive and implied supplement τὰ θειότατα or τὸ θειότατον, the plural being more likely because of the preceding τοὺς θειοτάτους (see also Rolfes' German translation and Zell's Latin translation). More recent translators and commentators (e.g., Peters, Chase, Rackham, Ross, Thomson, Ostwald, Gigon, Gauthier/Jolif, Apostle, Irwin, Rowe, Crisp, Reeve) prefer translations such as "and similarly with the goods" (Rackham), "Similarly in the case of good things" (Rowe), or "The same is true of goods" (Irwin). This kind of translation would have to appeal to the "genitive of connection" (Smyth 1956, n. 1381; cf. Kühner/Gerth 1898, II.1, 363 [§417, Anm. 11]). However this sentence is parsed, the association of *eudaimonia* with the notion of a divine good is implied also in the immediately following clause (ἀλλ' ὡς θειότερόν τι καὶ βέλτιον μακαρίζει).

33   The verb συνηγορέω (from συνήγορος, "advocate") belongs to the legal sphere. The sentence contains a clear hint at the contest for the first and second prizes, with *pleasure* as one of the contenders, in Plato's *Philebus* (22c–23a, *et passim*).

34   Literally, "is of" (objective genitive).

Yet before we go into the details, I need to justify my decision regarding where to end the Eudoxus testimonium. It is not possible to decide on grammatical grounds whether or not the words in the first part of (5), before "but to elaborate," are still part of the indirect speech governed by the verb "he held that" (ᾤετο) in (4).[35] We have to decide based on what makes the best sense for the reconstruction of the argument. The text in (5) begins with the statement that virtue is praised because it enables us to perform fine/noble deeds (πρακτικοὶ τῶν καλῶν). Yet Eudoxus, defending hedonism, would have argued that it is praised because it leads to pleasure. We have to conclude that the text of the testimonium does not continue beyond (4) and that (5) contains Aristotle's own reasoning. Once we start to treat (4) as a parenthetical remark or gloss (by Aristotle himself), we also see that (5) is a smooth continuation of (3) and belongs to the core of the argument in Part III.[36]

After these preliminaries, let us now try to disentangle this argument. It sets out with the promise that the higher form of speech adequate for "the best goods" can be identified through an appeal to what is intuitively plausible or commonly accepted (καθάπερ φαίνεται). To this end, Aristotle recycles (with some minor variations) the endoxic argument of the *Eudemian* passage T-1, which was based on division MEE. Segment (2) of Part III introduces felicitation (μακαρισμός or εὐδαιμονισμός) as the commonly accepted higher form of celebratory speech, listing two types of things that can be the objects of such "felicitation": first, gods and the most divine men; second, the most divine goods. Next, (3) singles out *eudaimonia* as a most divine good, arguing that felicitation (μακαρισμός) is reserved for it since it is viewed by all as a superior and more divine thing than objects of praise such as "that which is just" (or justice). Segment (5) adds that praise is given to virtue on account of the fine or noble deeds (τὰ καλά) that result from it.[37] It also briefly specifies the object range of the third type of speech act (*encomium*), but puts it aside as not directly relevant for the argument.[38]

---

35   This is so because the Greek text of (5) before "but to elaborate ..." lacks a verb.
36   Accordingly, the γάρ in (5) relates back to the reasoning in (3), not in (4).
37   Since this assertion is part of Aristotle's argument and reconfirms that not actions, but virtues (and the persons having them) are the objects of praise, Part III (1)–(3) cannot be used as support for van Cleemput's claim (2006, 127–157, 154 f and n. 860) that Aristotle considers secondary *eudaimonia* (in the sense of x.7–8) as merely *praised*, but not *blessed*. Secondary *eudaimonia* is also a form of activity, and it characterizes a life as a whole. Hence, in the conceptual framework provided by MEE, it cannot be an object of either ἔπαινος or *encomium*. I agree with van Cleemput that I.12 can be used as support for a dominant-end interpretation, yet he seems to me to overstate the case.
38   This remark at the end of Part III (1101b34f) is not a dismissive comment on the argument of I.12 as a whole, as some have thought (e.g., Joachim 1951, 61). The notion of *encomia* is

Part III uses, hence, a comparison primarily of the first two members of division MEE in order to identify the speech act that correlates with *eudaimonia* and to reconfirm that praiseworthiness presupposes a relation to some other good. It is, to be sure, a bit awkward that *eudaimonia*, rather than the person having it (the εὐδαίμων), is called an object of felicitation. Yet Aristotle probably thinks that in practical terms this amounts to the same, as the gods and "divine men" are felicitated on account of their supremely blessed condition. This ambiguity is analogous to what we encountered in the case of praise. In both cases, the person *and* the corresponding quality realized in this person (*eudaimonia* or virtue) are the object of felicitation or praise respectively.

What is the role of the Eudoxus testimonium in (4)? It does not seem to add anything important to Aristotle's argument. Rather, it is an acknowledgment by Aristotle that his own argumentative strategy agrees in part with an argument used by Eudoxus.[39] However, we also have to understand that the two authors pursue very different goals. Part III of Aristotle's argument talks about *eudaimonia* as such and its status as an ultimate and divine good above the praiseworthy goods. Eudoxus, on the other hand, wants to demonstrate that pleasure is the highest good in human life and that *therefore eudaimonia* must be a life of pleasure. The main point of agreement highlighted by Aristotle is that the things we praise are not highest goods and that, for this reason, the fact that something is *not praised* does not, by itself, entail that it is a lesser good. They also seem to concur in that the superior class of good things includes both the god(s)[40] and the greatest good human life can attain (which in

---

mentioned since it belongs to division MEE, but further elaboration of the difference between *encomia* and praises would be beside the point.

39 Gauthier/Jolif 1970, II, 87–8 view the entire argument of this chapter as an *ad hominem* reply to Eudoxus: Aristotle wants to refute Eudoxus by using Eudoxus's conceptual scheme to establish an anti-hedonist conclusion. However, the approving manner in which Aristotle refers here to an aspect of Eudoxus's argumentation is hardly compatible with the idea that Eudoxus is the primary target of this chapter.

40 The status of "the god" as a superordinate *relatum* of praiseworthy things in Eudoxus' argument remains uncertain. Perhaps "the god" serves as a paradigm of a joyous or blissful life that virtue allows us to emulate. Baker 2017, 1853 tries to draw some far-reaching conclusions regarding Aristotle from this part of the Eudoxus testimonium, claiming that it indicates that Aristotle assumes a hierarchy among the τίμια such that human *eudaimonia*, as a lower τίμιον compared to "the god," turns out to be an ἐπαινετόν relative to this higher τίμιον. Yet if Aristotle really meant to suggest that *eudaimonia* is *both* an ἐπαινετόν and a τίμιον, he would invalidate his argument by elimination. For the same reason, the καθάπερ-clause in 1101b26 is (*pace* Baker) certainly not meant as a suggestion that *eudaimonia* is also something praiseworthy.

the testimonium is referred to simply as "the good").[41] In other words, they both approximate the highest human good to the status of something divine.

Part III does not, like the *Eudemian* passage T-1, explicitly commit to a "back reference" from the objects of praises and *encomia* to *eudaimonia* as a life's overall τέλος (goal, fulfillment). In this regard, the only unequivocal commitment in *Nicomachean Ethics* I.12—stated and endorsed by Aristotle in his own words[42]—is the assertion that there is always a higher good in light of which we praise a person or a person's virtue: some kind of valuable action or achievement (1101b15 *f*) or fine/noble deed (b32). It is, to be sure, one of Aristotle's central tenets that virtuous action is essential to a person's *eudaimonia*, taking "virtuous action" in the broad Aristotelian sense that includes the activation of excellent intellectual qualities. However, he may have had second thoughts about linking the practice of praising directly to the goal of *eudaimonia*. As we will see, there are good reasons for believing that the argument of I.12 looks ahead to an argumentation in Book X that will establish that *eudaimonia*, as a venerable and divine good, has to be, first and foremost, a practice of scientific contemplation. Many of the activities and achievements in light of which a person's virtue or prowess is praised (and which are used as examples in Part II of I.12) are either not at all, or only secondarily, relevant for the contemplative life. Athletic exploits, for instance, are not relevant at all, while acting in accordance with the character virtues is indispensable, but does not define the happiness of the contemplative mode of living.

With the argument of Part III completed, Aristotle now states the overall conclusion, his QED:

Part IV   From what has been said it is clear to us that *eudaimonia* belongs to the [things] that are *prized/venerable* (τίμια) and *perfect* (τέλεια) [= QED]. (1101b35–2a1)

Since the preceding argument has associated *eudaimonia* with the notion of a divine good, it is now adequate to translate τίμιον also as "venerated" or "venerable." The QED includes the term τέλειον ("perfect/complete"). This has not been expressly justified in the preceding argument (as it does not even

---

41   According to the testimonium, Eudoxus allows for other, subordinate, kinds of goods. It is not uncommon in these debates to refer to the ultimate human good simply as "the good." Plato, for instance, does so repeatedly in the *Philebus* (e.g., 13b7, 14b4, 20b8, 21a2, 22c2).

42   In this connection, it is important to bear in mind that the clause in Part III (4): "and that the god and *the good* are of such a [superior] kind, since the other things are referred back to them" (1101b30 *f*) is still part of indirect speech governed by "he (Eudoxus) held that ..." and belongs, hence, to Aristotle's gloss on Eudoxus.

mention this term), but the combination of the notion of a highest good with the idea of completeness or perfection is familiar from the writings of Plato and Aristotle.[43]

It is not easy to pin down how exactly the conclusion stated in Part IV relates to the preceding argumentation. The "what has been said" certainly relates back to the entire preceding text of chapter 1.12. As I have pointed out in my comments on Part II, this chapter sets out as an argument by elimination and could have been completed on the basis of Conclusion A and the previously established result that *eudaimonia* is an ultimate good. Instead, the chapter takes an apparent detour involving Conclusion B and the subsequent argument of Part III that confirms, and further develops, Conclusion B. Part III fails to mention the term τίμιον or any of its cognates. It does, however, lay great emphasis on the divine character of *eudaimonia* as an ultimate good, and there is certainly a strong intuitive connection for the Greek audience that leads from the notion that something is divine to the claim that it is something prized or venerable in its own right. I submit that the main reason why Aristotle includes the argument of Part III is that it links *eudaimonia* to the notion of a divine good and thus suggests that it is a τίμιον *because it is a divine good*. As this same conceptual link is also emphasized in the final line of 1.12 (cf. Part V), we can be quite confident that this is here the guiding idea.

V

The last three lines of *Nicomachean Ethics* 1.12—Part V in my breakdown—are presented as an additional argument in support of the QED. This piece of reasoning is clearly no longer conceived as an argument by elimination, but purports to show directly that *eudaimonia* is something worthy of reverence.

Part V It [*i.e., eudaimonia*] seems to be thus [i.e., τίμιον] also because it is an origin/principle; for all of us do all the other things for its sake, and we hold that the origin/principle (ἀρχή) and explanatory ground (αἴτιον) of good things is something *prized/venerable* (τίμιον τι) and *divine*. (1102a1–3)

The gist of this argument can be rendered as follows:

---

43   In *EN* I.7, 1097a15–b6, Aristotle has offered an argument for why *eudaimonia*, among all human goods, is the only one that is unqualifiedly τέλειον.

(i) That which is a principle/origin of what is good is something venerable (τίμιον) and divine.
(ii) *eudaimonia* is a principle/origin of what is good (since humans do what they do for the sake of *eudaimonia*).
(CON) *eudaimonia* is something venerable and divine.

The argument resorts to the Aristotelian tenet that *eudaimonia* is, or should be, the over-arching goal of human life. This does not have to be read as a commitment to some strict form of moral egoism incompatible with altruistic motivation, since *eudaimonia*—as the *kind* of good to which all other practical evaluation refers back—may include, for instance, the well-being of loved-ones or the well-being of one's community, as Aristotle makes clear in other contexts. The reasoning in Part V nevertheless simplifies the more complex teleology of human action that we find in *Nicomachean Ethics* 1.7 (1097a24–b6) and other sections of his *Ethics*.[44] According to the more complex account disregarded here, there is an intermediate level of human goods that are worthy to be valued both intrinsically and in light of their contribution to human *eudaimonia*. Moreover, the argument is also quite unconvincing for the following reason: While it would be plausible enough (certainly for Aristotle's audience) to assume that the intelligent source, or also the "final cause," of the good order of the cosmos and its motions is something venerable and divine, the argument seems question-begging in how it assumes that the ultimate "final cause" of *human* action (its ultimate goal) has a divine quality just because it is an ultimate origin/starting-point (ἀρχή) and explanatory ground (αἴτιον) of goodness in the domain of human action. While one can certainly make a compelling case for the claim that this ultimate goal of human action needs to have *intrinsic value* for us, this falls short of proving that it is something "venerable and divine." If Aristotle had only used the expression τίμιον in the conclusion, we could read it simply as an attribution of intrinsic value. Yet he goes further by also attributing a divine quality to it.

To be sure, this attribution has been prepared by how Part III included *eudaimonia* among the divine goods. Yet we have to ask ourselves what motivates this move on Aristotle's part. If we can we detect the reason, this might allow us to explain why the arguments of chapter 1.12 are placed at the end of Aristotle's general discussion of the highest human good.

---

44 We encountered a similar issue in our discussion of the argument of Part II above.

VI

The place to look for an answer is *Nicomachean Ethics* x.6–8, the treatise on scientific study and contemplation (θεωρία)[45] as the element of supreme human *eudaimonia*. The idea of *eudaimonia* as something *venerable and divine* reemerges there. The treatise can be divided into a preliminary discussion in x.6, mostly dedicated to a critique of the life of gratification, and a main part, x.7–8. The latter contains a series of arguments that aim to prove that θεωρία is the most perfect form of human activity and that it is therefore the defining element of a supreme form of human *eudaimonia* ranking higher than even the most outstanding form of active life: the life of a virtuous political leader. The arguments offered employ various strategies, but one of the main strategies is to emphasize the proximity of the contemplative activity of a philosopher-scientist to a divine mode of existence, arguing that contemplation (θεωρία) activates the most valuable and divine faculty in us—the intellect (νοῦς)—in relation to the most noble and divine objects.

The gist of this argument is already expressed right at the beginning of x.7–8, in 1177a12–18. It is developed further in two separate segments. The first of these, 1177b26–8a23, involves a comparison of the contemplative with the active life. Whereas the active life of virtuous political leadership is the highest fulfillment of our ethical and social potential grounded in our nature as soul-body compounds, the contemplative life fulfills the highest aspirations of the human intellect, the divine element in us. The segment also connects the divine nature of the intellect with its status as a τίμιον, calling it the component that far exceeds all other components of human nature in its degree of venerability (τιμιότης).[46]

In the second segment, 1178b7–32, Aristotle argues that contemplation is the only activity adequate for a god and that therefore *supreme* human *eudaimonia* depends on our ability to engage in this kind of activity: The life of the gods is not active or political since they do not form a community that would bear any similarity to human society with its characteristic needs and vulnerabilities. Accordingly, their lives do not require social virtues such as justice or generosity. Nor do they need courage or moderation, since they have nothing to fear and are not influenced by inferior desires. Hence, it does not make sense

---

45 On the Aristotelian notion of scientific θεωρία (literally "viewing") as a form of active understanding of teleological or mathematical structures cf. Broadie 1991, 401.

46 Cf. 1178a1 f. The term τιμιότης is the abstract noun derived from the adjective τίμιον; compare the use of τίμιον in connection with νοῦς and its activity in *Metaph.* xii.9, 1074b15–35.

to project our moral virtues and corresponding activities onto the gods.[47] Yet we all assume, says Aristotle, that the life of gods is supremely happy (1178b8–9). Since neither the application of ethical virtues nor productive activity (which, for Aristotle, implies need) are fitting for gods, only the contemplative life associated with wisdom is left. Since, moreover, their happiness is supreme, a human mode of contemplative activity that comes closest to the contemplative activity of the gods is the happiest form of life for a human being (b20–24).

The segment then continues with the following additional argument:

T-3 (1) A sign/indication of it (*i.e., of the correlation of* θεωρία *and* eudaimonia*; JSz*) is that the other animals do not share in *eudaimonia*, as they are completely deprived of such an activity.
(2) For, in the case of the gods, life as a whole is blissful (μακάριος), whereas in the case of humans [it is blissful] only to the extent that it is realized as some kind of assimilation to such an activity [i.e., to θεωρία]. None of the other animals has *eudaimonia*, as none of them shares in contemplation (θεωρία). For *eudaimonia* extends just as far as contemplation (θεωρία), and the greater one's share in contemplation (θεωρία), the greater also one's *eudaimonia*,
(3) [and this] not just coincidentally (κατὰ συμβεβηκός), but on account of (κατὰ) [one's activity of] contemplation (θεωρία); for contemplation (θεωρία) is *per se* (καθ' αὑτήν) venerable (τιμία).
(4) Accordingly, *eudaimonia* is some kind of contemplation (θεωρία).
(*EN* 1178b24–32)

Let's first record the fact that T-3 talks about *eudaimonia* as such and that its conclusion does not seem to leave room for a secondary form of *eudaimonia* other than the contemplative life-style. Up to this point, the arguments of x.7–8 have been about "perfect" (τελεία) *eudaimonia* or the "happiest" (εὐδαιμονέστατος) mode of life and activity (1177a17, b24, 1178a8, b7, b23), which they equated with a divine mode of human activity in contrast with political and ethical achievements as the element of a secondary and more narrowly "human" type of eudaimonic life.[48] In order to reconcile T-3 with the general argumentative goal of x.7–8, we have to assume that it argues from a view-point according to which the notion of *eudaimonia* is *fully* satisfied only by one

---

47 This and other arguments in x.7–8 reflect a philosophical and rationalist conception of the gods roughly in line with Aristotle's conception of divine intellectual activity in *Metaph.* XII.
48 Cf. Long 2011, 111 *f*; Kraut 1989, 39–67.

specific mode of life, whereas any secondary form of *eudaimonia* could be called *eudaimonia* only in a looser application of this word based on some important shared feature.[49]

The reasoning adumbrated in this passage starts from the commonly accepted view that animals cannot attain *eudaimonia*, whereas the life of gods is always completely happy and humans may achieve some degree of happiness. The key move then is to identify a type of activity that is appropriate for gods, but animals are incapable of it, while humans can aspire to it. Since only scientific contemplation (θεωρία) fits this description,[50] the claim that such contemplation is the activity responsible for happiness has been corroborated. Moreover, the degree to which humans can have a share in happiness turns out to be a function of the degree of their participation in this kind of activity.

In (3) of T-3, Aristotle adds a consideration that aims to establish that this kind of correlation between contemplative activity and happiness holds essentially (*per se*) and not just coincidentally. For this argument to be valid, it has to include an implicit assumption. It is listed as premise (i) in the following reconstruction of the argument:

> (i) If *eudaimonia* is the correlate of a certain type of activity, and this type of activity **is *per se* venerable**, then *eudaimonia* correlates *per se* (and not just coincidentally) to this type of activity.
> (ii) [*established in (2) of T-3:*] *eudaimonia* is the correlate of contemplative activity.
> (iii) Contemplative activity **is *per se* venerable**.
> (CON) *eudaimonia* correlates *per se* (and not just coincidentally) to contemplative activity.

The phrase "*eudaimonia* is a correlate of contemplative activity" in this reconstruction is used as a shortcut for saying that the realization of *eudaimonia* both *depends* on the realization of contemplative activity and that the *degree*

---

49 The obvious point of agreement between primary and secondary forms of *eudaimonia* in x.7–8 is that they all represent forms of *rational activity* supported by ἀρετή. In my understanding, this does not warrant the claim that the practical reasoning of the φρόνιμος, resulting in practical truth, is itself "contemplation of a sort" (Richardson Lear 2004, 194–196, cf. 93–122). Practical reasoning, as analyzed by Aristotle, has a fundamentally different teleology, and therefore nature, than θεωρία, which is also the reason why "practical truth" (cf. *EN* VI.2) is not a specific form of theoretical truth.

50 Practical deliberation is not included since the life of gods (as conceived in this argument, and also in Aristotle's metaphysics) does not require it. Moreover, practical wisdom (φρόνησις) is inextricably linked to the character virtues, yet Aristotle has just argued that the gods don't need such virtues.

to which *eudaimonia* is realized varies with the degree (intensity, purity, etc.) of contemplative activity. Adding that this correlation obtains *per se* indicates that the dependency and co-variation is grounded in some *essential* link between the two phenomena.

The point of this reasoning, however, is not easy to capture. It will help if we explain what someone could have in mind who holds that contemplative activity is only *coincidentally* (κατὰ συμβεβηκός) responsible for *eudaimonia*. I suspect that Aristotle thinks of the following scenario: Assume a hedonist philosopher who holds that *eudaimonia* is a form of *supreme* pleasure and that contemplation, alone among all the causes of pleasure, brings about a supreme experience of pleasure. In this case, not contemplation but pleasure would be the essential constituent of a eudaimonic life. Yet since it so *happens* that contemplation elicits supreme pleasure, there would be a coincidental correlation between *eudaimonia* and contemplation. Aristotle, by contrast, holds that the correlation obtains not because of some ulterior consequence such as joy, but *per se* and on account of the nature of scientific contemplation as a *per se* venerable thing.

The phrase "*per se* venerable" functions as the middle term in this piece of reasoning, serving to establish that the correlation between *eudaimonia* and contemplation obtains *per se*. But what justifies premises (i) and (iii)? What, to begin with, makes contemplation something *per se* venerable (premise iii)? The underlying assumption here is certainly that a god, and everything essentially pertaining to a god, is intrinsically venerable (namely on account of the gods' supreme perfection), and that therefore contemplation, as the activity that defines the divine mode of actuality, must also be intrinsically (*per se*) venerable.

What could justify premise (i)? Chapter I.12 has argued that *eudaimonia* is something venerable and divine, and while it does not use the qualifier "*per se*" (καθ' αὑτό), adding it is unproblematic since classifications don't classify items on the basis of merely coincidental attributions. Given, then, that *eudaimonia* is *per se* venerable, the activity that essentially constitutes *eudaimonia* must also be something *per se* venerable. Accordingly, if we can identify an activity that not only correlates with *eudaimonia* but is something *per se* venerable (and there is no other such activity), we can infer that it must be what constitutes *eudaimonia* and that the degree of human *eudaimonia* corresponds *per se* to how close a human being approximates complete engagement in this activity. This is the idea asserted in premise (i).

The claims made in T-3 about the intrinsic venerability of contemplative activity can be usefully compared to what we find in some of Aristotle's remarks on metaphysics as the highest-ranking and most venerable branch of scientific knowledge. They spell out the higher rank of metaphysical studies (compared to other forms of theoretical study) in terms of a highest degree of divinity and venerability (τιμιότης) and thus confirm that Aristotle looks at contemplation (θεωρία) in general as something to be characterized in terms of intrinsic worthiness and a divine quality. Thus his discussion of "first philosophy" in *Metaphysics* I.1–2 identifies this first-ranked type of philosophy with σοφία (scientific wisdom) and adds in 983a4–11 that σοφία is the *most divine* and *most venerable* (τιμιωτάτη) form of knowledge on two separate counts: *first*, because it is the kind of knowledge a god would entertain; and, *second*, because it is a science of divine principles. In other words, it is most divine and most venerable both as an activity and on account of its subject-matter. Similar ideas are formulated in *Metaphysics* VI.1 (1026a10–22), which characterizes the highest form of theoretical science, dedicated to eternal divine principles, as the *most venerable* (τιμιωτάτη) branch of knowledge with the most venerable (τιμιώτατον) subject-matter. In *Nicomachean Ethics* VI.7, σοφία is likewise defined as "science and understanding[51] of the things that are by nature most venerable (τιμιώτατα)" (1141b2 f). In *Nicomachean Ethics* VI.13 (1145a6–11, cf. *EE* 1249b9–23), Aristotle adds that σοφία is grounded in the higher part of reason and that rendering service to it is comparable, roughly, to organizing the service to the gods.[52]

Nicomachean Ethics I.12 ended, as we recall, with the conclusion that *eudaimonia* is something venerable (τίμιον) and divine. This statement left open what kind of activity is most adequate for elevating the condition of a human life to such a level. The arguments in x.7–8 we have discussed provide an answer: for humans to reach this divine and venerable condition, they have to engage in an activity they share with the gods, and this turns out to be the contemplative activity of the philosopher-scientist.

---

51 The phrase "science and understanding" relates to the distinction between knowledge through scientific proof and understanding of the principles or starting-points of the proofs; σοφία combines both forms of cognition.

52 "τοῦ βελτίονος μορίου" in line 1145a7 takes up the distinction between two parts of reason prominent in Book VI (cf. 1139a5–15, 1140b25–26, 1144b14). It should therefore (*pace* Irwin, Inwood/Woolf and others) not be translated as "the better part [of the soul]," but as "the better part [of reason]," cf. Gauthier/Jolif 1970, I.2, 185; II, 443. The segment argues that practical wisdom (φρόνησις), seated in the lower ("deliberative") part of reason, makes choices on behalf of the exercise of σοφία, seated in the higher ("epistemonic") part of reason, but that it would be wrong to think that prudence thereby assumes a superior position vis-à-vis the epistemonic function. It also evokes a comparison with how the "political craft" organizes public life including public worship of the gods, without thereby assuming a position superior to the gods.

VII

The term "τίμιον" (which we have translated here as "prized" or "venerable") is semantically linked to the noun τιμή (worth, honor, respectability). Chapter IV.3 of the *Nicomachean Ethics* discusses τιμή, and worthiness to receive τιμή, in the context of an analysis of the virtue concept "greatness of soul" (μεγαλοψυχία). The chapter seems to contradict a key assertion in I.12 when it states that *complete virtue*, here also labeled as καλοκἀγαθία (1124a4), renders a person worthy of τιμή, whereas I.12 maintains that virtue is only a praiseworthy condition, not a τίμιον. Before concluding we should therefore look more closely at chapter IV.3 to see if we can find some form of resolution to this apparent inconsistency.

Chapter IV.3 classifies τιμή as an *external* good and argues that it is the greatest, or most significant, external good. The term "external good" refers to any kind of good that is neither a quality or activity of one's soul nor a quality of one's own body. A person's τιμή, understood as an external good, resides in the respect and recognition one receives from others. Aristotle describes greatness of soul as a form of *proud self-awareness* of a man who has complete virtue. On account of his excellent qualities, such a person *justifiedly* thinks of himself as worthy of receiving the greatest honors from those qualified to judge him (1123b26–4a9). Honors should not be granted because of noble birth, wealth, or political power, but as a prize of virtue (1124a20–29, cf. 1123b35). This stipulation acknowledges that there is a difference between *de facto* recognition and *worthiness* to be recognized, and that this worthiness is not an external factor, but supervenes on the quality of one's soul.

While IV.3 relates to τιμή as a social good that should be distributed among humans according to their ethical worthiness, there is another central dimension of τιμή in ancient Greek society. A Greek *polis* is more than just a community of humans. It includes the "gods of the city" and grants them a most elevated status, constantly expressing reverence for them during the many religious functions and festivities.[53] The idea of the superior venerability of the gods agrees also, in principle, with Aristotle's metaphysics of divine being, although his conception of the gods differs radically from Greek mythology. For Aristotle, their particular intrinsic worth (τιμιότης) is a function of their ontological perfection and their role as ultimate origins (ἀρχαί) of the orderly motion of the physical world. Regarding the comparison between gods and humans, we have to bear in mind that Greek polytheism did not conceive of a radical divide between the spheres of gods and humans as we know it from

---

53   This is acknowledged in *EN* IV.3, 1123b17–21.

monotheistic traditions. In Greek mythology, both the existence of persons who are of mixed divine and human origin and the divinization of certain individual humans are common ideas. Philosophy, too, developed new ways of understanding how human life could approximate a divine quality. Plato famously described the goal of human life as "assimilation to god" (*Rep.* 613ab, *Tht.* 176a–b). We have seen that Aristotle advocates his own version of this idea when he claims that the highest form of *eudaimonia* consists in a form of divine activity of a divine faculty within us. In this metaphysical and cosmological perspective, it is natural to say that humans become the more venerable, the more they assimilate themselves to the gods.

In the treatise on the great-souled man, complete virtue, or καλοκἀγαθία, is said to be the quality of the soul that renders a person worthy of honor. This is, as I have just pointed out, at odds with the argument in I.12, since the latter claims that virtue is praised, but not prized (τίμιον). To understand this discrepancy, we have to take into account the different perspectives at work in the two chapters. In IV.3, Aristotle takes up a traditional notion of distinction and respectability, καλοκἀγαθία, which originally had been used for the self-description of the aristocratic class who saw themselves as the "beautiful and capable people" (οἱ καλοὶ κἀγαθοί) worthy of respect and reverence by the populace. Aristotle reinterprets this term in the spirit of his own virtue ethics, claiming that social respectability should be a function of the full possession of virtue or excellence and no longer be associated with hereditary class membership or other such superficial criteria. Chapter I.12, on the other hand, and the arguments in X.7–8 it foreshadows, relate to a wider compass that includes the gods. Within this compass, it is obvious that the gods and their characteristic activities are what is most worthy of honor or reverence on account of their intrinsic worthiness (τιμιότης). Yet since humans can have a share in the contemplative activities characteristic of the gods, the supreme form of *eudaimonia* that humans can attain also partakes in divine worthiness and venerability.

VIII

How can we summarize, by way of a conclusion, the content of division TED and the purpose it fulfills for Aristotle? It has become clear that the class of objects referred to as things prized (τίμια) should be prized on account of their *intrinsic worth or venerability*. Praiseworthy people and their praiseworthy qualities, by contrast, receive praise on account of how these qualities relate to certain desirable activities and outcomes. The *powers* matter because they are assets that help the person with praiseworthy qualities to attain such outcomes. In Eudoxus's application of TED (if, indeed, he made use of it), qualities and actions are praiseworthy on account of how they lead to the prized outcome, namely, joy, which he views as the defining constituent of *eudaimonia* and probably also as the defining feature of the lives of gods. Aristotle's argument in *Nicomachean Ethics* I.12 refers to desirable activities and achievements as the good in light of which a virtuous person deserves praise; but he leaves open how, or to what extent, the various kinds of excellent activity and achievement enabled by praiseworthy qualities contribute to the prized or venerable state of *eudaimonia*. In Book X we learn that only certain intellectual activities fully realize this venerable condition and that *eudaimonia*, as a τίμιον, should therefore be identified primarily with the activity of scientific study and contemplation.

Against this result, one could object that *Nicomachean Ethics* I.9 already asserts that *eudaimonia*, as "the reward (ἆθλον) and goal of virtue," is an "optimal good (ἄριστον)" and something "divine (θεῖον) and blissful (μακάριον)" (1099b16–18). Pointing to this passage, one could argue that in the context of Book One, this characterization as divine must encompass *all* types of unhindered virtuous activity, not just contemplative activity (θεωρία), and that this carries over to chapter I.12, which should, hence, not be interpreted with X.7–8 in mind (thus, roughly, Long 2011). For a response, it will help to contextualize the assertion in chapter I.9. It is part of Aristotle's comparison of "established views" with his own theory presented in chapter I.7. His typical approach, in such a context, is to try to show that the various endoxic views all come close, in some way or other, to some aspect of the true account. Going through various suggestions about what causes someone to attain *eudaimonia*, he then also addresses the view that it is something "god-given." He cautions against this view and concedes only that *eudaimonia* may be called something divine, using the language just quoted. In a similar thematic context, the *Eudemian Ethics* (I.3, 1215a7–19) argues that *if* we assume that agents themselves are responsible for their *eudaimonia* through shaping their character and their actions accordingly, *eudaimonia* will turn out to be something "more divine" than if we attribute it to nature or luck. The underlying idea here is certainly that if we ourselves are, to a large extent, responsible for the attainment of *eudaimonia*, this condition must be grounded in reason, and to live by reason is something "more divine." This probably also explains why he is willing to admit in *Nicomachean Ethics* I.9 that *eudaimonia* can be called something divine, being the goal and reward of virtue. Yet as we can also tell from the *Eudemian Ethics*, such focusing on the rational basis of *eudaimonia* can go hand in hand with the idea that *eudaimonia* in the fullest sense is achieved by a life that excels in "divine θεωρία" (*EE* 1215b12 *f*, cf. 1249a21–b25). One should, moreover, bear in mind that the contemplative life-style of the philosopher-scientist does not make practical wisdom (φρόνησις) and the supporting character virtues redundant. Any form of rational organization of a life by a human being who is inspired by a noble goal requires these ethical virtues, but they are assigned a subservient role relative to the highest intellectual form of excellence. Thus there is no need to assume a conflict between the quotation in *Nicomachean Ethics* I.9 and the theory of supreme *eudaimonia* in X.7–8, and also no need to consider X.7–8 a poorly integrated piece of theorizing not to be connected with anything in Book I.[54]

As mentioned in the beginning, there are no indications that Aristotle was the author of TED. While we cannot exclude this as a possibility, we also don't have to assume it. I surmise that Aristotle saw TED as an opportunity to bring into focus the notion that *eudaimonia* is a *divine good* in humans. The arguments of I.12 don't yet specify what kind of activity would be most suitable for the full realization of *eudaimonia*. But they lend support to the idea that such an activity has to be venerable and divine. We have to wait until X.7–8 for the application of this criterion to intellectual activities. It stands to reason, accordingly, that this chapter was placed at the end of Aristotle's general treatment of the highest human good to serve as a forward-looking link to arguments in X.7–8, thus underlining the unity of the project of the *Nicomachean Ethics* as a whole.[55]

---

54 Regarding X.7–8, Long 2011 argues that the "abrupt emergence" of a theory of supreme *eudaimonia* in these chapters is "structurally flawed" since it applies "previously established criteria" to a kind of activity that "falls outside the main scope" of Aristotle's ethics and its intended political application (Long 2011, 113; see also Broadie 1991, 370–2). These claims are debatable, not just because of the forward reference to the θεωρία-treatise in I.5, 1096a4 *f*, but also in light of Aristotle's concluding comment on the relation of φρόνησις and σοφία in *EN* VI, 1145a6–11 (which emphasizes how φρόνησις, which cannot exist without the character virtues, fulfills an indispensable deliberative function for organizing a life dedicated to θεωρία; cf. n52 above) and his assurance in 1178b5–7 that such a life is still lived by a *human being in a social context* and thus requires the ethical virtues to succeed as a *human* life. As for the political applications, I see no reason why at least the ideal *polis* should not view the enabling of scientific study and contemplation as its noblest goal (cf. *Pol.* 1325b14–30, 1333a16–30, 1334a23–34).

55 My thanks to Colin King, Bryan Reece, and the anonymous peer reviewer for their helpful comments.

COLLOQUIUM 5

Commentary on Szaif

Colin Guthrie King
Providence College

Abstract

In this response I consider the implications of Jan Szaif's suggestion that there is a tight "conceptual affinity" between Books I and X of the *Nicomachean Ethics* (*EN*). I argue against one view which could claim such a thesis as an ally: the view which maintains that the *Nicomachean Ethics* is based upon the kind of conceptual cohesion supplied by a supposed metaphysical foundation for claims about happiness.

Keywords

acceptable premises – goods – ἔνδοξα – *eudaimonia* – metaphysical foundation

1

Jan Szaif (hereafter J.S.) has given us a paper with a clear exegetical thesis. He argues that the brief discussion of *eudaimonia* in *Nicomachean Ethics* I.12 within a three-fold division in the hierarchy of goods—goods which are prized, those which are praised, and powers—plays a larger role in the overall argument of the *Nicomachean Ethics* than previously appreciated. In particular he argues that there is a "conceptual affinity" between *Nicomachean Ethics* I.12 and X.6–8; and that I.12 prepares the ground for the famous claim in X.8 that θεωρία (the activity of contemplation) is the highest human good and the realization of *eudaimonia* in a complete form (*EN* X.8, 1178b7–8). There is little to add to this detailed analysis of I.12. The claim that this passage is related to X.7–8 also seems correct. Clearly, the term "prized" is (as J.S. notes) salient in both contexts, which share an occupation with the problem of the proper ordering of goods within a teleological framework. In the framework invoked in these two contexts, *eudaimonia* is first established formally as the highest good, and then successively filled in through an account of virtuous human activities and their relationship to the highest human good. As J.S. observes, the placement of *eudaimonia* in a proper ordering of goods is a feature of the 'architecture' of argument in Aristotle's *Nicomachean Ethics*.

In my comment on his paper, I wish to focus on the implications of this 'architecture' and how we should understand it. I will make a case against one particular understanding of the architecture metaphor, one which J.S. might accept without explicitly defending or endorsing it. It is an understanding based on an influential interpretation of Aristotle's ethics according to which his ethics are built on a metaphysical foundation which is itself not to be found in the ethics.[1] The background assumptions of such an interpretation are that Aristotle's ethics require such a metaphysical foundation to be philosophically well-founded, that Aristotle believes that his ethics require such a foundation, and that he actually has such a foundation in other works.[2] These assumptions form part of a wider claim regarding Aristotle's philosophical methodology. The claim is that Aristotle's methodology must go beyond the narrow coherence achieved through 'dialectical' procedures, that is, procedures based on ἔνδοξα, and achieve a wider coherence with metaphysical first principles.

This interpretation and the scholarly debate concerning it are relevant to this, and any other, exegetical thesis that takes a view on the metaphysical level of a given argument in Aristotle's ethics. As other interpreters have pointed out, it might be possible for Aristotle to invoke metaphysical principles dialectically—because they are accepted or acceptable (and not *qua* grounding or foundational metaphysical principles). This would not constitute a 'grounding' of ethics in metaphysics in the relevant sense required by those who support the thesis of the metaphysical foundation or grounding of Aristotle's ethics.[3] Statements about what is prized and statements about what is praised stand in strong relation to what is often called the basis of 'dialectical' method in Aristotle—ἔνδοξα, or acceptable premisses.[4] Thus the invocation of normative assumptions concerning goods and what is good by pointing out what is prized

---

[1] See Irwin 1980.

[2] These assumptions are critically discussed in Roche 1988.

[3] This seems to be the position of Roche 1988, who defends the thesis that Aristotle's method in the *Nicomachean Ethics* is dialectical. He bases his arguments against Irwin, i.a., on a premiss about the nature of the audience of Aristotle's argument: that they are properly morally habituated, and thus already share the most important background assumptions necessary for accommodating his ethical theory.

[4] In fact, we should distinguish between dialectic and argument from ἔνδοξα, and this for two reasons. First, dialectic, as Aristotle understands it, is a specific form of rule-governed interpersonal argumentation in which one interlocutor attempts to refute the thesis defended by an answerer. Aristotle's own texts do not meet this description (at least not straightforwardly) though they sometimes treat δόξαι. Second, as Aristotle himself states in *Topics* 1.1, not all

and what is praised is, *prima facie*, a likely candidate for a form of argumentation which is not grounding in a metaphysical sense, but rather in the rhetorical sense: for example, in the sense of grounding a thesis that is under discussion in another one, which requires no further justification for the audience in question because it reflects the basic practices of moral evaluation in which Aristotle's audience is regularly engaged and concerning which there is no significant disagreement. This would be the "weak coherence" criticized by the proponents of the grounding thesis; but it would be an appropriate sort of coherence if the aim of Aristotle's argument is directed to those who do not need to be convinced of the truth of metaphysical principles, but rather of the authority of certain normative claims (whether we choose to call such a form of argument "dialectical" or, as I prefer, "rhetorical").

I think this latter interpretation will be more appropriate to the invocation of "moral facts" about what is praised and what is prized. To show this and explore what implications it might have for J.S.'s project if true, I will consider a further context in which Aristotle considers divisions of goods that feature what is praised or what is prized, and compare this to the argument in *Nicomachean Ethics* x.8. We can recognize a general feature in these contexts and the one from I.12: we are presented with ἔνδοξα or δόξαι as reflected in linguistic practice and conventional presumptions, accompanied by an interpretation of what these practices and presumptions tell us about the proper ordering of goods which they concern. Let us first consider a passage in the *Eudemian Ethics* with a view to the key text for J.S.'s 'architecture' claim, *Nicomachean Ethics* x.8.

II

As in *Nicomachean Ethics* I.12, in *Eudemian Ethics* I.7 Aristotle introduces the view that *eudaimonia* is the highest good as a view which is already accepted: "It is agreed that this [*eudaimonia*] is the greatest and best of human goods" (1217a21–22). Aristotle explains the qualification "human" in remarking that there could be a *eudaimonia* of a higher entity (God), and that non-human animals cannot be said to partake in *eudaimonia*, since they have no share of the divine in their nature (a22–29). The importance of the predicate "divine" features thus also here, in the *Eudemian Ethics*. As J.S. rightly notes (26–27), Aristotle takes some argumentative pains in the *Nicomachean Ethics* to bind

---

argument from ἔνδοξα is genuine dialectic; and as he states in *Topics* 8.5–8.6, not all forms of dialectic involve argument from ἔνδοξα in an unqualified sense.

this property to the further one of being intrinsically valuable. In *Nicomachean Ethics* x.8, he employs a similar inference as a "sign" for the claim that the activity of the god is contemplative, and that of all human goods the one most related to divine contemplation is the most blessed or happy (1178b21–23). The inference there is "it is a sign that contemplation is the happiest human activity that none of the other animals have a share in happiness, since they are completely deprived of an activity of this sort [i.e. contemplation]" (b24–25). In *Nicomachean Ethics* x.8, Aristotle goes on to argue, in part on the basis of these claims, that θεωρία and *eudaimonia* are co-extensive and directly proportional: as far as the activity of contemplation extends, just so far is one capable of *eudaimonia*. The final conclusion of this argument is that θεωρία is an activity "valued in and of itself" (αὕτη καθ' αὑτὴν τιμία, b30), and that therefore happiness must consist in some form of θεωρία (b31).

We may note that the most robustly 'metaphysical' assertion from *Nicomachean Ethics* x.8—that all non-human animals are incapable of *eudaimonia* precisely because they are bereft of a faculty for contemplation—is invoked as a "sign" (σημεῖον, b24). This is a piece of evidence unlike that of a principle. A principle would indeed be the ground through which happiness and contemplation are connected. But as Aristotle himself notes, the co-extension of happiness and the faculty of contemplation could be accidental. He notes this after he has established a "sign" for the correspondence between happiness and the faculty for contemplation in the exclusion of both in one particular class of entities, namely "all the other living things" (besides gods and humans):

> It is a sign, too, that the other animals have no share in happiness, since they are completely deprived of such an activity [contemplation]. For, in the case of the gods, each of their lives is blessed; in the case of humankind, each life is blessed insofar as it has something similar to this activity. But none of the other living things is blessed, since none has a share in contemplation in any way. In fact the faculty for contemplation extends just as far as the ability to be happy, and to the extent that an entity is capable of contemplation, to that extent is it also capable of being happy. This is not an accidental correspondence, but occurs because of the faculty for contemplation, for this is valued in and of itself. Therefore, happiness will consist in some form of contemplation.
> σημεῖον δὲ καὶ τὸ μὴ μετέχειν τὰ λοιπὰ ζῷα εὐδαιμονίας, τῆς τοιαύτης ἐνεργείας ἐστερημένα τελείως. τοῖς μὲν γὰρ θεοῖς ἅπας ὁ βίος μακάριος, τοῖς δ' ἀνθρώποις, ἐφ' ὅσον ὁμοίωμά τι τῆς τοιαύτης ἐνεργείας ὑπάρχει· τῶν δ' ἄλλων ζῴων οὐδὲν εὐδαιμονεῖ, ἐπειδὴ οὐδαμῇ κοινωνεῖ θεωρίας. ἐφ' ὅσον δὴ διατείνει ἡ θεωρία, καὶ ἡ εὐδαιμονία, καὶ οἷς μᾶλλον ὑπάρχει τὸ θεωρεῖν, καὶ εὐδαιμονεῖν, οὐ κατὰ

συμβεβηκὸς ἀλλὰ κατὰ τὴν θεωρίαν· αὕτη γὰρ καθ' αὑτὴν τιμία. ὥστ εἴη ἂν ἡ εὐδαιμονία θεωρία τις. (*EN* X.8, 1178b24–31)

To put it in the language of the *Posterior Analytics*: there is a καθ' αὑτο predication between contemplation and happiness, such that contemplation is contained in the account of happiness as a genus, which is why happiness must be some form of contemplation. This is supported primarily by the statement that contemplation (like happiness) is valued "in and of itself." The fact (if fact it is) that all other living beings are deprived of happiness and contemplation merely establishes a correspondence that need not be an essential connection. It is the *per se* valuation of contemplation that establishes the possibility for what is valued (or prized) to be predicated in itself to what is blessed or happy.

If we are searching for a metaphysical principle here, it is most likely to be found in the statement that the faculty of contemplation is not only predicated of all the things which participate in happiness, but that there is an essential relation between the two: "This is not an accidental correspondence, but occurs because of the faculty for contemplation, for this is valued in and of itself" (1178b30–31). What is valued in itself can lay claim to being a highest good. Happiness has been established as this kind of good. Contemplation is here established as another such good. Since there can only be one ultimate good, these two must be essentially related. It seems appropriate to call this a metaphysical claim, but in the argument as formulated, it is supported by "empirical" claims about what is, in fact, valued in itself.

Let us now return to the *Eudemian Ethics* 1.7 and compare the argument there. In *Eudemian Ethics* 1.7, we find no explicit mention of θεωρία, but we do find a division of goods which seems to accommodate it. The division is a dichotomy: Aristotle distinguishes between those goods which are the object of human action, and those which are not (*EE* 1.7, 1217a30–32). The dichotomic division is justified in these lines: "we say this so, because some things do not partake in change and motion, and therefore do not belong to the goods realized by action. These are likely the best by nature. Other goods are practical, but only actionable by those more powerful than we are" (a32–35). Though there is no explicit mention of contemplation here, we might understand contemplation—and certainly divine entities—to belong to those things not subject to change (provided we can think of both as things not engaged in "action").

As many readers will recall, this passage directly precedes the part of the *Eudemian Ethics* (1.8) in which Aristotle trenchantly criticizes the Idea of the Good as a candidate for the highest good. The claim that what is prized should take precedence in the hierarchy of values is revealing in this connection. This claim provides a further reason for the rejection of the Idea of the Good, because this is—at least as Aristotle portrays it in *Eudemian Ethics* I.8—not an object of value "in itself," but a posit. In particular, the Idea of the Good is a thing posited through which those goods which really are valued are supposed to obtain their value. The lesson one may draw from this is that what is posited and indeed even what is an object of praise cannot be a proper candidate for highest good, because the highest good must be something which is really valued in itself, as made evident in what motivates our actions. The particular virtuous actions which are praised cannot even be deemed as candidates for such a good, as they are performed in pursuit of something which goes beyond them.

We can see a similar mode of argument at work in the *Nicomachean Ethics*. When for example in *Nicomachean Ethics* I.12 Aristotle considers the thesis of Eudoxus that pleasure is the highest good, he commends Eudoxus for having put his thesis in such a way as to make pleasure superior to the objects of praise. There we read:

> Eudoxus seems to have advocated well on behalf of the claim that pleasure belongs to the best things. For the fact that it is not praised as one of the goods indicated, he thought, that it was in fact something better than the objects of praise, and he thought that the god and the good were something of this sort. For the other things are related back to these.
> δοκεῖ δὲ καὶ Εὔδοξος καλῶς συνηγορῆσαι περὶ τῶν ἀριστείων τῇ ἡδονῇ· τὸ γὰρ μὴ ἐπαινεῖσθαι τῶν ἀγαθῶν οὖσαν μηνύειν ᾤετο ὅτι κρεῖττόν ἐστι τῶν ἐπαινετῶν, τοιοῦτον δ' εἶναι τὸν θεὸν καὶ τἀγαθόν· πρὸς ταῦτα γὰρ καὶ τἆλλα ἀναφέρεσθαι.
> (*EN* I.12, 1101b27–31)

I think, *pace* J.S., that this passage indicates a bit more than a partial agreement with Eudoxus in argumentative strategy. For the claim that the greater good and the divine are not proper objects of praise basically informs the theory of value at work in Aristotle's hierarchy of goods, and connects NE I.12 and NE X.8, as J.S. has convincingly shown. And this claim is attributed to Eudoxus here. More importantly for the interpretation of Aristotle's *Ethics*, however, we may see how the relativization of goods which are praised works together with Aristotle's theory of what is, as it were, the motivating value in the sphere of practical goods: those things which are valued in themselves. Aristotle's theory of such goods does indeed seem to be a foundational piece in the theory of the *Nicomachean Ethics*. It is based, however, not so much on a further metaphysical theory, but on a theory of value in which what is *actually* prized and praised is an important datum for theorizing the real hierarchy of practical goods. It is a theory of value which explicitly acknowledges certain particular existing values as a source of normativity.

One may still justly ask, however, whether the entire thesis is nothing but a philosopher's conceit. Are we really to believe that what all people really want is to live a life of contemplation? Empirical support for this, in our time and Aristotle's, would be hard to find. But the link between contemplation and happiness is not established this way, as J.S. aptly shows; and the claim which Aristotle seeks to defend is not empirical, even if part of his argument involves a claim about what is actually most valued (or "prized"). As we see in both the *Nicomachean Ethics* and the *Eudemian Ethics*, contemplation and happiness most clearly co-occur in the lives of the gods; and hence the importance of the property "divine" in those contexts, such as *Nicomachean Ethics* I.12 and X.8, where Aristotle is at pains to establish the relationship between contemplation and happiness. We find their co-occurrence in the *Eudemian Ethics* for example, where Aristotle mentions in passing that the good in the category of substance is "mind and god" (*EE* I.8, 1217b30–31), and in the argument of *Nicomachean Ethics* X.8, which establishes the co-occurrence of happiness and contemplation with a view to humans and gods. The (thoroughly Platonic) notion that contemplation is the activity which we share with the gods, and which is most divine, together with the conventional notion that the gods are the ultimate reference in terms of happiness, seem to be the two driving assumptions in the background of Aristotle's argument. They could be construed as metaphysical propositions, but they seem—above all—to function in the argument of the *Nicomachean Ethics* not as principles, but as acceptable premisses for the audience/readership of the *Ethics*.

III

By way of conclusion, two caveats are in order. First, I should note what follows from my criticism of the metaphysical foundationalist reading of Aristotle's *Ethics*, and what does not. In arguing that *Nicomachean Ethics* I.12 and its pendants in *Nicomachean Ethics* X.8 and *Eudemian Ethics* I.8 are rhetorical-dialectical, I am not arguing that ἔνδοξα or δόξαι are the epistemic foundation for Aristotle's ethics. Acknowledging certain propositions as acceptable but defeasible in a context of persuasive argumentation is different from saying that such propositions are the basis for our moral knowledge, or explanatory of moral truths. I think Aristotle often does the former in his ethical works without committing himself to the latter. And even if he should, under certain circumstances, do both, this need not be (and in my view indeed should not be) interpreted as an indication of 'method' writ large, a consistent or prevailing tendency. In this I am of a mind with the deflationary take on the 'endoxic method' espoused by Scott 2015. One acute observation from Scott's valuable study is that the *Nicomachean Ethics*, like Plato's *Republic*, is circuitous in its procedure: it begins with established norms and values, proceeds to reflect on them by philosophical means, and then returns to these conventional starting-points in order to explain something about them through the propositions won through reflection. Scott appreciates this feature of the *Ethics* while denying that, for Aristotle, the route thus taken is exact in the sense of a foundational or axiomatic procedure. This seems right to me, and J.S.'s interpretation of the relationship between goods which are prized and goods which are praised is a case in point. As J.S. shows, the linguistic practices of praising and prizing occasion a reflection on the ordering of goods, which such practices presume. This motivates a discussion of a non-conventional notion, that namely *eudaimonia* consist in wisdom as exercised in a form of θεωρία. Obviously, convention and the views of a majority do not directly support such a view, but as Aristotle thinks, such a view can cohere with and even make sense of norms presumed by convention.

Secondly, it should be noted that we have elided a large and contentious issue in the interpretation of the very passages with which J.S. is concerned. The issue concerns the question of whether morally virtuous activity is necessary or even sufficient for attaining *eudaimonia*, and whether θεωρία is both necessary and sufficient (as the passage NE x.8, 1178b24–31, cited above, seems to suggest). The discussion of this question cannot be entered upon here. But it is only fair to register that in a more recent discussion of this very question, Irwin did not bring the metaphysical foundationalist position to bear on it (Irwin 2012). In presenting a case for a 'pluralist' conception of happiness, Irwin weighs the textual evidence from within the *Nicomachean Ethics* and considers many passages which might also tell in favor of the view that Aristotle held happiness to consist in only one specific good ('monism'). But he does not cite *Nicomachean Ethics* I.12, which would seem to be evidence in favor of monism. The close connection which (as J.S. has shown) *Nicomachean Ethics* I.12 bears to *Nicomachean Ethics* x.6–8 thus could have wider implications for our understanding of the account of happiness in Aristotle's *Ethics*.

COLLOQUIUM 5

Szaif/King Bibliography

Aufderheide, J. 2015. The Content of Happiness: A New Case for *Theôria*, in *The Highest Good in Aristotle and Kant*, ed. by J. Aufderheide and R.M. Bader, 36–59. Oxford: Oxford University Press.

Baker, S. 2017. The Metaphysics of Goodness in the Ethics of Aristotle. *Philosophical Studies* 174.7: 1839–1856.

Barnes, J. 1980. Aristotle and the Methods of Ethics. *Revue Internationale de Philosophie* 34: 490–511.

Barnes, J., ed. 1984. *The Complete Works of Aristotle. The Revised Oxford Translation* (2 Vols.). Princeton: Princeton University Press.

Broadie, S. 1991. *Ethics with Aristotle*. Oxford: Oxford University Press.

Broadie, S. and C. Rowe. 2002. *Aristotle: Nicomachean Ethics. Translation, Introduction, and Commentary*. Oxford: Oxford University Press.

Burnet, J. 1900. *The Ethics of Aristotle, edited with an introcuction and notes*. London: Methuen.

Cleemput, G. van. 2006. Aristotle on *Eudaimonia* in *Nicomachean Ethics* I. *Oxford Studies in Ancient Philosophy* 30: 127–157.

Gauthier, R.A. and J.Y. Jolif. 1970. *Aristote: L'éthique à Nicomaque. Introduction, traduction et commentaire* (2 Vols.), 2nd edition. Louvain: Publications universitaires.

Grant, A. 1885. *The Ethics of Aristotle* (2 Vols.), 4th edition. London: Longmans, Green, and Co.

Joachim, H.H. 1951. *The Nicomachean Ethics*. Oxford: Oxford University Press.

Kassel, R., ed. 1976. *Aristotelis ars rhetorica*. Berlin: de Gruyter.

Irwin, T. 1980. The Metaphysical and Psychological Basis of Aristotle's Ethics. In *Essays on Aristotle's Ethics*, ed. A.O. Rorty, 35–53. Berkeley/Los Angeles/London: University of California Press.

Irwin, T. 1999. *Aristotle: Nicomachean Ethics, translated with notes and glossary*, 2nd edition. Indianapolis: Hackett.

Irwin, T. 2012. Conceptions of Happiness in the *Nicomachean Ethics*. In *The Oxford Handbook of Aristotle*, ed. Christopher Shields, 495–528. Oxford: Oxford University Press.

Kraut, R. 1989. *Aristotle on the Human Good*. Princeton: Princeton University Press.

Kühner, R. and B. Gerth. 1898. *Ausführliche Grammatik der griechischen Sprache*, vol. II.1, 3rd edition. Hannover and Leipzig: Hahnsche Buchhandlung.

Liddell, H.G., R. Scott, and H.S. Jones (= LSJ). 1996. *Greek-English Lexicon, with a Revised Supplement*. Oxford: Clarendon Press.

Long, A.A. 2011. Aristotle on *eudaimonia*, *nous*, and divinity, in *Aristotle's Nicomachean Ethics. A Critical Guide,* ed. J. Miller, 92–113. Cambridge: Cambridge University Press.

Ramsauer, G. 1878. *Aristotelis ethica Nicomachea, editit et commentario instruxit.* Leipzig: Teubner.

Rapp, C. 2002. *Aristoteles: Rhetorik, übersetzt und erläutert* (= Aristoteles, *Werke,* vol. 4.). Berlin: Akademie Verlag.

Reeve, C.D.C. 2014. *Aristotle: Nicomachean Ethics, translated with introduction and notes.* Indianapolis: Hackett.

Richardson Lear, G. 2004. *Happy Lives and the Highest Good.* Princeton: Princeton University Press.

Roche, T. 1988. On the Alleged Metaphysical Foundation of Aristotle's *Ethics. Ancient Philosophy* 8: 49–62.

Ross, W.D., ed. 1959. *Aristotelis ars rhetorica.* Oxford: Oxford University Press.

Scott, D. 2015. *Levels of argument: A comparative study of Plato's* Republic *and Aristotle's* Nicomachean Ethics. Oxford: Oxford University Press.

Smyth, H.W. 1956. *A Greek Grammar,* revised edition. Cambridge MA: Harvard University Press.

Stewart, J.A. 1892. *Notes on the Nicomachean Ethics* (2 Vols.). Oxford: Clarendon Press.

Szaif, J. 2006. Aristotle on the Benefits of Virtue (*EN* X.7 and IX.8), in *The Virtuous Life in Greek Ethics,* ed. B. Reis, 167–193. Cambridge: Cambridge University Press.

Szaif, J. 2012. *Gut des Menschen. Problematik und Entwicklung der Glücksethik bei Aristoteles und in der Tradition des Peripatos.* Berlin and New York: de Gruyter.

Index of Names

Alexander of Aphrodisias   151, 152n5, 153n11
Allen, Reginald E.   2, 5, 8, 13n18, 17, 18n26 20, 21n30, 27-28, 29, 30n46, 32, 34
Aristotle   29n44, 32, 43-83, 91n13, 96, 98n38, 112, 140-141, 144, 145, 149-188
Arius Didymus   152, 153
Aspasius   152, 153, 155n14, 159
Austin, Emily   122, 123, 130

Bailey, Cyril   124, 125n10
Broadie, Sarah   44n3, 45-46, 48, 55-56, 68n33-34

Cornford, Francis M.   13n18, 16, 18

Delbruck, Max   71, 75n2, 76
Diogenes Laertius   119-120, 133-134

Epicurus   119-148
Eudoxus   151, 163-166, 167n41-42, 177, 184

Furth, Montgomery   74

Galen   128
Gill, Mary Louise   3n3, 10n14, 11n15, 13, 15n19, 17, 23n31-32, 25, 27, 37n4, 38, 39

Heidegger, Martin   101, 111, 113

Lucretius   122n5, 124-125, 132-133, 136, 139

McCabe, M.M.   16
Meinwald, Constance   13n18, 39
Menn, Stephen   44n3, 45, 46n7, 56n19

Nietzsche, Friedrich   141, 144
Nussbaum, Martha   127n19, 139-140, 141, 144

Philodemus   120-121, 122n7, 125, 126, 127n19, 135
Plato   1-41, 44n3, 56, 57n21, 58n22, 85-117, 150, 163, 164n33, 167n41, 168, 176, 186
Plutarch   122n5, 132-134, 139, 141
Porphyry   131
Posidonius   128

Rickless, Samuel   6n8, 8n10, 15n19, 16, 26n34
Ryan, Paul   3n3, 10n14, 11n15, 13, 15n19, 17n24, 23n31-32, 25, 27, 37n4, 38, 39

Seneca   133, 141
Smith, Adam   141
Spinoza, Baruch   141

Tsouna, Voula   120n2, 127n19, 128